ABOUT THE AUTHOR

Edward Behr, brought up in France and England, served in the Indian Army before graduating from Cambridge University and joining Reuters. As *Time-Life* correspondent he covered the wars in Algeria, Lebanon and along the Tibetan border as well as the events in the Congo. He interviewed Mao Tse-tung for the *Saturday Evening Post*, covered the Chinese cultural revolution, the Soviet invasion of Czechoslovakia and the Vietnam war for *Newsweek*, and became European Editor of *Newsweek International*.

His prize-winning television films include documentaries on India, China, Ireland, 'The American Way of Death' (on the US funeral parlour industry) and the Kennedy family. His earlier books include: *The Algerian Problem*, *The Thirty-Sixth Way* (with Sydney Liu) and a novel, *Getting Even*.

Anyone Here Been Raped And Speaks English

A Foreign Correspondent's Life Behind the Lines

Edward Behr

NEW ENGLISH LIBRARY
Hodder and Stoughton

First published in the USA in 1978 by
Viking Press

First published in Great Britain in 1981
by Hamish Hamilton Ltd

Copyright © Edward Behr, 1978

First NEL Paperback Edition 1982
Sixth impression 1988

British Library C.I.P.

Behr, Edward

Anyone Here Been Raped and
Speaks English
1. Foreign correspondents
I. Title
070.4′33′092   PN4784.F6

ISBN 0 450 05360 1

Printed and bound in Great Britain
for Hodder and Stoughton
Paperbacks, a division of Hodder and
Stoughton Ltd., Mill Road,
Dunton Green, Sevenoaks, Kent
TN13 2YA.
(Editorial Office: 47 Bedford Square,
London WC1B 3DP) by
Cox & Wyman Ltd., Reading.

For some rather special friends: Tom Brady, John Gale, and Jim Mossman, who died; Larry Burrows, John Cantwell, Gilles Caron, Michel Laurent, Bruce Piggott, Paul Schutzer, and François Sully, killed in Vietnam, Cambodia, and the Middle East; Rick Merron, missing in New York. Not in sorrow but remembering the good times shared.

ACKNOWLEDGEMENTS

Anyone bold enough to write about journalism is in for a rough time because comparison must inevitably be made with Evelyn Waugh's *Scoop*, the best book ever written about the press and the only one to capture the quintessential absurdity of our calling. *Scoop* is essential reading for me still, about once every two years, and I have presented paperback copies of it to an assortment of people, including a United States Air Force colonel in charge of public relations in Saigon and Prince Sihanouk. Both, in their different ways, appeared to be in dire need of a quick primer on the vagaries of the Fourth Estate.

Waugh, in his later years, as in his posthumously published diaries, seemed determined to present himself in the worst possible light. But I find it easy to forget the tantrums, the rudeness, the grossness, the racism, and the reactionary posturing. Everything of this nature, I feel, was a mask behind which sheltered a sensitive pessimist and stoic. One of the sentences in *Put Out More Flags* should be framed and set above every politician's chair: 'It is a curious thing, he thought, that every creed promises a paradise that will be absolutely uninhabitable for anyone of civilise taste.'

If Waugh has been my patron saint ever since I first picked up *Scoop* while still at school, the editors of news-agencies, papers, and magazines were the real-life patrons who must be thanked for sending me on assignments in the first place and overlooking my appalling mistakes, especially Reuters, *Time*, *Life*, the *Saturday Evening Post*, and of course *Newsweek*. I must also thank *The New York Times*, for allowing me to quote from an article I wrote for its travel section on November 14, 1969;* Alan Williams, for his suggestions and encouragement; and last but not least, Vicky Elliott, who corrected my prose, unsplitting my infinitives, unravelling my punctuation, and eliminating my occasional Franglais.

CONTENTS

INTRODUCTION

By some process it would take a mathematical genius to explain, our past, scarcely caught up with, immediately begins to recede. Stacks of papers and magazines only twenty years old are now seen as vintage curiosities. And though I was born in 1926 and am thus hardly an old man, I feel that my childhood and adolescence are infinitely remote, belonging by rights to another life altogether, as do relatively recent events, like the Vietnam War.

It may be a question of outlook, for the world I was brought up in was a world which, for all the gathering storm of the Second World War and Nazism, still believed in the nineteenth-century liberal concept of perfectibility. In the Lycée Janson de Sailly, in Paris, where my Englishness stuck out like a sore thumb, it was never seriously questioned that humankind was set on a constantly perfectible course, that the present was better than the past, that Louis XIV was an improvement over Louis XIII, and that the benefits of the French Revolution, followed by the centralizing genius of Napoleon, made France, and perforce the world, a better place as time went on.

Later, at St. Paul's School in wartime Britain, the same myth of perfectibility was never seriously called into question. History was supposed to teach us that the tirelessly rising middle classes and virtuous British nineteenth-century nonconformists were progressively reducing the gap between exploited and exploiters, haves and have-nots, bringing justice and civilization not only to

Britain and Empire, but to the entire world.

This theory, which subliminally justified the arrant self-confidence of empire builders, was never one I blindly subscribed to. Perhaps it was the result of being educated with a foot in both British and French camps that made me somewhat suspicious of both systems, since I was more French than British when in England and more British than French in France itself. The strong anti-British syndrome in prewar France and the contemptuous dismissal of all things French in Britain made me, from the onset, wary and distrustful of all such generalizations. And if such theories of perfectibility were correct and universally applicable, how did one justify the 'Dark Ages'?

Gradually and inarticulately, experience began teaching me what philosophers of the absurd were justifying in more abstract language: 'As flies to wanton boys, are we to the gods; they kill us for their sport.'

It's difficult for me to date, even imprecisely, the emergence of my new private conviction, which it would be presumptuous to call nihilism, and the crumbling of the old. It could have been while I was still at school in England. A housemaster, to whom I had complained for being unfairly singled out for punishment I hadn't deserved, replied, 'But, Edward, the world is a very unfair place.' It could have come from watching the London blitz at close quarters: Why were some streets spared and not others? What possible explanation was there for my aged exiled Russian grandmother's horrible death in a Nazi concentration camp? It could have been in Sumatra, watching dead and dying village women and children being carried into a first-aid post after a mortar attack. Not being religious, I could not subscribe to the convenient notion of God's will, and I found the fatalistic attitude of the Indian troops I was with in wartime far more conducive to peace of mind than any Christian attempt to justify the spectacle of human folly around me.

For folly, greed, and hypocrisy seemed to me, at a very

early age, to be the fairy godmothers presiding over the destinies of our planet, and little has occurred since to make me change my mind. It seemed futile, from the outset, to attempt to fight injustice through political parties or ideologies, for since folly, greed, and hypocrisy were everywhere, they were nowhere more at home than inside institutions, parties, ideologies.

The only recourse, it seemed to me, was to try, where possible, to anatomize such instances, and what better way of doing so than by becoming a journalist?

But I quickly understood that the formula journalists labor under, whether through print or on the air, only imperfectly enabled me to achieve such a goal. Despite all the occasional crusading zeal of investigative reporters, most journalism is of an almost mechanical kind. For obvious reasons, which include the short attention span of readers and the economic necessities of publishers, what becomes news is not always, not often, what deserves to be singled out for publication.

Besides, the content of newspapers and magazines, like the shape of women's clothes, follows the vagaries of fashion. Thus, Nixon's visit to China in 1972 spawned a huge American interest in China and a vogue in all things Chinese. The end of the Vietnam war and the collapse of the Thieu regime in 1975 were followed by a tacit blackout of news out of the Indochina area; Americans just didn't want to know, just as they didn't, for some years after 1975, wish to read anything about the Vietnam War.

And because of pressures of space, of the constant need to compress and synthesize, what really happened is not always what we wrote about, even if our facts were indisputable, not because of an intent to deceive, but because we are compelled to deal in essentials. This book is an attempt to restore the balance; even the most trivial, nonsensical anecdote can be made to illustrate a general truth and sometimes more aptly reveals an 'ambience', a climate, than any careful marshaling of facts.

I have always been struck by the fact that reporters, relaxing and drinking together, are always swapping stories about what happened and that these stories are funnier, truer and more revealing than anything they write for their media. It is these nonessentials, often far more entertaining and, ultimately, significant, relegated to our tight little incestuous reporters' circle, becoming barroom gossip, often unprintable, usually scurrilous, and always self-deprecatory, that make any gathering of newsmen a hilarious and memorable occasion. It's the flavor of such stories, of this raw material out of which comes the barroom gossip, that I have long wanted to communicate to others, beyond our small exclusive circle.

For it's in laughter that some of the most serious points are made. Laughter is never gratuitous. It relates profoundly to our human predicament, as catharsis and means of survival.

One of the first serious books I read as a teenager, Henri Bergson's *Laughter*, caused a vivid impression. I remember his description of the chimpanzee, tumbling out of the tree and saving itself from hurt at the last moment and causing in its audience of apes the spasms of sudden anxiety followed by relief – chimp laughter. How scientifically valid Bergson's theories are today I know not and care less. For I have felt the chimp's escape from danger, and I know that laughter is indeed the surest form of released tension.

But there are other kinds of laughter, too. It's the essence of comedy to assert itself even in the most portentous, dramatic moments. Speaking personally, I cannot boast that my reporting career has in any way paralleled the spate of films about fearless reporters in tight-lipped, raincoated, and belted challenge against evil forces. In my world notebooks are lost, tape recorders jam, taxis break down in remote places, and on my way to the revolution noisy children throw up in crowded planes or drip through their imperfectly watertight hammocks. In short, it's a world of Woody Allen rather than Joel McCrea, with the reporter as victim rather than hero.

Not that there were always occasions for laughter, even bitter laughter. The Algerian and Vietnam wars were searing and, in some respects, degrading wars, even for observers. The massacres that took place at the time of Indian independence were unforgettable in their horror. Violence is seldom amusing, even if reporters become relatively immune to it. And the competitive nature of journalism is such that there are limits to camaraderie. Occasionally, pranks on our fellow reporters, designed to put our competitors on the wrong trail, boomerang straight back on the perpetrators. I'm reminded of a joke in bad taste, one of many, played by a group of reporters on one of their number who, constitutionally incapable of rising early, relied far too much on his colleagues to relay the news to him. We were in Rabat in 1955, and Sultan Mohammed V, exiled by the French for his nationalist views, had just returned in triumph. His puppet predecessor, Ben Arafa, had left, ingloriously, for France. At the hotel bar, a midday meeting place for correspondents, the story was duly planted.

'What happened this morning – anything?' our lazy friend asked.

'You must have heard about the zoo!'

' . . . ?'

'The sultan's furious. He's discovered that Ben Arafa has eaten all the animals in the palace zoo.'

'Why did he do that?' asked our friend, looking falsely casual.

'Because he'd never tasted lion before, that's why, and hoped it would make him strong.'

Having gulped down his drink, the young man rushed to his room and filed his story. A few hours later all reporters then in Rabat got cables from their news editors, saying, 'X – has filed superb story on ex-sultan eating palace zoo lions. Why unhave from you?'

If *chutzpah*, the ability to do without sleep, and a certain amount of low cunning are essential ingredients for a foreign correspondent, the greatest gift is an indefinable sixth sense, not to be in the right place at the right time, for this is sometimes impossible, but to be able to predict, in the most general sense, the long-term outcome of a given situation.

Here, without false modesty, I think I can say that I was right more often than I was wrong. Even before I became a reporter, in the aftermath of the Second World War in Southeast Asia, I felt, long before most of my fellow Indian Army officers, that we all were living on borrowed time, that independence was bound to come to the Indian subcontinent far faster than most people believed possible, and that in the aftermath of independence the British imperial heritage would flounder and, within years, become something of a joke.

Similarly, at the very onset of the Algerian War, when the prospects of Algerian independence seemed very remote indeed, I could almost sense the impending disaster about to impinge on the still blithely self-confident *pied-noirs*, the French settlers in Algeria, at a time when all but a tiny handful of observers were reluctant to admit that France would ever give up part of its sovereign territory. The feeling was even more intense during the Vietnam War, when – before Tet 1968 – the mood was generally, among U.S. officials at least, overoptimistic. It was the same instinct which convinced me that the May 1968 uprising in France would collapse if De Gaulle stuck to his guns and that the Socialist-Communist election agreement in France was doomed to end in bitter recriminations in 1978.

Finally, I hope to communicate what it really felt like to be on the inside of a huge, fast-breaking story, with all the attendant absurdities and anticlimaxes. As an example of fact's being stranger than fiction, I can do no better than recall my first visit to Cuba just after the 1962 missile crisis. I was one of the first reporters to enter Cuba then, and there were grim stories of suspected spies being arrested and held in dungeons for weeks at a time with no one the wiser. After clearing Cuban customs, I called in at the apartment of a British diplomat in Havana who had had advance warning of my arrival. I expected the mood to be grim and conspiratorial. Loud music could be heard on the landing. The diplomat's wife opened the door. 'I'm so glad you could come,' she said. 'Mr. Castro is teaching us how to tango.'

Any reporter worth his salt will admit that the chase becomes an end in itself, and I am no exception. It's this supposedly romantic crisscrossing in and out of trouble spots and remote places no one in his right mind would ever consider visiting that prompts outsiders to the cliché reaction: 'What an interesting life you must lead!'

There's seldom any proper rejoinder to this, beyond the self-deprecatory shrug. I have known only one adequate rejoinder. In 1969 Pope Paul VI visited the Holy Land and was taken on a visit of Jerusalem. A friend of mine, Georges Ménager, then a *Paris-Match* photographer, followed him through densely cheering crowds, so dense in fact that the Pope was unable to retrace his steps until police had opened a path through the fray. While they tried to beat back the faithful, Pope Paul VI and Ménager, isolated from the crowd and the rest of the press corps, eyed each other warily. Finally, the Pope said, in his fluent but heavily accented French, 'What an interesting life you must lead.' Ménager stared back and grunted, 'You haven't done so badly either.'

I. A PASSAGE TO INDIA

To PARAPHRASE Proust: For a long time, I used to get up early. Like many early risers, I find it difficult to witness the spectacle of others, more fortunate than myself, who are able to sleep on until a civilized waking hour. There is a compulsion to wake them and talk. This has led to the ending of any number of love affairs, to the brink of divorce, and to the fulfillment of a lifelong ambition: a house large enough for me to make all the noise in the world, in the early morning, without being tempted to disturb others.

Like many early risers, I hardly put these extra gained dawn hours to profitable use but usually fritter them away, reading the papers, walking the dog, making coffee. It was like that until recently, when, on a reporting assignment in Yugoslavia, in a late-night Belgrade nightclub of particularly Fellinian horror, my friend Colin Smith, of the London *Observer*, whom I had been regaling with stories about my early life in India and earliest experiences in journalism, said, 'Why don't you write about it? Soon,' he added with his customary tact, 'you'll be too old and senile, and you'll forget it all.'

So I began making notes in the early morning, and the exercise triggered off more detail than I had believed possible. And now I have come to that particular morning which is always a traumatic one of any would-be author: the insertion of the first page in one's typewriter. Chapter I, page 1 . But where does one go from here, and what does one do for words?

The simplest way is to start from the beginning, which for me was prewar Paris, where I was born. My father's profession is listed on my birth certificate as 'merchant' – as good a way as any of referring to his series of failed business ventures: An Amateur archaeologist, he was an indifferent moneymaker. An occasional diamond merchant and jewelry designer, born in Riga at the turn of the century, he might have remained rich had the 1929 stock-market crash not occurred and been followed soon after by a European recession of hideous severity. My first ten years were untroubled by money worries, and we lived in a large, spacious apartment near the Bois de Boulogne, with nanny, maids, and even, briefly, a butler in red-and-black-striped waistcoat. My parents had met in Brussels, shortly after my mother's precipitous flight from the Soviet Union in 1922. Her elder brother and my father were close friends, and both felt more at home in Paris than anywhere else in the world.

My father died, of a long, complicated kidney condition aggravated by an earlier car accident, before I was ten. Immediately our life-style changed. We moved into a minuscule apartment, and I began to realize that every minute item of expenditure had become, for my mother, a matter of acute concern. For a brief while she toyed with the idea of opening a flower shop. We depended on the generosity of her two brothers, my uncles. Echa, the older one, had become an important and influential figure in the South African diamond world. Her younger brother was a successful cancer surgeon in London. Uncle Echa and Uncle Zama reflected the opposite poles of the family diaspora. Echa, who helped support the Alliance Française in Johannesburg, was a wordly-wise, highly cultured Francophile, who never lost his Russian accent in French, English, and German, all of which he spoke perfectly. Zama, who was eventually knighted after operating on a number of crowned heads, became, in time, almost

2

aggressively English. He ended the Second World War as an air vice-marshal, one of the heads of the hugely expanded RAF medical services. He even looked the quintessential senior RAF officer, complete with thick, bushy mustache. For all that, he also retained a trace of his original Russian intonation and accent. What many people felt was sheer affectation – a patrician rolling of the Rs – was in fact the result of his learning English, as a medical student, at the age of twenty-two.

My mother had herself been one of Russia's first women medical students, and when the October Revolution of 1917 broke out, she was enrolled in the Red Army as a fully fledged medical officer. She spoke of those months with horror but had a curiously ambivalent attitude toward all things Russian: On one hand, she hated and feared what she called 'the Bolsheviki' and never referred to her birthplace as Leningrad but always as St. Petersburg. On the other hand, she became deeply emotionally committed to the survival of the Soviet Union during the Second World War and kept a detailed map on which she would chronicle the stubborn resistance, and the victories, of the Red Army.

It was almost impossible to get her to talk about her revolutionary experiences, except in the most elliptic utterances. 'I used to keep my spoon in my boot; otherwise, someone would steal it,' she told me once. Or, 'Trotsky was a very intelligent man and charming to talk to. But when he got up to make a speech, he always made a fool of himself.' Her familiarity with Trotsky led me, at one stage, to believe they might have been lovers. She denied this, but somewhat coyly.

Many times, in later life, I urged her to make a trip to Leningrad, if only to exorcise old memories. This she adamantly refused to do. 'They would arrest me,' she said. 'In their eyes, I'm still a Red Army deserter.' My mother begged me to give the Soviet Union a wide berth as a journalist. Finally, without letting her know, I transited

3

through Moscow airport on my way to India. The bored Soviet airport police showed not the slightest interest in the fact that my mother's maiden name was Kadinsky.

I grew up speaking both English and French but had no experience of British schools before I was fourteen. My earliest school memories are of a Paris kindergarten, from which I was removed after a particularly serious incident. In those days small children used real ink and real pens, with nibs, and a girl my age (I was six at the time), seated next to me at a long green-baize-covered table, was deliberately teasing me. Every time I tried to reach over to dip my pen in the communal inkwell, she would put her outstretched palm flat across it, to deny me access. At this considerable distance, it's clear that she was simply indulging in some innocent, unconsciously mild sexual play. What possessed me I shall never know, but after being denied ink several times, I suddenly flipped my pen so that its nib was upward, guarding the inkwell. Too late she brought her hand down and impaled it on the nib, which penetrated her hand and came through the other side.

She screamed, and was led away, my pen sticking to her palm like an arrow. My crime was too enormous for any kind of punishment save expulsion, and I never returned.

Eventually I went to a fashionable school called the Lycée Janson de Sailly. In retrospect it seems that I used to have to get up in the middle of the night in order to be there in time. A boy of my own age, Valéry Giscard d'Estaing, went to the same school, and we may have been in some classes together. I have no recollection of him then, and needless to say, he has no recollection of me.

When I think of the *lycée*, it brings to mind huge crammed classrooms, a highly formal atmosphere, remote teachers, and a daily competitive struggle to be first – a struggle I consistently lost, except for homework involving the English language. The atmosphere of the school was fraught with tensions. France, in the thirties, was unabashedly anti-Semitic and Anglophobe. Being both

4

caused me a few problems, such as being beaten up occasionally on my way home from school. I soon discovered that there was more playacting than real aggressive determination among my school colleagues and that a head-on confrontation was preferable to ignoble flight, a lesson useful in later life.

At the *lycée* I helped edit my first newspaper: a four-page offset production of cartoons and school news, bankrolled by the father of one ·of my schoolmates, which we endeavored to sell in the schoolyard with only indifferent success.

Came the war. At first nothing changed, but then, just after my fourteenth birthday, Hitler's blitzkrieg began.

It was just as well for me, academically speaking. Apart from English, history, and geography, my grades were abysmal. Most of my teachers, I recall, were remote, obviously bored, and savagely contemptuous of all but their brightest charges. My mother successfully bribed a taxi driver to take us to Vichy, then to Bordeaux. A First World War veteran with waxed mustaches, he insisted on taking along his wife, who kept repeating, 'Daddy, Daddy, why can't we go home?' At Vichy he succumbed to her persistent nagging and would take us no farther.

The whole of France appeared to be on the roads, moving in the same direction. Occasionally we would come across French Army trucks struggling in the opposite direction against overwhelming traffic odds. I remember sitting in a crowded hotel lobby in Vichy, listening to the bleak news on the radio. A well-dressed, middle-aged man spoke up. 'Pétain's the man we need,' he said. 'He'll save us from the Germans. He's the only one who can. This defeat is a blessing in disguise.'

I shrilly disagreed. 'Britain will fight on,' I said, 'and in the long run will save you all.' I was angrily shouted down. It was well known, said someone, that the British would fight only to the last Frenchman. In weeks Britain, too, would have surrendered. 'I bet you're wrong,' I said, left

5

the room, and burst into tears.

Another taxi driver agreed to take us to Bordeaux. Before we caught the last ship to England, a small coal freighter which, unknown to us all then, ran the gauntlet of German submarines and was very nearly sunk, I spent hours trying to find us (my mother, my elder brother, and me) a hotel room in which to spend the night in Bordeaux itself.

Standing in front of one of the town's leading hotels was a sleek dark Frenchman whose white silk tie, contrasting with his dark suit, made me take him for a hotel clerk. 'Have you any rooms?' I asked. He grinned.

'My young friend,' he said, 'the senators are in the attic; the deputies are in the cellars. I take it you are neither.' Someone pointed to him and said, 'There's Pierre Laval.'

I spent a few weeks in my uncle's house in Harley Street that late summer of 1940. I remember watching the antiaircraft batteries being set up in Regent's Park and the white puffs of smoke as they took aim at an isolated German daylight bomber. Later on there were to be some close shaves: One night at the height of the blitz, I stood in the middle of Harley Street during a school vacation and watched a big department store on Oxford Street called D.H.Evans fiercely burning after a direct hit. Bombs also landed close enough to my uncle's house to shake the very foundations of the building, knocking down some basement shelves housing prized, and pickled, carcinoma specimens, which for some reason he had preserved— perhaps to display to students, perhaps simply as macabre souvenirs. My mother and I swept up the hideous-looking objects in their foul brine and threw them away. My uncle grieved over their loss as a gourmet might have mourned the loss of some precious wine.

I was taken to St. Paul's School, which had been evacuated from London to a Berkshire mansion, and was given the once-over by the highmaster, Walter Oakeshott. Probably because I was that exotic rarity, a bilingual schoolboy with a French *lycée* background, I was enrolled, and a year later I managed to win a scholarship there.

Paulines were housed in a variety of boardinghouses and private billets in and around a village called Crowthorne, whose only claim to fame was that it was also very near the Broadmoor 'criminal lunatic asylum.' Here were detained, so the formula went, 'during His Majesty's pleasure,' all those convicted murderers and murderesses whose lawyers had successfully pleaded that their clients had been insane at the time of their criminal acts, as well as many whom the prosecution had determined were really insane and 'unfit to plead.'

Many Paulines lived in the homes of the Broadmoor warders, of whom very few fitted the cliché image of tough guards. Indeed, my most vivid memory of school is of cycling through some fields while wild-eyed men with sharp farm implements walked in single file nearby, followed by a plumped, uniformed figure sweatily keeping up with them as he wheeled his cycle.

There were pathetic attempts at therapy: Every year St. Paul's School played Broadmoor (a mixed team composed of warders and inmates alike) at cricket, and on one occasion I found myself obliged by the school to attend a concert party staged by the patients, who had organized themselves into a troupe calling itself The Broadhumorites. There were comedians making the usual jokes about the blackout and rationing and some less usual jokes, involving arcane references to their own confinement, which drew roars of laughter from the carefully selected inmates allowed in the audience. A woman with only one hand (she herself had chopped the other off after killing her baby) quaveringly got through the rendition of a song entitled "Twas in a Little Spanish Town upon a Night like This,' with warders hovering in the wings, visibly alarmed at her condition. This was England. I was not all that surprised. Had not my French schoolmates and teachers repeatedly charged that all the English were mad?

I felt oddly out of place in my first year at St. Paul's, so much so that I attempted to enlist in De Gaulle's Free French forces. De Gaulle was short of men, but not that short. A kindly French captain urged me to remain at school and come back in three years—if the war lasted that long.

By that time I had developed other compelling interests: a passion for Empire and for India in particular. I read all I could about India, including most of Kipling. I was determined to visit places with such names as Ahmedabad, Waziristan, Quetta, and Chittagong and to walk the Grand Trunk Road.

It proved surprisingly easy.

For this was the time various branches of the armed forces were going after their quarry with all the thoroughness of talent scouts seeking out promising Harvard Business School graduates at the height of the sixties boom.

To attract recruits, the British War Office sent its most glamorous representatives to the public schools, which then were still the repositories of 'leadership' and 'officerlike qualities,' whatever these may have meant.

There were Fleet Air Arm pilots, ecstatically describing the good life aboard His Majesty's aircraft carriers; there were bemedaled tank commanders, vaunting the merits of their armored regiments; there were Royal Air Force heroes galore, some on crutches, all pushing their particular form of sport. Even Air Marshal Sir Arthur 'Bomber' Harris took time off from planning carpet-bomb attacks on cities to talk to us about the glamorous life of a bomber pilot, and last, but for me certainly not least, there were recruiting officers offering a career in the Indian Army.

The fact that such exciting prospects ended, actuarially speaking, with sudden death was never emphasized. So just as bemused and somewhat apprehensive housewives, reeling from irresistible sales talk, appose their signatures to documents entitling them to countless volumes of the *Encyclopaedia Britannica* in exchange for 124 easy monthly payments, so many British schoolboys, who should have known better, signed up as volunteers for a quick but exacting training course, an early officer's temporary commission, and sudden demise, all because of this highly sophisticated version of the eighteenth-century press-gang.

The alternative, in those heady, superpatriotic days of 1942–43, was too horrible to contemplate: compulsory service in the British coal mines as a 'Bevin Boy,' named after Ernest Bevin, the Labour leader, who had given his seal of approval to a scheme to recruit school leavers as miners as an alternative to military service. Increasingly, as the war progressed, the need for coal had begun to outweigh the need for cannon fodder. In the public schools no one volunteered for such a fate, though several of my friends, ignoring the special recruiters until too late, found themselves so drafted—among them Tony and Peter Shaffer, of *Sleuth* and *Equus* fame respectively, whose coal-miner experience, to hear them tell it later, made T.E. Lawrence's agony in the RAF seem like a lighthearted caper.

For me there was never any doubt. Even before an Indian Army brigadier with a sallow, malarial complexion called General Twining appeared at St. Paul's, I was deaf to the entreaties of any other services. I had chosen, though I didn't know it, one of the easiest courses to follow. Repeated Churchillian disasters in the East had led to the capture or annihilation of hundreds of thousands of Indian Army officers and men in Malaya and Burma. Huge efforts were being made to reconstitute the Indian Army with more than a million volunteer recruits; all this required large numbers of 'junior leaders,' and what better source than Britain's public schools?

I needed no prompting, and it was only much later that I discovered that Twining was not only a general but also a brand of Indian tea and that this probably explained the general's almost maniacal vested interest in the continuation of British rule in India. So, in my final year at St. Paul's, I became exclusively concerned with passing the three-day 'selection board' held in a requisitioned London hotel. It consisted of a series of not-very-demanding physical and intelligence tests, supplemented by a question-and-answer appearance before a panel of civilians, some of unmistakable Indian Army origin. The exception was a psychologist, who later made quite a name for himself as an expert sexologist.

The payoff came a few months later, in a buff envelope containing a travel warrant to Maidstone and announcing my incorporation into the Queen's Royal Regiment. On arrival, it became clear why the original selection board had been so lax. The real selection, we learned from the group of recruits just ahead of us, occurred at Maidstone barracks. It was a no-lose situation for General Twining. His volunteers either made the grade, and were shipped to India, or else they failed, and went on to swell the ranks of the Queen's Royal Regiment, becoming cannon fodder of another kind.

The courtesies of the earlier selection board were light-years away from our new, abject condition. All accounts of army life tend to be tediously similar, meaning little to those who have avoided this particular hurdle. Three vignettes will sum up those wretched months.

The first centers on our platoon sergeant, a failed boxer turned failed professional footballer with a cauliflower face and slicked-down black hair. His most intense pleasure consists of making his squad run endlessly, if possible in full battle order with packs and rifles. Running is something he has done all his life and does well. He takes particular pleasure in noting the stragglers and reporting them to his superiors.

His other habit is a compulsive tendency to tell rather bad dirty jokes. I can remember only one. An Irishman goes to the doctor because he doesn't want his wife to have any more children. The doctor tells him to use his head. The Irishman returns a few months later. 'That's fine,' he says. 'The wife's not pregnant. But don't it hurt your fuckin' ears?'

Paradoxically, it is the sergeant who proves to be the first dropout. One evening he collapses in the latrine, vomiting and pissing blood. We watch, silent, as he writhes on the sticky white tiles, soiling himself; then an ambulance comes and we never see him again.

The second is a frozen flashlight picture, taken in the kitchens of Maidstone barracks in the middle of the night. I have been detailed, while on guard duty, to fetch tea. As I wait, I watch, in the dim light, an endless line of cockroaches climb up a table leg, along the table's surface, and up a wall. Occasionally a cockroach breaks ranks and heads for a mound of butter, where it remains, trapped as on flypaper. The army cook, skimpily buttering slices of bread, flicks some of them to the ground, but some severed and mutilated cockroaches remain embedded in the butter, and presumably the missing parts have been spread on the bread. At all subsequent meals I attempt to verify that I am not eating cockroach spread.

The third has to do with our final grading, determining whether we leave for India or remain ingloriously in England as privates or, worse still, go through the entire course again. There are some relatively straightforward tests and an Urdu exam—for we have been spending two hours a day learning Urdu from an elderly Indian Army officer, specially brought out of retirement and wearing the insignia of a long-defunct cavalry regiment, the Deccan Horse. He uses a dog-eared primer with simple sentences and stories that bear little relevance to the war and seem designed for kindergarten infants. The first story in the book begins, '*Ek rajah tha. . . .*' ('There was once a maharaja. . . .') Years later, making a TV documentary film on India for Swiss television, I film an open-air classroom in a northern Indian village, and the eight-year-olds intone the same sentence. Things change slowly in the East. . . .

I do well in the Urdu exam, adequately in the other tests, including a 'trick' test to appraise our combativity. We are summoned, one by one, before an instructor and asked what we would do if while leading a patrol, we were to come across a couple of wounded enemy soldiers. The question is meant to discover whether we would allow humanitarian considerations to interfere with the task at hand. 'I think I'd shoot them, sir,' I reply with grotesque, cheerful self-confidence.

'Are you sure?' Of course, I'm not sure, but it's only a game, and the object of my game is to get out of Maidstone barracks, out of the cold and the dirt and exhaustion.

I know I have passed when General Twining makes his final, ceremonial appearance. He shakes me by the hand. 'Good show,' he says. 'Kill a few Japs for me, won't you, dear boy?'

We return briefly to the London hotel where the selection board occurred. One is going on as we arrive, and we feel immensely superior to these amazingly puny-looking schoolboys. One of them sidles up to me and asks, 'What's it really like?'

'Cockroaches for breakfast,' I tell him.

There followed a brief limbo existence. We were relatively free, living four to a room in what, after Maidstone, appeared to us to be the ultimate in luxury, but during the day we were on call, ready for departure.

I spent some time at Marylebone Public Library across the road, and one evening, on my own, I went to see Ralph Richardson in *Peer Gynt*, a performance, and a production, so staggering that it has been the yardstick for all future comparisons. On leaving the theater, I was for the first and probably last time in my life propositioned by a man. 'Come and have a drink,' he said.

'Where do you suggest?' I asked.

'There's a YMCA round the corner, and afterward we

could go to my place.' He was small, with glistening eyes, and even in my extreme innocence I sensed his sad lust. I began walking away from him fast. He ran after me. 'What's the matter?' he said. 'Aren't you interested in queerness?'

Another evening, returning from a visit to my family, I witnessed a strange drunken ballet in a crowded underground train. Three soldiers in battle dress and two ATS girls, the women army auxiliaries, sat in a stench of spilled beer, all unmistakably drunk. One of the ATS girls was enormous. A soldier suddenly grabbed her and started bouncing her between the two rows of seats facing each other. As she was thrown back and forth from one soldier to another, her fat thighs shaking, her skirt hiked up to show outsize khaki underwear, the group sang, 'You can *have* her, I don't *want* her, she's too fat for *me*!' The rest of the crowded train looked on with awkward tolerance. They were still at it when I left.

The following morning, in the anticlimactic, muddled flurry which, I later discovered, characterizes all troop movements, we loaded ourselves and our belongings on trucks, then onto a train at Liverpool Street Station, and finally, eight hours later, onto a huge, battered, steam-erupting converted passenger liner called the *Empire Pride* conveniently tethered to the railside docks in Liverpool itself.

As officer cadets ('the lowest form of animal life') we were given the worst quarters on board, for it was assumed that we at least were unlikely to complain. Home now was a dark row of tables on E Deck, with hammocks for most of us and tiered bunks for the privileged few. Crowding us into E Deck with our packs and kit bags was like squeezing sixteen students into a Volkswagen. Apparently it couldn't be done. In order to put up hammocks to sleep in, it was necessary to proceed one by one and row by row, for once they were up, it was impossible to move between them. There was just no space. On either side of me at night, I felt the sausagelike shapes of my two neighbors at my hips. In heavy weather, which duly came, the rhythmic creaking and groaning of the hammock hooks and straining woodwork were deafening.

The full horror of our new fate—the trip was to last a full month—struck home within minutes of boarding. From the upper decks, the Liver bird statue on Liverpool's tallest building, looking like a bedraggled refugee from Notre-Dame Cathedral, mocked us through the fog and icy rain.

We remained confined aboard, but motionless, for three days as the *Empire Pride* took on stores, crated vehicles and troops, Red Cross nurses and mysterious civilians. It was a singularly class-ridden ship. On the upper decks, Goanese stewards tended to the needs of officers and nurses in luxurious cabins. There was a dining room shimmering with starched tablecloths and silverware. These areas were theoretically out of bounds, and we ate our meals in our mess deck out of foul containers. There were lines all day before six washbasins (one for 100 men), and the hot salt-water showers functioned only a few hours daily. After the first week there was no salt-water soap.

It was not, for other reasons, a happy ship. The officer commanding troops was not on speaking terms with the ship's captain, a remote figure (occasionally seen wearing a beret) with an alcoholic's mottled complexion. As we froze (later we were to boil) at interminable boat drills, I noticed a captain in the uniform of the Free French forces. Eventually, since we stood side by side at boat drill, we began exchanging banalities. He was on his way to Calcutta and eventually to Indochina, he told me, though he didn't know what kind of reception a Gaullist captain was likely to receive at the hands of the Vichy French in Saigon—to say nothing of the Japanese. 'My chances of survival,' he said with a shy smile, 'are rather slim.' His name was Pierre Messmer, and when I next met him, he was the French prime minister, but he still had the same stiff, shy, soldierly bearing and clipped tones that made him an ideal butt of smart Parisian jokes.

At our daily boat drills we agreed that conditions were deplorable. 'You're all right,' I told him. 'You should see where we live.'

Occasionally some upper-deck passengers, including nurses, would come and gawk at our Brueghel-like surroundings. We drove them away with lewd insults. On the deck above was a battalion of Lowland Scots, of simian appearance, under-sized but immensely tough, the generation of the Great Depression. Theirs was a real hellhole, too, but rumor had it that no ship's officer dared enter it and that any other ranks straying in by mistake or out of curiosity were beaten up, robbed, and raped. Halfway through our long voyage, a young lieutenant made the mistake of 'inspecting' their living quarters during their evening meal. 'Any complaints?' he asked, and was immediately knocked senseless and covered with the remains of beef stew. The insurrection had far-reaching consequences. On arrival in Bombay, the Scots were marched away under guard. Most of them were to be posted straight to units in the thick of the fighting in Burma. Few survived.

The first ten days our convoy circled Spain in an unremitting storm. The entire ship stank of vomit and disinfectant. The latrines and washbasins became clogged, the air was unbreathable, but it was too cold, and too wet, to stay in the open air for long. Then, gradually, it became warmer and calmer. As we crossed the Strait of Gibraltar, we cheered loudly. The worst seemed over.

This, it turned out, was not the case. There was more to look at: flying fish; immobilized French Navy ships at the entrance to the Suez Canal (they had refused to take sides during the war and were being held under guard, the crews surly, defiant, and ostentatiously hanging civilian wash out on their expensive guns); boys exposing themselves on either side of the Canal and making obscene gestures. Small boats defied the MPs to come close, and there was much haggling over fresh fruit and dates, most of them crawling with weevils.

We were even promised a picnic. It turned out to be another of those exhausting, aimless marches, with rifles and full packs, along the deserted Egyptian shore. We took no food with us, assured that a mobile army canteen would meet us somewhere along the road. It never materialized. Back on board, as we tried to sweep our mess deck clean of accumulated sand, we were told that our day's rations had been taken ashore for our picnic and that there was no food for us on board that day.

This was the stuff mutinies are made of. There was no doubt in my mind then, nor is there any now, that somehow those rations had found their way onto the Alexandria black market, thanks to an unscrupulous crew and their necessary army accomplices. My faith in Empire was shaken. That such things could happen in other people's armies was a source of satisfaction. But that they should also occur in the British Army was unbelievable, like catching a headmaster cheating. My naïve anger was a source of considerable merriment, not among fellow officer cadets, who shared my bewilderment, but among the rest of the troops on board, who heard of our plight and laughed. To them what had happened only confirmed the Army's crooked ways. Nor was there any indignation, only admiration for those who had perpetrated this latest outrage.

I decided to complain, formally, through the proper channels. I made an appearance before the elderly colonel, whose fate it was, after God knows what appalling blunder or act of cowardice which had removed him from a more active command, to travel backward and forward on the *Empire Pride* with his tired herds. He was evasive, and I quickly realized that this filching of rations for a nonexistent picnic was an event that occurred regularly near Alexandria, like a toll levied as one passed 'go.' The thought even occurred to me that the colonel himself might

16

be involved. His promise to hold a court of inquiry (which was still meeting when we left the ship at Bombay) was the practiced response I was to recognize later on in my travels as a reporter; it was the posture of the bureaucrat establishing his first line of defense, secure in the knowledge that this time around, the natives could be fooled.

My Platonic dream of British India crumbled still further when, after agonizingly airless days in the Indian Ocean, we finally arrived at Bombay. The coast looked impressive, and there was the Gateway to India arch just as I had imagined it. All of a sudden the ship was full of coolies, bone-thin, in faded blues and pinks. Another squad of ragged civilians, working with maniacal haste, began hammering corrugated iron sheets flat with frenzied hammer blows. To what purpose? I never did find out.

But the ladies in flowered print dresses serving us tea and biscuits as we stepped off the ship could have been doing so in Tonbridge or Harrogate. Only Bombay's railway station, that superb example of Indian nineteenth-century Gothic, failed to disappoint me. For the rest of it, Bombay was more like a big English town than I had imagined, but with brown people, no blackout, and curiously old-fashioned billboards advertising Indian watches, soap, and radios.

Once more we were settled into a train, this time a wooden third-class coal-fired museum relic. It slowly made its way through appalling slums, so slowly that hawkers jumped on and off, their wares pathetic flick knives and lighters made out of scrap metal. Fearing an assault on the train, one hysterical cadet loosed off a round from his rifle. He was threatened with an immediate return trip to England.

Apart from the welcome heat and the discomfort of the slippery wooden benches, I have a vivid recollection of one stop, one early Indian morning pungent with woodsmoke and burning dungcakes. Out of nowhere some Indian peasant girls crawled between the couplings to gather coal droppings from the tracks. They were the first Indian girls I had seen at close quarters. Their saris were grimy, but their midriffs were bare and their light-brown skins pleasing. One was outstandingly beautiful: a tall, slim girl with enormous eyes. She was graceful in her movements as she grubbed for pieces of coal, her buttocks taut, her long fingers reaching out under the wheels.

Suddenly on the scene appeared an old man, the caricatural villain of Indian movies, crafty and white-bearded, with broken, betel-stained red teeth. With his long stick, he began flogging the girls, hitting them hard on the back and buttocks as they scavenged on their knees. There seemed to be no purpose in his savagery. Was he intent on driving them away or on getting them to increase their efforts? We watched passively as he swung his stave again and again; we heard the thud of the blows followed by the girls' breathless whimpering.

The tall girl he spared. A wife? A slave-concubine favorite? Not a daughter, for as she worked, he bent and patted her rump in an unequivocal gesture of possession, and she turned, expressionless but submissive, and nuzzled against him as he ran his hands over her body, slipping one hand between her legs, all the while looking up at us with wild, brazen eyes.

Then he shouted something, and the strange party broke up. The girls scampered down the culvert, put their baskets on their heads, and began walking away from the train. From time to time the old man swung at them with his stick, hitting them cruelly, and even from far away we continued to hear his hoarse, angry cries. The girls clung to their baskets with both hands in order not to stumble. Alone, the tall girl was allowed to walk behind him. The scene, which lasted only a few minutes, provided us with endless speculation. It has remained, in various forms, a recurring erotic dream.

Bangalore was another world. After our sordid travels,

the Officers' Training School appeared indescribably sybaritic and a reminder that the British Raj still offered its 'sahibs' a privileged life. Gnomelike grinning bearers washed, pressed, and starched our uniforms. The mess was huge, airy, and cheerful. We were almost as pampered as in the days of young Winston Churchill, who used to be shaved in bed, while still asleep, by an acrobatic barber.

Compulsory sports in the afternoon included horse riding in the barracks of the Mysore Lancers, a state force regiment (i.e., a locally raised militia party paid for by the Maharaja of Mysore) whose duties were exclusively ceremonial. We learned the old-fashioned Indian Cavalry way, and for those who showed promise there was even the opportunity to learn to play polo on tough little ponies owned by the Mysore Lancers, to practice the art of tent pegging and even pig sticking. I was not gifted for polo. Communication with our instructors was a little difficult since they spoke only Malealum, a rich, complicated southern language utterly different from the Urdu we were learning.

The course itself, though moderately taxing, was scarcely the ordeal that Maidstone had been. The main weeding-out process had occurred before our departure from England. For ambitious overachievers, the main goal now was to obtain sufficiently high grades to get the posting of one's choice. Inevitably, the Gurkhas were the most coveted, with the Sikhs and Pathan regiments a close second. Lower grades led to postings to the less glorious Indian Army Service Corps (supplies and transport), and it was still possible to flunk the course altogether. In this case unsuccessful ex-officer cadets were posted as privates to British regiments already in India.

Rightly or wrongly, it was also assumed that low marks led to postings to more recently raised (and lower-caste) regiments composed of the so-called scheduled classes, otherwise known as untouchables. And officer cadets with family connections to Indian Army regiments were virtually guaranteed a commission in the 'family' regiment, often returning to regimental centers in towns they had been born in. In short, the system defied logic, was clumsy, cumbersome, and peculiarly English. Somehow it seemed to work.

Halfway through the course I felt I was doomed to get a bad posting after losing my way during a night exercise. I compounded my ignominy on this occasion by failing to stop my truck, on the way home, to give a lift to one of our instructors, who had waited all night for us to report to him in some remote spot and whose motorcycle had broken down. I simply hadn't seen him. Realizing I was in trouble, I determined to do better, and my next exercise, a river crossing of some complexity, was successful. My language teacher, Mr. Fitrat (inevitably we called him Footrot), gave me top marks.

My gradual improvement from my earlier low point in the course enabled me not only to survive but to get the regiment of my choice: the Royal Garhwal Rifles.

This was perhaps the most prestigious of all Indian Army infantry regiments. During the First World War its members had won more Victoria Crosses than any other Indian regiment. The Garhwalis, from the northernmost province of India bordering on Tibet and Nepal, shared some of the ethnic features of the Gurkhas and wore, like them, the sharp, curved, black-holstered kukri knives. Garhwal and Nepal had been locked in wars for centuries before British rule, and some Garhwali names had distinct Nepali overtones. But the Garhwalis were, it was believed, quicker to learn than the Gurkhas, more adaptable, in a word more intelligent. I realize now that we spoke of Gurkhas, of Sikhs, of Pathans, of Jats, of Punjabi Moslems like so many racehorses, with exclusively physical characteristics. We generalized from what little we knew, or gossip we had heard, stressing their physical qualities to the exclusion of their other characteristics.

The Garhwalis' environment ensured that all those

20

selected from the large pool of available volunteers (for joining the Army was also an escape from the direst form of poverty) were formidably tough specimens.

At that time Garhwal was still considered by the British government in India as a form of native reservation, to be shielded from contact with the outside world at all costs. There were few roads, and no good ones. It was common for Garhwalis, mostly small hill farmers with flocks of mountain goats, to walk from 12,000-feet to 6,000-feet levels several times in the course of a single day. As a result, they had endurance and staying power beyond belief and actually preferred moving over mountainous countryside to flat surfaces, though they also moved easily through thick scrub and jungle, which were to be found at the bottom of those steamy narrow valleys in their native habitat.

They were small, with short torsos, incredibly sturdy legs, shaved heads with a small single lock of hair at the back, and a less marked Asian appearance than the Gurkhas, whom they otherwise resembled physically.

There were, however, major differences between them. The Garhwali riflemen were moodier than the Gurkhas, more difficult to handle, more introspective. But they made superb soldiers, being cheerful, loyal, and on the whole indifferent to the taboos of the Hindu religion, whose festivals they observed with an immense amount of rum drinking, but whose other injunctions they conveniently ignored. Throughout the war Garhwalis ate bully beef (when available) and accepted their officers' white lie that it was mutton, even when labels on huge cans showed a species of horned animal that could by no stretch of the imagination have been a lamb.

Their culinary habits were indeed primitive. As a new arrival I was soon invited to an informal drinking party by the Garhwali officers (a class apart, and existing only within the Indian Army, of commissioned officers in an intermediary limbo between officers and NCOs; elsewhere

21

they are known as VCOs, or viceroy's commissioned officers, and the term exists to this day), and I gagged on one of the small dishes I was supposed to eat. It was raw goat, cut up into bite-sized chunks in a potpourri of meat, fat, offal, and intestine, all marinated in chillis so powerful that the meat had to some extent been cooked as a result. Later I found it almost palatable and was about to develop a taste for it—until I actually watched it being prepared. Later on, when in Sumatra I had bartered some bottles of rum against some splendid Australian Merino sheep, I was criticized by my company cook for their poor quality. '*Huzoor* [Lord],' he said, 'these animals not good. Too much meat, too much fat. Not enough gristle.'

The one physical weakness of this patient and enduring mountain people, who made excellent scouts and enjoyed an instinctive sense of direction (which certainly palliated my own weaknesses) and extraordinary eyesight, was a propensity to tuberculosis. This was really a British crime, a consequence of neglect owing to nonexistent public-health budgets in such remote parts of India. During my stay in the regiment at least two people I knew well—one Garhwali officer and a senior NCO—died of tuberculosis. Subadar Ram Singh was our battalion's motor-transport officer, a tough little Mr. Fixit with fingernails perpetually black from poking into the entrails of fully amortized trucks. He went on leave, returned ill, and died of galloping TB six weeks later. We were in Sumatra at the time, and I suppose I helped him die. He wouldn't eat, and I brought him a bottle of rum at the field hospital where he was. We drank most of it at one sitting, and Ram Singh, who knew he was going to die and was no drunkard, said, 'This will help me go feeling good.' He worried about his trucks and who would maintain them after he was gone, but though he wasn't in any sense a practicing Hindu, he believed in reincarnation and was quietly confident that he would be reborn in an improved setting. After his death we incinerated him in the orthodox Hindu fashion: His body was placed between logs smeared with ghee (clarified butter) and incense and set fire to. His skull exploded with a small plop.

Before entering the regiment, most Garhwalis were completely illiterate, and indeed, the recruiting officers distrusted the 'plains' Garhwalis, who could read and write and were familiar with the big cities, rejecting them when possible on often flimsy health grounds. At one time, in my own infantry company, there were twin brothers whose only known language, before they joined up, was Tibetan. They said they came from the Indian side of the Tibetan border, but I learned later that they were indeed Tibetans from across the border and had sold their goat flocks to take the long trek to volunteer. I asked one of them once why he had done so. 'We wanted to see the world,' he answered. 'Also my brother and I had girl trouble.' In contrast, one of our best NCOs was a former Patna taxi driver, and another excellent soldier in my company had been a Calcutta hotel groom.

With no roads to speak of, it was usual for Garhwalis from the remoter mountain areas to walk for as many as fifteen days from the regimental center in Lansdowne to their village. Leave was always a serious affair, and a lengthy one; in some cases, travel time—all officially worked out on the basis of so many miles per day—exceeded leave time.

It was to Lansdowne that I went on being commissioned. The train stopped (and still does) at a small town called Kotdwara. From there a crazy mountain road led to Lansdowne, more than 6,000 feet above sea level. Wildly suicidal bus drivers, honking furiously all the way, could cover the distance in just over an hour. Apart from the ravines and the loose gravel and rockfalls, herds of wild monkeys provided another form of hazard. Beyond Lansdowne were no roads to speak of at all.

The regimental center had literally been carved out of the mountainside. The only flat surface was a huge parade and sports ground. There was a small village, with shops kept by retired soldiers, some bungalows, rows of barracks, and an officers' mess with a spectacular view of the Himalayas, whose snowcaps were seemingly near enough to touch. I returned to Lansdowne nearly twenty years later, and it had scarcely changed, except for the introduction of electric light. We used gas-pressure lanterns.

For all the turmoil of the war, the basic instruction of Garhwali recruits seemed timeless—and indeed, it hadn't changed much on a recent visit. Drill, physical education, weapon maintenance, elementary tactics, and reading and writing classes took up most of the recruits' time. There were football and basketball games every day. And during my stay, apart from serving on two courts of inquiry (a theft of ammunition and a recruit who hanged himself), I had little to do and was extremely impatient to get to an active battalion in operations. 'You're here for us to have a look at you,' said a major with a limp. 'Don't worry about the war ending. There'll be lots to do.'

There was. Beneath the surface and the unchanged daily routine, a whole new set of problems loomed. With the war almost over, the inevitable question of India's independence was posed in a way no government could avoid, and indeed, one of the first decisions of the Attlee government after the war was to state that the principle of full independence was agreed. Independence affected the Regular British officers in the Indian Army far more than myself, who was there in any case on temporary sufferance. It also posed huge problems for those regiments where 'Indianization' had lagged behind. The Garhwalis had a reasonable record; in Lansdowne half the officers were Indian, and when I joined the 1st Battalion, the proportion of Indian to British officers was roughly the same.

But by far the biggest and most immediate problem was what to do with the returning members of the so-called Indian National Army once the war was over. These were prisoners of war recruited out of Japanese and German POW camps by the Indian nationalist firebrand Subhas Chandra Bose, who was to die in a plane crash somewhere in Burma in the closing stages of the war. Bose had split with the Congress party nationalists such as Nehru over the issue of violence. He believed that open war should be waged against the British imperialists, and in POW camps he found hundreds of thousands of potential recruits. He also represented an authoritarian, quasi-fascist type of nationalism, abhorrent to Nehru. It was innately conservative and based on the support of the wealthy. Finally, he was a spellbinding orator and a skilled propagandist, and he succeeded in building up an army of tens of thousands, nearly all of them Indian Army prisoners of war, to fight alongside the Germans and the Japanese. The INA members had been subject to intense propaganda of a highly original kind. Psychological warfare was still in its infancy, but Subhas Chandra Bose was probably one of the first revolutionary leaders to invent a new form of warfare, one involving a 'battle for hearts and minds.'

Bose's operation was in essence a simple one: He attempted to persuade POWs that they were the unconscious victims of imperialism and that Japan, which had pledged Indian independence to Bose, should be assisted in driving out the colonial invaders and putting an end to 'the oppressive British yoke.'

It was pretty crude stuff, but effective. In former times British Indian Army officers had simply assumed that their own patriotic values were those of the men they led. They discovered, with Bose, that this was not so. As far as the Gurkhas were concerned, it was not patriotism that motivated them, but personal loyalty and the implementation of a contract, for—technically speaking at least—Gurkhas were mercenaries and Nepal was a strictly neutral country.

As far as non-British Indian Army officers and men who were not Gurkhas were concerned, the situation was a

25

complex one. Many of the more educated servicemen had been nationalists at school or the university and had joined the Army for a mixed bag of reasons, including social promotion or even ambition of a far-seeing kind. Most of them realized that the INA was a trap. Some heroically resisted brutal attempts to compel them to join. And most Indian Army officers I have kept in touch with have considerable contempt for those who did join Bose.

There were also some soldiers whose understanding of the political implications of the INA were hazy. One Gurkha was repatriated after the war from Europe proudly wearing both the British Military Medal and the German Iron Cross. Both were awarded for bravery in knocking out tanks. The side he happened to be on at the time proved of relative unimportance.

There were also cases of career Indian Army officers who had committed themselves to Bose's INA. Their postwar trial ended in acquittal, and their prestigious defense lawyers included Nehru himself. But Nehru's own later efforts to rehabilitate these ex-officers and reintegrate them in the Indian Army failed because of the immediate outcry that was raised from within the Indian Army itself. Some of those who did join the INA after their capture by the Japanese turned out to have had almost as bad a time as collaborators of the Japanese as they would have had as their prisoners.

For after their initial propaganda had worn off and as the supply difficulties of the Japanese forces began, the INA was left to fend for itself, with virtually no logistical support—which, by any means, was woefully inadequate for the Japanese themselves as the war proceeded. Toward the end of the war the Japanese in Burma were in any case desperately short of everything except sheer animal courage. And many INA volunteers, realizing they were on the losing side, simply sat tight, waiting to surrender, and where possible got rid of their insignia.

When my battalion liberated Rangoon in May 1945, it

was met at the dockside by a milling crowd of happy people, Burmese and Indian, and some of them were INA. For all their demoralization, their lot was enviable compared to that of the British and Indian Army prisoners kept in another town in an improvised POW camp, under the guard of the Kempitai, the dreaded Japanese special military police. One Garhwali rifleman was found there, dying. A recent prisoner, he had tried to escape, and the Kempitai had simply broken his leg at the knee. Other prisoners were almost as weak and as thin as Belsen inmates. Many Kempitai were later tried for war crimes, but some of them never got back to Japan. There was some expeditive justice—with kukris—while the officers looked the other way, during those last few days of the war. There was also some last-minute carnage as fleeing Japanese, trying to escape by sampan and any kind of small boat, were blown away by artillery fire and navy guns as they desperately tried, in the thousands, to paddle away.

To everyone's surprise, a large number of Garhwalis, it turned out, had enlisted in the INA. Two of the regiment's best battalions had been captured in Malaya at the fall of Singapore in 1942, and the majority of the prisoners had become INA men. It was a private shame to many in the Lansdowne regimental center. It was also incomprehensible to them. In the immediate postwar months a reception center classified returning POWs as 'white,' 'gray,' and 'black.' The black category had been intensely politicized and actually fought side by side with the Japanese, with considerable effectiveness.

What this should have told the British government in India was that 'politicization' of the Indian Army had not, after all, been avoided and that the stalwart Sikh and Punjabi farmers, Garhwali goatherds, and Pathan tribesmen, who—it was commonly assumed—had nothing but contempt for urban politicians and for the Congress party's independence drive, were in fact much more sensitive to the political situation than was commonly believed. This was to become tragically clear at the time of partition, two years later. Perhaps the lesson was learned, up to a point, for independence for India, after 1945, was no longer in doubt. The question was not when, it was how?

All my real wars have taken place in peacetime. My first, in Sumatra, was the zaniest of all.

Indian Army units converged on Indonesia (then the Dutch East Indies colony) to disarm the Japanese there at the very end of the war, after the first atomic bomb explosion on August 6, 1945. Japanese troops in Indonesia were not the half-starved, desperate fighters they had been in Burma. Throughout the war elite Japanese troops, superbly equipped and extremely well fed, had remained in Indonesia not because the population needed subduing (acts of overt resistance were few, and even Sukarno's was verbal) but simply because there was no Japanese shipping left, after the Allied command of the sea was complete, to take them anywhere. So they lived off the rich, fertile land, alternately cajoled and terrorized the Indonesians, and when the time came to obey the emperor's command to surrender, they did so with dignity.

Those they surrendered to were numerically so grotesquely inferior to them that had the Japanese decided to fight it out, we all would have been massacred. Fortunately nothing of the sort happened. Huge stacks of ceremonial swords piled up on their barrack squares. Japanese colonels with slight knowledge of English became interpreters for the 'liberation forces.' Japanese troops, still formidable-looking without their arms, were pressed into service as dockers, drivers, and hospital orderlies. One unit even found itself assigned a Japanese doctor in the field, and on at least one occasion, deplored and hushed up at Mountbatten's express command, Japanese artillery went into action alongside Indian Army troops against the Indonesian 'rebels.'

Only the Kempitai, whose atrocities had been committed mainly on Dutch and Eurasian settlers, were arrested and held in solitary confinement. They would bow ceremonially from the waist whenever a British officer passed their cells. The Japanese accepted their new status with seeming equanimity, and even the repatriation delays (some were to spend almost a year in Indonesia before going home) didn't faze them.

To say the Dutch were pleased to see us is a wild understatement. They, and the Eurasian community, which had identified itself with the colonizers, literally threw themselves at our necks. Things had been horribly tough for them; to the original humiliation of a speedy capitulation (which caused the Dutch in Indonesia to lose all face with the 'natives') were added shortages of food and medicine and completely severed contacts with home.

Some Dutch settlers and their families had been put in camps that were little better than Nazi concentration camps, but the 'good life,' as it had been lived in the balmy days of prewar colonization, was so compelling a memory that many Dutch settlers would have stayed on after the war had the Indonesian nationalists not made it clear that those days were over for good and that there was no place for old-style settlers anymore.

In the few months following the Japanese surrender, life for a young Indian Army officer was paradise: There were beach parties, swimming parties, dances. I met a Eurasian girl of singular beauty whose father's occupation record had been ambiguous, to say the least. He had worked with the Japanese, using his influence with them to pay off local scores. He was jailed by the British military authorities. For her safety, she decided to move in with me. She was delighted to be rid of her father, who, in the days of the Japanese occupation, would follow her to the beach and lash out at any Indonesian who dared look at her too closely. Later she married a young Dutch officer and moved with him to Eindhoven. I imagine a staid, by now plump Dutch housewife with a trace of Oriental blood in her almond eyes and soft, uniformly sunburned skin, a Philips executive for a husband, and a brood of children.

The delights of Sumatra were not confined to officers. But, as a wit noted one day, 'it was always VD Day in Sumatra.'

There was a shortage of penicillin, and treatment for even mild cases of gonorrhea was long and painful—and reduced the battalion's effectiveness considerably. Our Bengali medical officer, a small shy man with a stammer, was ordered to lecture the troops on its perils. Since he barely spoke Hindi to begin with and since he insisted on lecturing the Garhwalis as if they were first-year medical students, the talk was scarcely a success, punctuated as it was by crude catcalls in Garhwali dialect from the back of the audience. At one stage, to make a point about the virtues of prophylaxis, he unwrapped a condom and inserted it on his middle finger, to show how use of contraceptives cut back almost all infection risk.

Alas, our battalion VD rate, no higher than others, but no lower either, continued to be the despair of our commanding officer, 'Jock' Maclean, and we soon discovered why. Having interpreted the little doctor's instructions literally, Garhwalis, before actual penetration, were pausing to slip their army-issue contraceptives over their middle fingers. It was only after Maclean had threatened to inform next of kin and cut local pay and allowances for all the time spent in treatment that the rate dipped a little.

I had suggested setting up a medically controlled army brothel in our compound, both to cut down sickness and to swell our canteen and battalion funds. The idea was turned down, not solely on moral grounds. Maclean had growled that 'we were here to soldier, not to pimp.' A realistic judge of men, he added that this was the kind of project everyone would want to have a hand in. 'I don't want all my officers to spend their time recruiting suitable candidates,' he said.

In this immediate postwar period the economics of Sumatra were a classic illustration of Gresham's law [about bad money driving out good]. There were so many currencies that many were unidentifiable. Prewar Dutch East Indies guilders, Japanese yen, Japanese-occupation guilders, and, finally, some Allied postwar 'mad money,' printed, by the looks of it, on a home press in the back streets of Calcutta, all circulated simultaneously, with rates varying from day to day.

In addition, there were pounds, rupees, dollars, gold Maria Theresa talers, Chinese paper money of incredibly high denominations but of almost no value, and occasional notes from Malaya, Thailand, and even Australia. To this hotchpotch of existing currencies I was responsible, in a very small way, for adding yet another variety: Monopoly money.

It happened this way: The Indonesian nationalists, when they were sure that the postwar Dutch government was not prepared to grant them immediate independence and that the British government was not going to help, either, quickly took the offensive. This consisted not just in a guerrilla war on us Indian Army 'occupying forces' but also in an attempt to enforce a food-supply embargo by threatening to kill any farmer caught selling fresh vegetables or rice to Indian Army units.

The embargo was variously obeyed and enforced. In my capacity as mess secretary (a burden I had been made to assume in addition to my other duties as battalion intelligence officer, largely because I was the junior officer around) I was under constant pressure to acquire as much fresh food as possible. It wasn't always easy. Much of the time I spent haggling with Chinese shopkeepers in back rooms of dingy shops. In exchange for canteen rum, whiskey, and gin (for supplies of alcohol at duty-free prices were again available in small quantities, and Garhwali troops were entitled to a daily rum ration) I would acquire sacks of fresh fish and tomatoes, and chillis, onions, and dozens of squawking live chickens.

But I had to cast far and wide for fresh supplies, as pressure on the shopkeepers increased. One such foray took me to a small island off the Sumatran west coast, where there was practically no nationalist agitation to speak of. I went in a small craft manned by the Royal Navy and realized too late the possibilities of a bonanza. For here was fresh food in quantity, but I had nothing to offer in return. The islanders rejected my Japanese-occupation guilders, and I could not persuade the crew to part with any of their precious liquor supplies. Suddenly, I had a brainwave. Promising to replace a Monopoly set, I bought it off the Royal Navy. I then explained to the island headman that I could let him have some of the new currency that was being introduced elsewhere in Indonesia, but that—since the release date of the currency was to come only in a few days' time—he was not to mention this to anyone.

The Monopoly money looked a good deal more genuine than anything he had seen during the Japanese occupation, and he parted with a sizable amount of chickens and vegetables in exchange for some Monopoly bills. A few days later I got another officer to go back to the island, with my remaining stock of Monopoly money, and he made more important purchases. The fact that different people would brandish Monopoly money and handle it as though it were the real thing put the islanders' suspicions to rest. There is a happy ending to the story: Six months later, when an acquaintance went back to the island, the Monopoly money was in circulation there and had completely driven out not only the plummeting Japanese-occupation guilder but the Japanese yen as well.

My forays for food were also the occasion for trips into the interior. Relying on somewhat faulty local intelligence, I would drive to a village which I had been told was secure to negotiate the purchase of food. I removed my army insignia, and only my batman, with a concealed Sten gun, came with me. In this fashion we kept not only the officers' mess but also the battalion reasonably fed. But the risks were real. The Indonesian nationalists eventually heard of my free-lance expeditions, and their game was to wait until I had made my deal with the village and was loaded down with food and then to ambush me. This happened on several occasions. After loading up my jeep, I would drive like hell, usually taking a different road from the one expected of me. Once my windshield was smashed by a bullet, and on another occasion small Japanese grenades bounced off the jeep but failed to explode. On both occasions my batman, sprawled over sacks of onions and chillis, failed to react. Back in the comparative safety of open country, I turned on him in fury.

'Why didn't you open fire? We were nearly killed.'

'And lose these?' he replied, holding up the trussed chickens he was clinging to with both hands.

The propensity of the Indonesian nationalists' arms and grenades to misfire was our most effective secret weapon. The town of Padang, where we were based, was patrolled all night long, but various outposts and bunkers on the town's perimeter, including the airport and several bridges, were guarded by permanent detachments of Garhwalis. Nightly they were deluged by grenades, very few of which exploded, however. It became a ritual. In one of my daily intelligence 'situation reports' to brigade headquarters I no longer quoted figures but wrote instead, 'An average number of grenades was thrown during the night.' No one apparently read these reports, for I received no rebuke.

Every morning I would make my rounds, collect the unexploded grenades, and either explode them, preferably with an expert firing the fuses for me, or dump them in a river, whence, I suspect, the nationalists would rescue them, dry them out, and recycle them. In retrospect my handling of these grenades was foolhardy and irresponsible. I simply couldn't believe they represented a real threat.

Our Sumatra period also had its darker side. One

33

operation, mounted against an Indonesian 'rebel' headquarters, led to some unexpected casualties. During this battle I found myself squatting in a jungle clearing with a platoon of Garhwalis. On the other side of the bushes I could hear the crackle of radio sets and the colonel talking to the adjutant. Some firing was going on, some of it quite close by. I eavesdropped. It seemed that a patrol was needed to spy out the land to find out whether a neighboring hill was occupied by some rebels or not. If not, it was an ideal vantage point from which to rain down mortar shells on the enemy. I heard the colonel say, 'I can't afford to lose an experienced officer. I'll have to send that young fucker Behr.'

While hostilities were still in the intermittent stage, two British sailors and two Red Cross nurses went for a beach picnic in a jeep—and never returned. A grenade—which did go off—was thrown into another jeep in the center of the town, killing four officers of another Indian Army battalion. Dutch settlers were kidnaped, held for ransom, and murdered. We freed a group of Dutch hostages from a guerrilla-held concentration camp in the middle of the jungle. As time went on, there was increasing guerrilla activity around the town perimeter, and the road from Padang to the capital, Medan, on the other side of the island, became virtually impassable as our joke war escalated.

I didn't knowingly kill anyone until the carnage of partition, and my activities, while I was intelligence officer, were at one remove from the firing line. But I had my share of nausea after the sailors' disappearance. The Garhwalis combed the area, and finally, the putrefied bodies and their jeep were dug up, not far from where the murders had taken place. There followed a series of reprisals—burned villages, deportations, arrests, and even summary executions—which would have branded us as war criminals had any publicity been forth-coming. What our remote divisional command wanted to know was why the sailors

34

and their girlfriends had been killed. They had been unarmed. The jeep had not even been stolen. The nearest village had no record of nationalist activity. One witness, who denied taking part in the actual murder, said that there had been nothing political in it. The villagers, he said, had been shocked at the spectacle of two naked couples making love in broad daylight and had hacked them to death with their knives.

Was there in fact some obscure taboo that they had violated? Prudishness was not a marked Indonesian characteristic, but open-air sex may well have been a repugnant concept. Certainly nakedness was not; the area was full of Batak tribespeople, occasional cannibals still, who habitually wore no clothes at all. But then they never copulated in public either.

It would have required a skilled anthropologist to tell us. Unfortunately our only expert on local customs was of no use whatever in this case. He was the harbormaster, a former career officer in the Dutch Navy, a man of caricatural Dutchness, who had lived most of his life in Sumatra. Married to an Indonesian and surrounded by a brood of half-caste boys of such beauty they would have made Somerset Maugham's mouth water, he had been hidden from the Japanese by his relatives. Our return, in 1945, enabled him, alas, to resume drinking—his favorite occupation.

Forever extolling the virtues of Dutch colonial rule, this prodigious bore was indeed, as he claimed, much loved by the local population. I suspect they loved him because in his drunken abjection, he could be mocked and mimicked; in a word because he was an excellent symbol of the decline of the Dutch colonial empire. It was embarrassing to have to deal with so shaky a representative of colonial rule—for he was the only permanent link between us and the Dutch government. On the other hand, he was so dependent on our hospitality that he would no more have thought of crossing us than he would have refused a drink.

35

As harbormaster Captain X had in his charge a couple of boats. One was a solid Rotterdam-made tug; the other, a flat-bottomed Japanese boat of uncertain vintage. This fleet was his pride and joy. An avid student of military strategy, Captain X was constantly telling us what we should be doing to crush the rebellion. His views would have been considered extreme by those British officers who, after the Indian Mutiny in 1857-58, tied their erstwhile mutinous sepoys to guns and blew them apart. But one day he came up with a proposal which sounded promising, and I made the mistake of listening to him.

Some thirty miles down the coast was a sizable rebel enclave. Its men had ambushed us repeatedly in the past. They were known to hide out in a fishing village and to keep their weapons there. This village was singularly well placed. Access to it from land was difficult. It could be reached with ease only from the sea. Since any major troop movement on our part invariably got reported to the Tentera Republika Indonesia (Indonesian Republican Army) well in advance, why not, I suggested, follow the harbormaster's advice and use one of his ships to make an undetected landing from the sea, surround the village, and search it?

The plan materialized. On the dawn of Queen Wilhelmina's birthday, a date deliberately chosen by the harbormaster to strike a blow for colonial rule, one infantry company was smuggled aboard the flat-bottomed boat in conditions of ludicrous secrecy. I was with them. The operation was designed to occur in two phases. Should we discover any arms or should we be fired on, a second company, in the tug, would materialize, and the rest of the battalion would seal off the escape routes behind the village.

Captain X, looking as manic as Humphrey Bogart in *The African Queen*, took us on a wide parabola before moving close to shore. The company commander briefed his men. The Garhwalis were excited; this operation reminded some

36

of them of their landings along the Arakan coast a few months earlier. This time there was all the romance of amphibious warfare with almost none of the dangers.

The operation looked good, too good, for some 500 yards from the shore, we hit a coral reef and became hopelessly marooned. We had become impaled on a clearly visible protuberance, and Captain X, who had neglected to verify this most elementary of hazards, behaved true to type. He ranted and raved. Almost in tears, he agreed to call off the operation—if we could raise some help to get out of there.

We remained stuck on the coral reef most of the day. Fishermen came out and circled our wrecked craft. Hastily ordering the Garhwalis to conceal their arms, I made everyone pretend we were on a holiday outing. Stripped to their undershorts, the men swam about and mingled with the swelling throng of tiny fishing boats. It became extremely hot. In local dialect, the captain explained that we had taken the trip because it was Queen Wilhelmina's birthday and therefore a public holiday. The fishermen became bolder, inspected the damage at closer quarters, and shook their heads.

It had been my painful task to explain to the colonel, over the radio, what had happened. The rest of the battalion was recalled, and the tug eventually showed up. Garhwalis and fishermen with, presumably, some nationalist rebels among them, pushed and hauled, and we were towed, ignominiously, back to Padang.

From this fiasco onward Captain X went into a marked decline. I escaped lightly; for a couple of weeks the colonel sent me to guard a small bridge along the Pedang-Medan road. 'I think you might be more successful on land,' he said.

No subsequent NCOs' rum party in the 1st Battalion at which I was present was complete without a retelling of the story. The coral-reef saga was a watershed. Events, in retrospect, were referred to as occurring before it or after it. In the shorthand gossip of the officers' mess, it was referred to as Behr's Second Front or as The Teddy Behr Picnic.

The lowest point in my Sumatra soldiering, however, was not this disastrous experiment in amphibious warfare. It occurred with the visit of high brass. Mountbatten, the 'Supremo,' had been infuriated by reports that Japanese units had been used alongside Indian Army units to fight the rebels. He was aghast and incredulous, and he sent his senior corps commander to the area to investigate the rumors.

Our own battalion's conscience was clear. Other Indian Army units were indeed compromised. A Japanese artillery battery, with an English-speaking captain, had been used on at least one occasion to give supporting fire to attacking Indian infantrymen, and another unit had 'requisitioned' a Japanese medical officer when its own failed to return from leave. He turned out to be skilled, efficient, and cheerful—a remarkable improvement on the previous incumbent. Our own battalion might have had a Japanese dentist with it still, had wiser counsels not prevailed. This was a Japanese soldier taken prisoner shortly before the end of the war in a coastal village on the Arakan coast. He had been found curled up and asleep in a shack near a railroad and was almost killed in his sleep by a panicky young officer whose first long-range patrol this was. His first words, on being prodded awake, were: 'Am I glad to see you guys!' He was an American nisei (and California dental student) who had had the bad luck to attend his grandfather's dying days in Japan shortly before Pearl Harbor. Conscripted into the Japanese Army, he had been trying to desert ever since.

Delighted by this new pet, the battalion at first toyed with the idea of concealing the 'Yank' in its midst and providing him with the tools of his trade. He was dispatched eventually to headquarters for interminable debriefings, but succeeded in being kept apart from the rest of the

Japanese in British hands. He must have been the only Japanese prisoner of war to be demobilized in California.

For the corps commander's visit, I was put in charge of his personal security—and since my 'liberated' white Packard convertible was considered worthy of VIPs, it was assigned to the general throughout his stay—with me as driver.

In vain did I plead that it badly needed a tune-up and that it could be relied upon to start only intermittently. Such excuses were brushed aside, with the result that early one morning, at the airstrip, I sat behind the wheel, the engine chugging over, waiting for the general to land and inspect our guard of honor.

Our brigade commander was the kind of man who suspected that all Indian Army soldiers were inferior 'native troops' and their officers unemployable. He was an artillery-man, recently out from England, and our relations were far from cordial.

'Turn that engine off!' he shouted.

'Won't start, sir, if I do that?'

'Did you hear me or didn't you?'

I switched it off. Needless to say, when the corps commander finally got in, the Packard wouldn't start. There is nothing quite so comic as two senior generals being pushed in their car by droves of grinning Indian troops.

'Where did you get this car?' the corps commander asked me, after it had finally started.

Had I been more experienced I would have said, 'Don't know, sir. Pool of civilian vehicles, sir.' As it was, I said, 'Took it off a Jap, sir.'

'You what?'

'It wasn't really his to start with, sir. Belonged to a Dutchman who died.'

There was a silence at the back. Then I could hear the brigadier saying, 'You see, that's the kind of thing we have to contend with.'

That night, to celebrate the corps commander's visit,

twenty Kempitai war criminals escaped from Padang jail because Rifleman Bal Sing Bisht fell asleep at the wrong moment. Bal Sing belonged to my intelligence platoon.

In the last few months of our Sumatra stay an on-again, off-again *modus vivendi* was attempted between our Indian Army brigade and the Indonesian rebels. There were to be 'no go' areas on both sides and an end to urban terrorism. There was also a secret clause, in what was already a secret and largely verbal agreement, to the effect that the TRI (Tenera Republika Indonesia) was to help us recover not only Japanese deserters (and escaped POWs) but also Indian Army deserters, whose motive in deserting had been to go and live with their Indonesian girlfriends. This sounds like the typically vindictive action of a brutal military bureaucracy. But as I remember it, those Indian Army deserters who did return to the fold were treated leniently. By a fictional manipulation of dates, many of them were considered to have been simply absent without leave. Our Garhwali unit was exceptional in that it had no deserters to start with. A handful of Indian soldiers and a sizable number of Japanese did, however, stay on after our departure.

The detente brought about by our temporary truce had considerable impact on our lives. There were low-level meetings between local nationalist leaders and army officers. Byzantine negotiations, often through third parties, were necessary to bring about face-to-face meetings. The difficulty consisted largely in getting them started in the first place. As Henry Kissinger was later to find out when he began seeking secret contact with Hanoi, there is never any dearth of willing third parties—but as in Henry's case, our third parties, many of them, turned out to be wildly indiscreet, or mythomaniacs with no real knowledge of the rebels' whereabouts, or *agents provocateurs*. On one giddy occasion, however, a couple of truckloads of TRI guerrillas showed up in Padang to play the Garhwalis at football on the field we also used as an impromptu airstrip for small planes. Press as we might, there was no return match.

And our communications with the other side were tenuous at best. One faintly absurd reason was that the Indonesian nationalist guerrillas were forever changing the names of their formations to make them sound more martial. Today's 'Flaming Moslem Tigers' would become overnight the 'Golden Tigers for Total Independence' and then metamorphose themselves into the 'Death-or-Dishonor Islamic Freedom Fighters for Ultimate Self-Sacrifice.' Such frivolity complicated my intelligence task, but I was not wrong in a rule of thumb I invariably applied: The more vainglorious the name, I explained in briefings, and the longer the title, the less of a threat any particular guerrilla unit represented.

There were rivalries within the Indonesian nationalist units themselves. I once drove out to an agreed rendezvous in some remote spot to settle details of a temporary local truce and met the guerrilla chief as arranged. He was an amiable, moon-faced ex-student from Medan. We brought out our respective maps. Suddenly, from uncomfortably close by, we heard the sound of rifle fire and realized that some of it, at least, was coming our way. 'The firing isn't coming from my men!' I shouted as I rolled over into some tall grass.

'It's not from my men either!' my opposite number shouted as he did the same. The meeting broke up in panic, disorder, and an aura of mutual distrust.

A Dutch soldier of fortune, Kurt Westerling, who later led a rebellion of Amboinese soldiers from the Dutch East Indies island of Amboina against newly independent Indonesia, and still later wrote a somewhat garish account of his numerous adventures, described in his book, but without naming me, how I once challenged him to seek out and kill the leader of a well-known nationalist guerrilla group in Sumatra.

His version is that he brought back the rebel's head in a

41

sack which he dumped on my desk, whereupon I fainted. Though I vaguely remember Westerling, the prototype of all those later 'centurions' who were to fight losing battles against the emerging Third World, I recall little about him, except that his brutal behavior toward the civilian population resulted in a brigade order to have nothing to do with him. However selective my memory, I feel I would have recalled the incident of the severed head had it actually occurred. I was never, to my knowledge, the timorous uniformed *Salome* he depicted. Years later, when Westerling was engaged in various entrepreneurial activities in Tangier, some of them on the fringe of legality, I sought him out—both to satisfy my curiosity and to write a story about him. He was as elusive then as some of the Indonesian nationalists I sought out in 1946, and we never met.

Our peacekeeping role was drawing to a close: Dutch troops finally came in large numbers to try to resume control of their rich colonial empire. In November 1946, a crack Jagar battalion relieved us. We had been first into Sumatra, and we were last out. On the eve of our departure, with the Dutch troops taking over night patrols for the first time, they contrived to shoot eighteen people, all civilians, in the streets of Padang.

More than twenty years later I returned to Medan and Padang on a reporting assignment for *Newsweek*. The places had scarcely changed through years of Sukarno's misrule, and there had been little new building, so that old landmarks were still visible and instantly familiar. It was difficult to imagine that Britain had ever been involved in a holding operation here or that Indian troops had ever fought the Indonesian rebels. Indonesian troops, in their smart, starched uniforms, were as unlike the guerrillas of old as possible.

At a crossroads I watched a well-dressed young Chinese drive a white convertible Packard of incredibly ancient vintage. Surely that was *my* Packard, my single piece of wartime loot? I introduced myself and asked him about the car. It was mine, all right. His father had bought it off a Dutchman when the Dutchman left. The Dutchman had bought it from a Dutch Jagar battalion officer. It was still running reasonably well, he said, but even in America it was impossible to get spare parts for cars like these. Anyway, he said, it was time to leave Indonesia; the Chinese were unpopular here, and many had already returned to China. He would join some relatives in Malaysia. What were his chances of getting to the United States?

II. PESHAWAR

> Wellington is supposed to have said that
> the Battle of Waterloo was won on the
> playing fields of Eton. It may be that the
> historians of the future will say that India
> was lost in the public schools of England.
>
> SOMERSET MAUGHAM
> *A Writer's Notebook*

IN THE movies made by that mediocre film director Jean
Negulesco, a switch in scene to Paris was invariably
indicated by a shot of the Eiffel Tower, panning down to a
bearded artist in smock and beret carrying French bread
and whistling '*Auprès de ma blonde*' to a bal musette
accordion accompaniment. In *City Lights* Chaplin used the
torn-off pages of a diary to suggest the passage of time. My
own particular cliché, to illustrate my move from Sumatra
to Peshawar, should ideally be that other favorite symbol of
film directors of the old school: the blurred and
superimposed shots of railroad tracks shot as from the front
of an imaginary train.

It was the longest train journey ever: ten days in a low-
priority troop train after our troopship had docked in
Madras. Still in jungle fatigues suitable for the tropics, we
moved slowly, imperceptibly, from the hot and sultry
summer of southern India in December to the biscuit-
colored and icy wasteland of northern India.

Even taking our low-priority status into consideration

(for we went into sidings to let everything else go by), it was an interminable journey, made palatable for me by sufficiently ample stocks of books and scotch and a cavernous leather-bound, wood-paneled first-class compartment built in the nineteenth century.

For three days we were marooned by floods. We spent hours in railroad stations, then as now the best vantage points to see India from. All major stations still had separate Moslem and Hindu dining rooms, a reminder of the uneasy co-existence of different races and religions, soon to end in conflagration.

For reasons best known to himself, our battalion commander insisted that the battalion assemble and carry out a formal march-past immediately after arriving in Peshawar in the dead of night, and a shivering, demoralized Garhwali battalion paraded unsteadily outside its new barracks, which would have been familiar to Learoyd, Mulvaney, and all the other heroes of Kipling's Indian barracks-room tales.

For though the British Raj was about to fall apart with terrifying suddenness, Peshawar, capital of the North-West Frontier Province and only forty miles from the Afghan border, was still a bastion of tradition and Kiplingesque behavior. It was neatly divided into two separate cities. The cantonment, entirely surrounded by barbed wire, was as spick-and-span as an English country village. Most of it was a series of army barracks impossible to heat in winter, with huge parade-ground surfaces, built well before Kipling's time. There were bungalows with well-tended lawns, one of the most luxuriously appointed clubs in the whole of India, and every week the Peshawar Vale Hunt met to chase, not foxes, but jackals, complete with mottled English squires in red coats and horse-faced ladies.

The center of Peshawar Cantonment was the Mall, a superb example of successful neocolonial-cum-English-country-town planning. It was a somewhat narrow street, with hedges and trees on either side and shops set back behind the trees. I can forgive anybody almost anything, but not Mr. Zulifkar Ali Bhutto, Pakistan's former prime minister, for uprooting the Mall and its trees to turn it into a two-lane highway more suitable to his Roman triumphs. There were well-groomed horse-drawn tongas, for the same English ladies who went hunting jackal on Sundays were active members of the local branch of the Royal Society for the Prevention of Cruelty to Animals and would ruthlessly persecute any tongawalla found ill-treating his horse. There were dances and hunt balls and Scottish reels galore at the Peshawar Club. All the sahibs and memsahibs were aware that their privileged lives in India were coming to an end, and they were determined to make the most of it while they could. Pipers were provided by one of the battalions in the garrison, the 2nd Black Watch, whose soldiers, whenever they left their barracks off duty, had to step onto a mirror embedded in the floor of the guardroom to prove to the guard commander, who inspected them before they were allowed to leave, that they were wearing nothing under their kilts. I have told this story repeatedly to my French friends, who refuse to believe that this ritual ever took place.

Across the railroad tracks lay Peshawar City, so different from the cantonment it was difficult to believe the two towns were in the same country. Peshawar City then was still an exotic medieval walled city, with eleven massive gates abutting a huge fort. Inside was a maze of shops, markets, tiny workshops, and hole-in-the-wall restaurants, and the narrow streets were jammed with Pathans, mostly armed with home-made Lee-Enfield rifles.

The Pathans are tribesmen who straddle the Pakistan-Afghanistan border. They number about 2 million and are among the toughest, hardiest people in the world. They speak a language of their own, Pushtu, and eke out a living by tending meager herds of sheep, by marginal subsistence farming, by smuggling, and more recently by hiring themselves out as laborers both in Afghanistan's capital,

Kabul, and in the main towns in Pakistan.

Those Pathans inhabiting the North-West Frontier were then still only half reconciled to the imposition of British rule and were plagued by vendettalike feuds among themselves. For generation after generation, warring Pathan families fought and murdered one another over some obscure quarrel whose initial cause, like that of the Montagues and the Capulets, had often been forgotten. Pathans carrying their rifles at the ready as they walked in the streets of Peshawar City on a shopping expedition were a common sight.

Nor did they confine their aggressions to one another. Most of the family and tribal disputes were over firewood gathering and grazing rights, but the Pathans were still, on occasion, not averse to playing games with the British Army. Throughout the Second World War a tough old tribal leader called the Faqir of Ipi kept a sizable number of British and Indian troops mobilized in tribal territory, and the troops were still trained in techniques to counter Pathan sniping and sneak raids. This involved, when they were on the move in tribal territory, rushing up steep hills and occupying all the potential sniping positions as the rest of the column marched by below.

The homemade version of the Lee-Enfield army rifle was as essential an attribute to the adult Pathan then as was his turban. Years later, when President Ayub Khan started building small factories in the North-West Frontier Province to wean the Pathans away from their warlike ways, he was met with two unexpected demands: The Pathans wanted rifle racks inside the factories and payment by the day. For with blood feuds at their level of intensity, who knew what tomorrow would bring?

Experts on Pathan vendettas could reel off in endless detail the rivalries among different subtribes of Waziris, Afridis, and Mahsuds. Most of the mountain areas, as tribal territory, were outside the normal jurisdiction of the British Raj. Instead, British pragmatism had devised a scheme whereby, in return for substantial amounts of cash, regularly delivered in notes and (originally) gold coins, tribal leaders, or maliks, were empowered to administer their own tribes and keep the peace. These subsidies were withheld if the tribe indulged in attacks on British or Indian troops. Within the tribe such justice was of an extremely rough-and-ready nature: Maliks had their own jails and their own brutal ways of keeping the peace. But woe betide any malik who failed to share the subsidy with the rest of the tribe. Strongly egalitarian, the Pathans were quick to eliminate any tribal leader who showed any signs of greed or overweening pride, and this, in turn, was the starting point of more family vendettas.

Yet another reason had to do with women's honor. Though many Pathans were bisexual (most outposts of the Frontier Corps, the locally raised militia led by specially selected British career officers, included a small, floating population of Pathan boys with rouged cheeks and kohl-blacked eyes to minister to the needs of the militiamen), there was no fooling around with Pathan women. Outside the streets of Peshawar City, where raddled old Pathan ladies and very young girls occasionally showed their faces, I can't remember ever having seen the face of a Pathan woman; they all wore the burka, which covered them from top to toe, with only a tiny slit for eyes and some dots to breathe through. Though this was a male-oriented society par excellence, Pathan women, for all their constraints, were not subservient to their menfolk, to judge from the peremptorily shrill, nagging sounds that came from under their burkas when they were in the company of brothers or husbands.

Shortly after our arrival in Peshawar, Regular Indian Army officers with far more claim than I to command companies, some of them former Japanese prisoners of war, returned to the battalion, and I found myself demoted and virtually jobless. A vacancy arose in the Peshawar Frontier Brigade Group for a brigade intelligence officer. I applied and got the job, though not without the misgivings of the brigade commander, John Morris, who made no secret of the fact that he would have preferred a more senior, a more experienced, and above all, a Pushtu-speaking officer, preferably from the Frontier Corps.

I was on probation. My sole asset was that I had become so fascinated with Peshawar City and its inhabitants that I had spent most of my spare time since my arrival roaming its streets and knew it well. Shortly after I took up this appointment, the brigadier summoned me to show him the city, and wherever we went we were greeted by shopkeepers, carpet merchants, restaurateurs, police informers, and beggars, all of whom seemed to be on familiar terms with me. 'At least you seem to know your way around,' he said. 'You may conceivably be of use to me after all.'

Morris was a career Gurkha officer who had spent part of the war with Orde Wingate and the Chindits in Burma, earning a DSO in the process. Like most officers who had fought the Japanese at close quarters, he was ambivalent in his attitude toward them, but he reserved his hatred for Wingate, whom he regarded as a half-crazed maniac. 'I survived Wingate and the Japanese, in that order,' he would say. His experience behind the Japanese lines with Wingate in Burma had left him with a considerable distrust of young, inexperienced officers like me. 'You young people all crack up in the end,' he said after discovering my age. Constantly on the watch for signs of an incipient nervous breakdown which never came, he gradually came to trust me and even, on occasion, to ask my advice. We became friends and corresponded long after he left the Army to head a successful paint firm in northern England. 'Bloodthirsty little beggar, aren't you?' he said at the time of the communal massacre of Hindus and Sikhs, a few months after he had taken command. I knew him well enough by then to realize this was his highest form of praise.

My predecessor had confined himself to writing prim and dull reports culled from those provided by battalion intelligence officers. I determined to do something different. The political situation in the North-West Frontier in 1947 was fascinatingly complex, and I felt that I could contribute more than mere reports on army morale and Pathan tribal movements.

It was apparent, by this time, that partition was a likely eventuality. But the North-West Frontier, though solidly Moslem, was a bastion of Congress party strength, and many Pathans, especially in Peshawar and nearby Charsadda, were under the spell of a remarkable man, Khan Abdul Ghaffar Khan, the 'Frontier Gandhi,' who preached the Gandhian ideals of self-sufficiency, poverty, and austerity, even spinning his own cloth like Gandhi's disciples farther south.

The Frontier Gandhi was resolutely opposed to Pakistan. Instead, he advocated Pukhtunistan, a separate Pathan state or—at worst—an autonomous Pathan province within a greater India. Khan Abdul Ghaffar Khan's sway over the Pathans of the plains and the inhabitants of Peshawar was considerable. He had little influence in the tribal areas, where his Gandhian preachings were regarded as the masochistic mouthings of an eccentric. His headquarters was a small town near Peshawar, Charsadda, where he ruled over a devoted private army, the Redshirts, who had built themselves a permanent camp where they drilled, spun cloth, and held indoctrination courses.

Khan Abdul Ghaffar Khan's relations with Nehru were close, and in local elections a Redshirt majority had enabled him to appoint one of his relatives, the Khan Sahib, as chief minister of the North-West Frontier. The Khan Sahib, also a member of the Congress party, was thus firmly opposed to Mohammed Ali Jinnah's partition plans, with the result that an important and turbulent province risked siding with India and wrecking Jinnah's chances of creating a separate state of Pakistan.

It was in this climate, and with communal massacres already occurring in parts of the Indian subcontinent, that I became brigade intelligence officer. I was never asked to help win the Pathans around to the notion of Pakistan. This was done by the British Political Agents who disbursed funds in the tribal areas. They went from malik to malik, assuring them that the subsidies would continue after the end of British rule, so long as their tribes threw in their lot with the notion of Pakistan. The warnings had due effect, and from the moment the 'tribals' were won around to Pakistan and partition, the Frontier Gandhi's cause was lost.

With Morris's approval, I decided to try to establish contact not only with the Peshawar police but also with the local politicians, including Khan Abdul Ghaffar Khan. After several fruitless attempts, I finally succeeded in getting inside his Charsadda camp and in talking to him. I found him a somewhat naïve but admirable fellow. 'I am not in the dirty game of politics,' he told me. 'I am a social reformer.'

Realizing the looming eventuality of Pakistan, he now tried to exact from Jinnah some formal promise that Pukhtunistan would be established within Pakistan, but Jinnah, a shrewd and wily man, was careful never to allow himself to be inveigled into putting anything about Pukhtunistan into writing, though his verbal promises, if vague, were reassuring. Because he continued to campaign for an autonomous Pukhtunistan, Khan Abdul Ghaffar Khan was to spend eighteen years in jail after independence.

I became the only British officer tolerated within the Redshirts' camp and duly reported the Frontier Gandhi's apprehensive state of mind to my brigadier. Khan Abdul Ghaffar Khan knew that I did so but was responsive to my argument that the more people knew of his plans and views the better. It was, of course, useful for the Army to know

51

just how militant the Redshirts were prepared to be in the cause of Pukhtunistan. It turned out that though the Peshawar chief of police, Khan Abdul Rashid, had his own informers inside the Redshirt movement, my information was invariably more reliable.

The rank and file of Khan Abdul Ghaffar Khan's movement may have been Gandhian in spirit, but his followers were not averse to violence to make their presence felt. It became clear that some kind of showdown was bound to occur, and troops began training in what the Army euphemistically called 'action in aid of the civil power.' This was riot control, including what to do when called upon to open fire on a crowd. In typical army fashion, a rigid drill had been devised to ensure that such action was carried out in soldierlike, orderly fashion, its key element being that written permission had to be obtained from a magistrate on the spot. Soon, all over Peshawar Cantonment, Indian troops could be seen rehearsing such psychodramas, with little Garhwalis acting out the role of threatening crowds with considerable artistry.

To test the degree of support for Pukhtunistan in Peshawar City itself, Khan Abdul Ghaffar Khan was prevailed upon by his more militant aides to stage a huge demonstration. Crowds surrounded the railroad station, blocking trains in and out. Then, encouraged by this success, they began advancing on the cantonment. The local police failed to stop them. Two companies of Garhwalis were ordered out. A magistrate shouted warnings from a megaphone, then hastily signed the 'fire' order as rocks were hurled. A Garhwali rifleman fired three shots, and the crowd dispersed, leaving two wounded men behind.

I asked the Garhwali rifleman later why he had picked those particular Pathans. 'They were ahead of the rest, beating their breasts, and shouting, "Shoot me, shoot me,"' he said with considerable logic, 'so I shot them.'

This demonstration was soon followed by another huge

rally of pro-Pakistan Pathans, called to coincide with the visit in April 1947 to Peshawar of Lord Louis Mountbatten, the new viceroy. In their book *Freedom at Midnight*, Larry Collins and Dominique Lapierre imply that Mountbatten took considerable risks in attending the rally and was saved from the tribesmen's ire only because of his presence of mind in wearing his olive-green military uniform, green being the symbol of Islam and Pakistan.

Nothing could be further from the truth. The demonstration, as the local governor of the North-West Frontier Province, Sir Olaf Caroe, and all his Political Agents well knew, was carefully orchestrated by the British to demonstrate that the majority of Pakistanis—unlike the Frontier Gandhi's supporters—favored Pakistan. By the tens of thousands the 'tribals' had been trucked in by their maliks and performed with considerable enthusiasm.

As the date of partition approached, tension between the communities increased. Our main problem now was not the reaction of the Redshirts but the attitude of the Pathan, Moslem majority to the 30-percent Hindu and Sikh minority in Peshawar. Far more than in the rest of India, Hindus and Sikhs had felt secure in this predominantly Moslem area for one very good reason: Cutting through religious differences had been a common allegiance to the Congress party. So, unlike Lahore, where racial tensions escalated into killings as soon as the notion of partition was discussed, many Hindus and Sikhs in Peshawar had believed that they might stay on in Pakistan. Almost all were prosperous, middle-class businessmen, shopkeepers, lawyers, or bureaucrats, with strong ties of friendship with their Moslem, Pathan counterparts. Most had been in the area for generations.

But as the date of partition got closer and closer, news of the communal massacres in the rest of India began to have their repercussions in Peshawar. We hoped against hope that the uneasy calm would last, despite the Pathans' propensity for violence and the fact that all were armed.

53

One day in July, a month before partition, an ominous incident occurred. By this time I had established close links with the Peshawar police, and little happened in the city without my being told. One afternoon the phone rang. 'There are some Hindus being butchered in the Old City, near a police station,' a Peshawar police officer told me. 'It looks ugly and has been going on for some time.' He told me the street, and.I drove to the nearest city gate in my jeep, with my driver, a Pathan regular soldier from the crack 19th Lancers Cavalry Regiment—which was one of the regiments earmarked for Pakistan. I had picked him for his brawn and reliability rather than for his driving abilities, which were minimal, and in fact always drove myself. Now, and subsequently, I was glad he was with me.

For when we reached the scene of the incident, a small but growing and interested crowd was standing over a heap of bodies. A small car, recently looted, stood outside a house. One of the men lying on the ground was conscious. The other two, in pools of blood, looked as though they might die at any moment. I stooped and asked the conscious man to tell me what had happened, meanwhile ordering my driver to get to the nearest phone for an ambulance.

The three men were career officers in the Indian Army. One of them, a surgeon, owned the house in Peshawar city in front of which I now stood. He had been in the process of packing his belongings with two army friends, for as a Hindu he had no option but to transfer to the Indian, as opposed to the Pakistani, Army. A mob had gathered and began looting their belongings. Some twenty yards down the road was a police station; none of the policemen had done anything to stop the looting and had, in fact, looked the other way throughout. When the army officers tried to protest, they had been attacked by the mob, beaten, and apparently stabbed.

The crowd—like all Indian crowds—grew and grew, and I was grateful for the presence of my Pathan driver, who

54

held them at bay.

The ambulance arrived, but the crowd muttered and began blocking the narrow streets to prevent it from getting through. In contravention to all the army rules on handling crowds, I ordered my driver to fire a Sten gun burst over their heads. They dispersed briefly, and the noise finally attracted the attention of the police, who could scarcely keep pretending that nothing had happened after hearing the shots. In Urdu I told them what I thought of them and promised dire punishment for all if they failed to keep the crowd at bay. Reluctantly they cordoned off the crowd, but my driver kept his Sten gun trained on the mob as I helped load the men into the ambulance. The three men had stab wounds, but as I lifted one unconscious man, I put my right hand behind his back and straight into a hole where his right shoulder blade had been. He had been blasted by a shotgun at close range.

Soon afterward I was on the phone to Khan Abdul Rashid, the chief of police, who had become a friend. I pointed out the dangerous implications of the day's incident. I begged him to investigate the behavior of the policemen who had watched the mob's attack without interfering and to punish them. Otherwise, I said, the pattern would repeat itself, the policemen would use this precedent to keep aloof from all clashes involving Hindus. He agreed, grimly, though I never did find out whether any of the police were ever disciplined.

Independence Day passed peacefully. It was the last appearance of the pipe band of the Black Watch, which performed on the vast parade ground outside Peshawar Fort. From August 15 onward the Black Watch in Peshawar, like all remaining British units in India and Pakistan, was forbidden to take any part in any peace-keeping duties and remained confined to barracks until its departure.

My own battalion of Garhwalis had departed, to my considerable sorrow, a few days before independence. The whole of the brigade was in the process of change; a battalion of Gurkhas had also left. The Sikh squadron of the 19th Lancers was about to leave. Peshawar Frontier Brigade, whose normal strength was five battalions, was down to two and a half battalions, a battalion of the Frontier Force Rifles, a superbly disciplined, crack army unit with an all-Pakistani officer command, two Pathan squadrons of the 19th Lancers, and a battalion of the 8th Punjab Regiment, newly arrived from New Delhi, which was in terrible shape. It was through this battalion, whose officers were almost all new arrivals from other units, that Nemesis finally struck.

I was in my bungalow early one Sunday morning, September 7, when I received a phone call from a hysterical Pakistani officer of this Punjab battalion. 'There is fighting,' he said over and over again. He was unable to say anything else. I put on my uniform, drove my jeep around to Brigadier Morris's house, and found him in white tennis shirt and shorts, about to have breakfast on his lawn. 'I think the balloon has finally gone up,' I said. 'I don't think you have time to change.' As I spoke, we could both hear the crackle of small-arms fire not very far away. The brigadier grabbed his army hat with its distinctive red band, jumped into my jeep, still in his tennis clothes, and away we went.

What had happened, we found out later, was this: The barracks and the parade grounds of the 19th Lancers and the Punjab Regiment were side by side. The guardroom of the 19th Lancers was manned by the Sikh squadron, which was still awaiting departure. To enable the Pathans in this unit to be used for more mobile duties, their commanding officer had quite rightly made the Sikhs responsible for the security of the battalion installations.

A truckload of Punjab Regiment infantrymen was patrolling the cantonment perimeter road that Sunday morning, and as it drove past the 19th Lancers guardroom, a shot was fired by one of the Sikhs on guard duty. Precisely

56

why the shot was fired was never discovered, beyond the fact that the loosing off of the one round was almost certainly accidental. But the bullet hit the truck of the patrolling Punjabis. They immediately assumed that they were under attack, rushed back to their barracks, and alerted the rest. Within minutes the Punjab Regiment had launched a classic infantry attack on the 19th Lancers, and by the time we arrived on the scene both sides were deployed in war. A machine-gun section of the Punjab Regiment was giving covering fire to the rest of a platoon, which was advancing on a flank. On the 19th Lancers' side, the Sikhs were deployed, too, and firing back.

This was the scene we came across as we neared the parade ground. 'Drive straight down the middle,' said Morris, and he stood up, clutching the windshield of my open jeep.

In their book *Freedom at Midnight*, which describes the scene, authors Collins and Lapierre, who invariably seemed to be privy to the innermost thoughts of the characters they write about, refer to me as 'terrified.' When I protested, they changed the adjective, but only in the French translation, to *interloqué* (disconcerted).

As I remember it, I had no time to be either terrified or *interloqué*. Out of the corner of my eye, I was watching the Punjab flanking operation, wondering whether the apparition beside me would be startling enough to make the troops come to their senses and what a lucky accident it was that the brigadier had decided to play tennis that morning, since he was even more striking a figure in white than in his usual uniform.

I kept the jeep slowly moving until we were in the middle of the parade ground shared by the two battalions. 'I'll walk over to the Nineteenth Lancers,' said Morris. 'You go over to the Punjabis and make them stand up.'

The firing had died down. I heard behind my back the brigadier's firm but conversational tone. 'Now then, what's all this nonsense? Get up, all of you,' he said, as though

57

addressing schoolboys refusing to get out of bed. I decided to do the same. To my relief, soldiers did begin to stand up. But whereas the brigadier's authority and the superior discipline of the 19th Lancers enabled him to get them under control almost immediately, I found myself surrounded by furious, shaken soldiers, convinced that they were in the right.

'Let's all move over to the guardroom,' I said, and was relieved when, leaving his lancers' side, the brigadier came over to join me. By now some of the Punjabis' officers were on the scene and were volubly defending their men's action.

The brigadier was superb. He allowed them to say their piece. Turning to the seniormost Punjabi officer present, he said, 'If you intend to stay in the Army, I advise you to get your men disarmed and under control. Otherwise, I'll have you out within twenty-four hours.'

I left the brigadier with the Punjabis to try to extract some information from the dying Sikh soldier, the only casualty of the morning's shooting. By all accounts, he was the one who had fired the fateful shot. A young man, he lay on a stretcher waiting for an ambulance, and a fellow lancer was trying to keep the flies away from his appalling wound. From chest to crutch, his stomach was like a model used in medical school for anatomy lessons; his liver, intestines, kidneys, and spleen were clearly visible. I sat with him. He remained unconscious until he died.

I drove back to brigade headquarters to warn the police chief of what had happened. We all obscurely knew that the uneasy peace in Peshawar was over, but we hardly expected what followed. Within an hour the rumor had spread all over the North-West Frontier Province that Sikh soldiers had run amok in Peshawar Cantonment and had killed Pathans and civilians. And within three hours Pathans from neighboring villages had begun entering the cantonment and were killing Sikhs and Hindus in a bout of frenzied savagery unparalleled anywhere on the subcontinent.

Elsewhere the weapons of communal killings had been knives, Sikh swords called kirpans, and, occasionally, shotguns. But the Pathans used their homemade rifles, indistinguishable from real army-issue Lee-Enfields, to considerable effect. Many had seen American gangster movies and emulated Bogart or Cagney. They stole cars and went from one Hindu house to another, killing and looting as they went. All over the cantonment the crackle of gunfire could now be heard.

That first day there was little that could be done to prevent the massacre. The Peshawar police fulfilled my apprehensions. Nowhere was contact made, either because the Pathans vanished whenever they spotted armed police or—more likely—because the police simply didn't wish to get involved. Army units we committed to the streets were almost as unsuccessful. To try to repel the Pathans, now coming in by requisitioned buses by the thousands from the countryside, the brigade had only one battalion of Frontier Force Rifles and a couple of squadrons of 19th Lancers, with armored cars and tanks. The Punjab battalion could not be used, for obvious reasons, and neither could the Black Watch. The artillery and some engineer units raised a few platoons of men totally unfamiliar with either riot control or street fighting.

Phone messages poured in from all over town. Shopkeepers pleaded for protection, which we were unable to give. Sikh and Hindu officials and businessmen begged for some kind of action.

I toured the cantonment in my jeep, trying to locate police units and work out some form of coordination between them and the Army. One police officer flagged me down and showed me, inside a government compound, the bodies of thirty-three Hindus. The men had been shot. The women had first had their breasts cut off.

Slowly Brigadier Morris got his shaky and depleted brigade into a better posture. An emergency refugee camp for Hindu and Sikh families was opened inside the fort.

Although conditions there were unbelievably squalid, those taken there did know at least they were physically secure—for the time being. How we were ever going to move them to India was a problem yet to be dealt with.

A pep talk with officers and NCOs of our only truly operational unit, the 1st Battalion of the Frontier Force Rifles, had an immediate effect: They started engaging the Pathans more successfully in street battles. Since the battalion had had considerable wartime experience in Africa and Italy, the Pathans soon found themselves on the defensive and, occasionally, in flight.

I was sitting in brigade headquarters with all our reserves committed, save a ten-man section of engineers, when a surprisingly calm voice on the phone informed me that the Pathans were attacking the military hospital, only a few hundred yards away, and were butchering the largely Hindu hospital staff.

Yelling to the engineer section to follow me, I ran to the hospital. I realized, a little late, that the men I was leading were themselves Pathans. As we tried to enter the hospital front gate, we were fired upon, and before taking cover, I caught a glimpse of corpses in the courtyard. There were shots and screams.

After scrambling around to the back of the building, we let ourselves in through a window. I knew the layout of the hospital well, and sprinting like mad and hoping not to meet any Pathans inside the building en route, I took the army section with me onto the roof. Cautiously we crept out, hiding as best we could, to look down on the courtyard and to see the Pathans in the act of dragging out and killing hospital orderlies and nurses.

I gestured to the man with the Bren gun in the section to give it to me, and aiming carefully, I shot three of the Pathans in the courtyard in quick succession, making sure that I didn't aim anywhere near the civilian staff. No sooner had I fired my single shots than two things happened simultaneously: The Pathans ran for cover across the road and started firing back. And the sergeant whose Bren gun I had taken leaped over to where I was and began wrestling the gun away from me, shouting incomprehensibly but with unmistakable fiery passion in Pushtu.

My immediate reaction was that I was about to relive the 1857-58 Sepoy Mutiny and that he was going to kill me for shooting his fellow Pathans. I cursed myself for using the section in the first place. Then I noticed that the rest of the section was firing away with great gusto into the road below. What the sergeant was saying, in fact, was: 'Let me have a go, too.'

I knew that a company of the Frontier Force Rifles was in the vicinity. In slow English, which one of the Pathan soldiers translated into Pushtu to the rest, I explained that I was going to leave them on the roof, that they were not to fire away indiscriminately, but only to keep the gang across the road from murdering any more civilians. In the meantime, I would try to get the Army to block both ends of the road and round them up.

With my revolver drawn, I made my way down the stairs and out the window at the back. No Pathans appeared to be inside. Outside, I debated whether to rush back to brigade HQ and get my jeep or to proceed on foot. A tonga clip-clopping by saved me the trouble. But ignoring my instructions, the tonga driver, impervious to any of the firing still going on, wheeled his horse around and turned into the very street where the Pathans I had fired on were now gathered, most of them in a ditch. I hid my revolver and assumed an innocent expression. Watching the scene from the roof, the engineers held their fire.

Spotting a British officer, the Pathans, who had minutes earlier been murdering people, now rushed into the street to talk to me. Hindus and Sikhs were up on the roof, shooting innocent passersby, said one excited Urdu-speaking Pathan. Three innocent bystanders had been killed, and what was I going to do about it? I promised to notify the police and hissed to the tonga driver to

61

move out fast.

Eventually I found the company, paid off the tonga, and got the road cordoned off. The Frontier Force troops moved in with guns blazing, and the Pathans in the ditch surrendered.

We gathered in more than twenty rifles, and the Pathans were taken away to the cells of the 19th Lancers' barracks. It was extremely warm. Packed in cells, they suffered. The brigadier was amused by my caper. It was, he said, the first bit of good news that day.

That night, near the Old City, Pathans set fire to a large tenement block housing more than 1,000 Sikhs and would have burned them to death had not the engineers blown up a number of surrounding buildings to prevent the fire from spreading. Even then it was impossible in the darkness to get the Sikhs to evacuate the building and allow themselves to be taken to the fort. Despite the gallantry of a Sikh officer of the 19th Lancers, who volunteered to act as go-between—and was shot at several times—we had to wait until morning.

The second day the situation was almost as bad. Overnight Hindu shops in the cantonment had been taken over by Moslems, and Moslem names in bright new letters were painted over the former—and whitewashed—Hindu names.

I received a message from Khan Abdul Qayum Khan, the new—pro-Jinnah—chief minister of the province, who had succeeded the Khan Sahib. Qayum Khan was a former Congress party supporter who had sensed which way the wind was blowing, recently defected from Congress, and joined Jinnah's Muslim League. He had strong local support and had been duly rewarded with this key post.

Now, as I approached his house, I understood why I had been summoned. On his lawn hundreds of Sikhs and Hindus waited patiently. The minister saw me hurriedly in the hall. 'I want you to take these people away,' he said. 'It is not safe for them—and it is not safe for me.' These were colleagues, fellow members of the Congress party, officials, barristers, judges, and civil servants he had known all his life. He had not provided them with so much as a glass of water.

I summoned up some trucks and got them out and off to the fort. Then I went back inside the house, saluted, and said, 'You're safe now, sir. I have taken all your *friends* away.'

Something had to be done about the marauding gangs in stolen cars. The brigadier decided on an effective but singularly ruthless course of action. The police furnished us with descriptions of the most wanted cars, whose occupants had, some of them, killed more than 100 people apiece in less than two days. We positioned tanks of the 19th Lancers at some key intersections of the cantonment. Without warning, and to make a deliberate example, the tanks opened fire on the stolen cars and blew them up. The gory remains were left on the streets. Soon the cantonment was littered with abandoned cars, still crammed with loot.

It was while I was standing on the veranda of the 19th Lancers' headquarters that I heard wailing sounds, followed by shots. A bearded man, presumably a Hindu, came into view, running terrified from left to right. Pursuing him a short distance away was a Pakistan Air Force enlisted man, on a big black bicycle, firing a Sten gun at him from over the handlebars.

My driver-bodyguard was with me. We closed in on the cyclist. I aimed at the bicycle with my boot and knocked him over. With precise, careful gestures, my bodyguard removed the magazine from the Sten gun and hit the cyclist across the back of the head with it. There was a noisy clang. In all the movies I have ever seen, people to whom this happens fall unconscious. Not so in this case, and soon we were a mass of arms and legs, trying to restrain the crazed airman. Finally, we stood on him and the bicycle, while the Pakistan Air Force HQ down the road was summoned to take him away. The airman could not understand he had done anything wrong. 'But he was a Hindu,' he kept saying.

Later I attempted to find out whether he had been charged with any offense. The Pakistan Air Force officer I talked to was charming but made light of the whole matter. 'One of our chaps went a little wrong in the head, so we sent him to hospital,' he said. 'He's up and about now. He's quite recovered.' I wished my bodyguard had hit the airman a little harder.

Cholera now broke out in the refugee camp inside the fort, and it became urgent to move everyone out as soon as possible. But how? Other convoys on their way south to Rawalpindi had been ambushed. We decided to do things differently. Our first convoy, straight down the Grand Trunk Road, was a dummy. There were some Sikhs in it, well in evidence, but these were Sikh soldiers, all of them volunteers. Most of the convoy consisted of two completely concealed companies of the Frontier Force Rifles. When the Pathans attacked as we expected them to, our soldiers sprang out of their trucks and routed the attackers. From then on, we had no more trouble with our refugee convoys and lost not a single refugee—though what happened to them after they reached Rawalpindi I never found out.

I went up in a small spotter plane and witnessed the welcome sight of Pathans streaming out of Peshawar. Gradually the killings diminished. How many people lost their lives will always remain unknown. But local police statistics showed that some 6,000 bodies were recovered in the course of ten days, and there must have been many, many more. At this time Peshawar had a population of only around 200,000.

So far I have given a blow-by-blow, worm's-eye view account of what actually happened in one little-known part of the subcontinent, where almost no reporters came to visit. Whatever else it revealed, it must have shown just how unprepared and inadequately staffed we were to prevent anything of this kind. The massacres hardly came as a surprise, and all over the Indian subcontinent other witnesses might have told the same grim story.

The question, then, must be asked: Why were such massacres allowed to occur? Whose responsibility was it? I am not alone in laying most of the blame for what occurred fairly and squarely in Mountbatten's lap.

As soon as the principle of partition was raised, it was obvious that communal and religious stresses would erupt into violence and that every available army and police unit would be needed to prevent such violence from degenerating into massive killings. Indeed, a year earlier, killings on a large scale had occurred in Calcutta, and it had proved almost impossible to put a stop to them, even with the large numbers of police and army at hand.

For this reason, army commanders all over the Indian subcontinent begged Mountbatten to defer Independence Day until both the Indian and Pakistan armies and police forces had been reorganized and were functioning as new, separate Indian and Pakistani entities. Even so, it was by no means certain that they would have been able to restrain the fierce anger of both communities. They might at least have avoided the worst.

Peshawar was a fairly typical example of a garrison suddenly reduced to less than half its size, with pockets of Sikh and Hindu troops left in Pakistan for as much as a month after independence. The attack of the 3rd Battalion of the 8th Punjab Regiment on the 19th Lancers was also a classic example of the excesses that occurred as a result of overhasty transfer. Before arriving in Peshawar, this battalion had been in Delhi and had witnessed the massacre of Moslems by Hindus which occurred in the very week of independence. The Punjabis' motive in attacking the Sikhs of the 19th Lancers was revenge, and it was fairly typical of what happened in the wake of partition all over the subcontinent.

Yet, apart from a 50,000-man 'boundary force' on the newly created Pakistani-Indian border, which proved totally inadequate, Mountbatten refused to heed the advice of his subordinate commanders on both the Indian and Pakistani sides. He even refused to entertain the notion of deferring Independence Day to January 1948, which would have proved completely satisfactory to both Nehru and Jinnah—and given everyone six extra months. And he ignored the flexibility implicit in the instructions of the Attlee government, which had suggested that Independence should occur 'no later than December 1948.' Why?

The official answer, as told to Larry Collins and Dominique Lapierre in *Freedom at Midnight*, a book, in my opinion, so uncritical of Mountbatten as to lose some value as an impartial record of what really happened, is that the last viceroy felt that unless independence were granted immediately, civil war would break out. This is somewhat along the lines of the argument put forward by the American officer at the town of Ben Tre in Vietnam during Tet 1968 who said that 'to save the town, it became necessary to destroy it.'

Some students of the period feel that Mountbatten badly wanted to return to Britain to take up an active naval command. Others suggest that he became bored with India after his first few months as viceroy and that his attention wandered. Others again feel that Mountbatten simply picked August 15, 1947, because it was the anniversary of August 15, 1945, when he had taken the unconditional surrender of the Japanese High Command at the end of World War II—and indeed, Mountbatten has never denied that he saw the two dates as symbols of his unbrokenly successful career.

Perhaps the answer is a mixture of all three hypotheses. Certainly, Mountbatten's retreat to Simla after August 15, 1947, and his reluctance to return as governor-general of India to help pick up the pieces at the request of Nehru and Vallabhbhai Patel (India's first interior minister after Independence) show that he was strangely insensitive to the chaos he had contributed to. That partition was

66

inevitable remains debatable, but that it should have occurred in its actual form was tragic. No one will ever know how many people died as a result of this ill-planned and grotesquely ill-executed division of the Indian subcontinent. But surely one of the least wholesome of its aspects has been Mountbatten's post facto insistence that he was right, that all deaths that ensued were inevitable, and that no other course of action was possible. Many Indian Army and police officers, from the highest ranks to the lowest, know differently and see in Mountbatten, even after all these years, not the glamorous leader of the Burma campaign but a man tarnished by hubris, with blood on his hands.

While I still reflect with some disugst on this display of callousness, I was not surprised by it. The French, with some justification, would simply describe what happened as another example of 'perfidious Albion.' But there was more to it than that. What made the dismantling of the French Empire so difficult, and emotion-fraught, was the French investment in the re-creation of a French ideal overseas, of the conscious molding of alien races and entities into a recognizable French pattern. In the quick, *sauve-qui-peut* British withdrawal from India, one was conscious only of the mercantile aspect of British imperialism. As long as the few boxwallahs, the traders and businessmen, remained, the rest of the subcontinent would revert to its fragmented state, and no one seemed to care.

At a distance, I also wonder at my own callousness and still more at my lack of remorse for my own behavior in Peshawar. In other circumstances, my actions might have brought me to court as a war criminal, for in a technical sense it could be argued that I gunned down civilians in cold blood. They were armed, of course, and they were criminals, too, and I can feel no more remorse now than I did then, though the events in Peshawar may have taken more of a personal toll than I imagined at the time. For no sooner had I left Peshawar than I fell ill with a bad bout of hepatitis, and for months after my return I was unable to walk into a butcher's shop. The smell, reminiscent of the sickly-sweet, meaty smell of Peshawar during the September carnage, nauseated me.

My personal effects, sent on ahead of me before the September massacres began, vanished without a trace. Included were some valuable antique silk carpets I had bought from Peshawar dealers with whom I had become friendly. Needless to say, insurance failed to compensate me for any loss, for the partition, all insurance companies claimed, had been tantamount to 'an act of war'—and I suppose that in a sense they were right.

Very recently I visited the scene of my youthful crimes. Peshawar Cantonment was smaller than I remembered, like a house one has lived in as a child. The army barracks were the same, but shabbier, and the flat parade-ground surfaces were no more. Now they were dotted with bungalows, office buildings, apartment blocks.

The military hospital where I had dueled with the Pathans was still there, now a hospital for army dependents. How had I ever managed to stay balanced on such a slanting roof? It, too, was smaller than I remembered, and my field of fire was now obstructed by new buildings and trees which hadn't been there in 1947. The tongas remained, but the Old City, spilled over beyond its old limits to beyond the very fort itself, was almost unrecognizable. The eleven beautiful historic gates and the city wall had been pulled down by some philistine bureaucrat. I got humiliatingly lost.

Peshawar city had changed in other ways, too. It was still an animated medieval market, but it was less prosperous than it had been. There were Pathan beggars in the streets. A doctor friend I had known in the old days told me that Pathans in urban areas were now dying of heart disease—an unthinkable end in 1947.

The rich merchants with their priceless old silk carpets had disappeared. So had the flat parade-ground surface outside the fort, now a mammoth parking lot. Here I had stage-managed the independence parade, and the Black Watch pipe band had played 'All the Blue Bonnets Are over the Border' for the last time on Indian soil.

I wandered along the Saddar Road in the cantonment, now Avenue Reza Shah Pahlevi. Down one alley I had fired my revolver at a looter—and missed. Green's hotel-restaurant, once the hangout of the younger British set, looked deserted. Here an elderly *rotisseur* had squatted over his tandoor stove, occasionally garnishing delicious plates of mutton and chicken 'tikka' with strands of his own white beard. Peshawar Club was also much the worse for wear, drab and decaying. Had Kipling's India ever existed, except in my imagination? Had I dreamed it all? But the Frontier Gandhi, still hale and hearty at eighty-nine, bless him, grasped me with both long simian arms, held me close, and said, to my surprise and silent, incredulous joy, 'Welcome back. I remember you well.'

III. THIS ONE, I FRAME

I SAT at the end of a table in Reuters News Agency newsroom, a 'trainee correspondent.' All around me were mature men in shirt sleeves, scrawling on news agency material with thick pencils. I did nothing for more than an hour. Then the man at the end of the table, obviously in some position of authority, thrust a typewritten page at me. 'Gimme two paras on that,' he said.

The copy I turned in, after the kind of shilly-shallying which only Woody Allen could have done justice to, was obviously not to my new master's liking. He looked at it with distaste and spiked it on the huge spike in front of him. 'We're not the London *Times*, remember,' he said.

Another hour passed. Shifts changed, but I didn't dare leave. The man in authority at the end of the table left and was replaced by a milder, grayer man of gentlemanly mien. He eventually noticed my presence. 'Try to do something with this, will you?' he said, thrusting a couple of pages at me. Mindful of the earlier rebuke, I decided to pull out all populist, gutter-press stops. He looked at the finished piece, visibly appalled. 'I don't know where you're from,' he said gently as he spiked it, 'but you must remember we're not the *News of the World*.'

Gradually the dismal craft of rewriting agency copy came to me. It wasn't very different from writing out army orders or giving instructions to one's platoon: information, intention; objective, in this case replaced by who, how, why, age, what happened. Originality was not encouraged.

Speed was. Every day supervisors, rather like quality-control foremen in automobile assembly plants, noted the hour, the minute, and probably the second that Reuters had announced a major news break, comparing it with monitored reports of the same story from Associated Press and the old United Press.

How had I ended up in this predicament? On demobilization, I returned to England in an army troopship in conditions of squalor almost equal to those of my outward journey, to find that as an ex-serviceman I was entitled to a sizable student grant—if only a university would have me. I determined to sit for both Oxford and Cambridge University entrance exams—or rather, for the entrance examinations set by various groups of colleges in both places. After some weeks of intense reading and self-imposed cramming in the British Museum reading room, I did well enough to be offered a vacancy both at University College, Oxford, to study law, and at Magdalene College, Cambridge, to study history. I chose Cambridge for two reasons: My Uncle Zama pointed out that I would have far more fun as a barrister than as a solicitor—but that a barrister's first years in practice were proverbially lean ones. He was willing to support me for the necessary period, he added, but I should know at the outset that few barristers were self-supporting before they were thirty. What really clinched matters was that most of my closest St. Paul's School contemporaries were at Cambridge. I did enough work to get a reasonably good honors degree, wrote occasionally for the *Cambridge Review*, tried my hand, disastrously, at university amateur theatricals, and helped run the French Club—the only easy way of meeting attractive French girls in Cambridge to learn English.

I became a Reuters correspondent almost by accident. My studies supervisor had determined that I was the stuff of which research students were made, and I had almost embarked on a research project when I panicked; at the last moment the idea of spending the rest of my life in academic

71

surroundings, even as delightful as Cambridge, filled me with claustrophobia.

Having rushed around to the university placement bureau, I was asked, by a gaunt, unsmiling man, what I had in mind. Since I had written for the *Cambridge Review* and done some broadcasts for the French service of the BBC, how about journalism? I proposed timidly. Hopeless, he said. 'Everyone who has nothing else to offer wants to be a journalist—I can't think why. There are two trainee vacancies for Reuters and over two hundred and fifty applicants. Do you still want to try?'

It seemed worth it, if only for a quick visit to London. I was interviewed by the editor of Reuters, a huge man bearing an uncanny resemblance to the late King Farouk. My Indian Army experiences and my mastery of French appealed to him. He made a phone call in front of me, obviously to the Reuters correspondent who had covered the Indian independence aftermath in 1947 and was now a senior editor somewhere in the building. My daily briefings to a handful of correspondents in Peshawar had not been in vain, for I walked out of the building with the job.

After my first few weeks with Reuters I almost wished I had been turned down. But then I was sent to Paris, and my real life as a reporter began.

At first the same agency routine applied as in London, but with the additional barrier of the French language. Who really makes the news? I began asking myself. In London, Agence France-Presse (AFP) correspondents rewrote Reuters' copy, as fast as they could, and the finished product ended up as part of the AFP news service. In Paris we shamelessly rewrote Agence France-Presse copy, serving it up as Reuters' fare. All over the world lesser news agencies were writing up *their* versions of Reuters' stories and serving them up as authentic Indian, Spanish, or Brazilian news-agency stories. Somewhere, at the bottom of this inverted pyramid, someone was getting a story at first hand. But who was he, and how did he set

72

about it? The mystery was complete and remained so for some weeks.

Gradually I discovered that some of the infinitesimal parts of our global news agency compost heap were of our own making. There was the case of an African MP, in French-speaking West Africa, who had disappeared after a particularly hectic and disputed bye-election. Rumors abounded, in the lobbies of the French National Assembly, that he had been eaten by his still occasionally anthropophagous constituents. Still timid and unused to the phone as an extension of a reporter's aggression, I phoned the leader of his parliamentary group at the French National Assembly. Shocking rumors, I said, had been spreading concerning the unfortunate demise of Mr. A. Was it at all possible to confirm—er—that he might possibly—er hum—have come to a singularly strange end? There was an uncontrolled burst of rich African laughter. 'I think,' said the voice, 'it's highly likely he ended up in the pot.' I found the quote, in a dozen languages, in press cuttings sent to us from all over the world.

But one of my first ventures into agency journalism ended in disaster. This was the time ex-Marshal Henri Philippe Pétain lay dying in a jail on the Ile d'Yeu off the Atlantic coast. For some reason the news of Pétain's actual death looked as if it would be a landmark in agency journalism, and all the major news agencies, and indeed most major French papers, were intent on securing secret and exclusive information which would enable them to scoop their competitors on this inevitable denouement. At Reuters a senior correspondent had visited the island and made a deal with one of the jailers, apparently an eminently bribable lot. Our man was one of a team of male nurses with daily contact with the unfortunate ex-marshal. He had promised to phone Reuters as soon as Pétain died, at considerable risk, as he had pointed out, to his own career. The code was to be: 'The parcel left at such-and-such a time.' But this apparently foolproof arrangement contained a number of hidden snags. First, the ex-marshal, in an extremely weak state, habitually fell into prolonged fainting fits in the morning, outwardly indistinguishable from death itself. More ominously, I was unaccountably left out of the conspiracy altogether (too junior? too blabbermouth?), and inevitably the predictable catastrophe occurred: Pétain fell into a particularly death-like trance, the corrupt gendarme assumed he was dead and phoned through his phrase, and I, at the Reuters end in Paris, failed to understand what he was talking about.

'The parcel left at eight-thirty A.M.,' said a voice with a thick Marseilles accent.

'I don't understand,' I said.

'Are you completely dumb or what?' said the voice. And then, as an afterthought, he added, 'Pétain died at eight-thirty this morning,' and promptly hung up.

Bewildered, I sought out the news editor. 'Someone on the phone just said that Pétain's dead,' I said.

'Well, send it, you damn fool.'

I did, covering myself by adding a word or two. 'According to unconfirmed reports,' I wrote, 'ex-Marshal Pétain died this morning.' An equally inexperienced Reuters man on the other end, disregarding my cautionary clause, sent back a news 'flash' (reserved for top-priority news): 'Flash—Pétain dead,' it said. And then followed an interminable obituary piece on the 'victor of Verdun' and his later controversial career.

Meanwhile, I was watching the AFP teleprinter machine, which was bound, sooner or later, to come up with a matching story—if true. Nothing of the kind emerged from the AFP wire. Our scoop was going to be a vast one—too vast, as it turned out, for Pétain didn't die for another six months. I at last managed to phone our initial source. 'He looked dead as a doornail,' he said, 'but revived later on.' It was useless to argue, and an embarrassing 'rowback' ensued. Well in character, the

74

Reuters bureau chief in Paris, Harold King, managed to shelve all the blame onto his inexperienced trainee correspondent, who, needless to say, was made responsible for the whole lamentable affair. And when Pétain did finally die, we were the last to announce the fact.

This was the era of French 'yellow press' photo-journalism par excellence, and competition was also fierce for deathbed pictures of the marshal. Here Reuters was not directly concerned, but the French press was, and there then occurred an almost similar embarrassment involving two French leading papers, which had spent considerable time—and money—acquiring the services of 'inside' men on the prison staff.

For hours at a time a prison guard had been coaxed in the art of taking deathbed pictures, using a reporter lying on his hotel bed to practice on. An expensive camera was left in the guard's trust. Came the day of Pétain's death, and the paper waited in vain for a roll of film that never came. The guard, it subsequently turned out, none too bright, had taken the pictures all right but had forgotten the name of the Paris newspaper he was to send them to. Eventually, a day late, they showed up in a rival newspaper.

Another Reuters story, which provided me with my first insight into the peculiar workings of French justice, occurred when I was on duty as deskman in the early hours of the morning. It was just after one of France's numerous Cabinet crises, and a new government had just been formed, after much interparty bickering. The new government had proudly posed in the ritual group photograph around the benign portly figure of President Vincent Auriol. One of the new ministers, a junior secretary of state for youth and sports, was a relative newcomer to politics, Pierre Chevallier, a member of a tiny middle-of-the-road radical splinter group, the UDSR. Chevallier got into his car, drove to Orléans, where he was mayor, and ran up the steps of his house, calling out to his wife, 'Darling, I've just been made a minister,' or words to that effect.

It was the last thing he ever said, for she was waiting for him with a ·45 revolver, which she proceeded to empty in his direction, ending with a coup de grâce in the head as he lay already mortally wounded on the steps of his house. Convinced that her husband was cheating on her—when, in fact, he was only attending party caucuses in smoke-filled rooms—Madame Chevallier had decided to take her revenge in exemplary fashion. The trial was the social event of the year—and she was acquitted.

It was in the Elysée's main ballroom that I was privy to one of the more unusual comic scenes. The Vatican nuncio in Paris, later to become Pope under the name of John XXIII, had just been made a cardinal, and in renewal of a custom which went back to the seventeenth century, it had been agreed that the French head of state, the one-eyed President Auriol, was ceremonially to present the portly Cardinal Roncalli with his red hat. A small group of correspondents, of whom I was one, was convened to witness this historic occasion. What we watched would have made a perfect self-contained episode in a Jacques Tati movie. Cardinal Roncalli lowered himself to his knees on a fragile prie-dieu, which creaked alarmingly. President Auriol, seizing the red hat with both hands and hopelessly miscalculating the distance because of his one eye, planted it firmly on the prelate's head at an extraordinarily rakish angle. Roncalli then attempted to rise and found that, owing to his great weight, he could not. Struggling aides brought him to his feet, still wearing his hat at a cowboy angle, so that he looked like a drunken prelate under arrest. Suddenly powdered lackeys in white breeches appeared on either side of Auriol. One of them held a tray of insignia of the Legion of Honor, which were to be distributed to various members of the Vatican Mission. The other held a tray of petits fours for the champagne reception that was to follow. I watched Auriol, by now so thoroughly confused he seemed not to know whether to pin a petit four on the future Pope or to eat a Legion of Honor.

It was still the pre-TV age, for TV was slow to develop in France. The size of the press corps, for major events, was therefore more manageable. For Winston Churchill's last visit to France as prime minister (in 1953) relatively few correspondents filled the press room in the French premier's office, the Hôtel Matignon, while Churchill dined in state with the then French premier, René Pleven. Unfamiliar with the topography of the Hôtel Matignon and seeking a toilet, I got lost.

I emerged into a small courtyard from a side door, and as I stood, trying to get my bearings, another door opened, and Sir Winston Churchill, in white tie, tails, and decorations appeared. He must have been engaged in a similar pursuit, for with immense aplomb, he proceeded to unbutton his fly and relieve himself interminably on the cobbled stone pavement. I watched with fascination, and finally, the great man realized that he was not alone. Giving his immense organ a final shake, he slowly coaxed it back into his trousers with an undisguised air of having accomplished something necessary, enjoyable, and naughty. As he did so, he spoke. 'I was last here in 1917, young man,' he said in that deep, much imitated voice. 'Mister Clee-mon-so was prime minister then. Let me tell you [shake, shake], things were very, very different then.' And with a courteous nod, he turned on his heels and went back inside to resume his dinner.

This was the heyday of a French weekly called *Radar*, of unbelievable brashness, combining the worst features of the *News of the World* and the *National Enquirer*. Its front page invariably showed a gory, shocking, or unusual picture, taking up most of the page, with huge screaming headline reading: 'Radar *était là*.' The staff of *Radar* were *paparazzi* before the term became fashionable: tough, cynical, leather-jacketed young men with powerful motorcycles, rhinoceros hides, and glamorous girlfriends. I teamed up with a couple of them in 1952 during the first official visit to Paris of Princess Margaret. It was a remarkable education.

Radar wanted exclusive pictures of Princess Margaret. It got them, with my occasional, straight-man assistance.

From the first, Princess Margaret's visit was a public-relations disaster. 'It's a private trip, really,' said embarrassed, plummy British Embassy voices. 'So we can't tell you anything about her program.' As a result, whenever her car emerged from the British Embassy gates, it was followed by a swarm of my *Radar* friends on motorcycles and *Paris-Match* teams in fast cars, swerving in and out of Champs-Elysées traffic to dive-bomb her with cameras.

Two incidents stand out. I am, in the company of a *Radar* man, about to pass myself off as a waiter hired for the evening by the former ambassador, Duff Cooper, in whose Chantilly mansion the princess is being entertained. Amazingly we pass as additional hired help—in rented waiter's clothes. We perform for most of the evening. I chicken out after dessert, having nevertheless got myself an exclusive story. The *Radar* man stays on, is caught trying to take pictures of Princess Margaret playing the piano, and is humiliatingly ejected.

The other incident involved my active participation as a decoy. The evening has not been without strains. It is the princess's last evening in Paris, and it's correctly believed that the party she is with will end up in a Paris nightclub. But where? An eavesdropping waiter at Maxim's tells me that everyone is going to the Nouvelle Eve in Pigalle. I phone the nightclub. 'The princess is coming?' I ask interrogatively. I hear grunted assents in somewhat Levantine French. Impeccably turned out in my rented tuxedo, I arrive on my motorcycle, which I park at some distance from the Nouvelle Eve. There I find the management lined up and realize, to my horror, that I am regarded as a kind of advance man, probably a superior kind of security guard. I am shown the princess's table and

78

am placed strategically at a smaller one. Champagne is brought. I wait—and wait. Finally, the enormous maître d' arrives.

'You did say the Princess Margaret, she come?' he asks.

'No, I asked *you*,' I reply, and leave hurriedly, before his minions throw me out.

Meanwhile, *Radar*, of course, has found out where the princess's party is really going, a somewhat staider *boîte* called the Monseigneur. The *Radar* objective is to take a picture of Princess Margaret dancing in the arms of some suitable escort and to splash it on the front page ('Radar *était là*') along with a plausible account of her latest romance. We arrive at the Monseigneur nightclub. No one with cameras is allowed in, at the princess's express request. We sit, and the two *Radar* men, their cameras concealed, dance with their girlfriends. Finally, the princess rises and starts dancing, too.

This is my cue. I leave the nightclub and make for the *Radar* car. On the back seat is an enormous Speed Graphic of the kind used by the press in the thirties. I don a shabby raincoat, seize the Speed Graphic, and blunder back into the nightclub at a run, making a beeline for the still-dancing Princess Margaret. Needless to say, I am immediately submerged by a variety of French and British detectives, pummeled by the nightclub's own villainous bullyboys, and ejected with professional dexterity.

Meanwhile, I have distracted attention, and even as I am being removed, struggling and protesting, one of the *Radar* men whips out his camera from beneath his *smoking* and takes picture after picture of a startled, frozen-faced princess still dancing with her escort, an émigré Yugoslav prince, as they both watch my humiliating exit. The camera is then thrown across the room, to the other *Radar* man, who catches it and, like the ex-Rugby ace he is, dives through more policemen, through the staff exit, and into the street. We meet at a prearranged point a few moments later and laugh hysterically. 'Radar *était là*,' and Princess

Margaret's Scotland Yard detective is sacked.

Such Chaplinesque nonsense seemed to be my lot. Chaplin himself arrived in Europe by liner, one step ahead of the McCarthyite lobby which wanted him investigated. I was sent to meet him, boarded his ocean liner, the *Queen Mary*, at Cherbourg. It was scheduled to arrive in Southampton the following morning. Chaplin, nervous, tired, and rather drunk, was nevertheless astute enough to realize that much of his public sympathy would depend on this first contact with the European press. Most of the press aboard were French, and I acted as interpreter. Chaplin invited me to tour the ship and then to dinner. As usual, my departure had been a last-minute business, and it was only after Chaplin's press conference, while the ship was still docked at Cherbourg, that Reuters told me to stay aboard—and travel to London with him. Meanwhile, I had phoned my story from a wharfside café, and as I rushed back to the liner, I skidded and fell. The seat of my trousers split wide open, leaving a ten-inch gaping tear. For the rest of the evening I went through an elaborate Chaplinesque ballet to conceal my predicament, insisting that I be last up the stairs and into the restaurant. Chaplin tired a little of my elaborate courtesies, until I explained the reason.

Another memory: a huge Communist rally in the now-demolished Vélodrome d'Hiver in Paris, which had been preceded by weeks of campaigning, culminating with a '*Tous au Vél d'Hiv*' banner headline across the front page of *L'Humanité*.

Perhaps because I arrived by motorcycle in neoproletarian garb, or else because, without knowing it, I was the ringer for a real middle-rank party official, I was whisked through the crowded entrance by tough men in leather coats and red ribbon armbands. Instead of sitting with my colleagues of the bourgeois press, I found myself in a small box overlooking the speakers' gallery full of delegates from 'brotherly parties' and a few French CP officials, obviously acting as hosts. Just as the meeting was about to begin, one of the leather-coated men who had been on duty outside came to me and whispered in my ear, 'Comrade, do you happen to know where the snacks are for the security detail?' I shook my head.

Later on Jacques Duclos, one of the CP's ranking leaders, toured the booths and shook my hand with every sign of being delighted to meet an old friend again. Later still, in the middle of Duclos's speech, one of the French comrades turned to me and said, 'What's the matter? You're not clapping?' I never did find out why I had been given this privileged prosition but decided to hang in there. The leather-coated men would probably look askance at me if they were to spot me, halfway through, ensconced in the 'bourgeois' press box. All I can remember of this meeting is Duclos announcing that Maurice Thorez, recently hit by a paralytic stroke, was on his way to treatment in the Soviet Union—and such was my inexperience that I omitted to mention this fact in my lead.

Throughout this period Reuters assumed that the kind of experience thus provided was so invaluable that any salary could only be a token one. 'You should be paying us,' Harold King used to snarl. As a result, after my meager army gratuity ran out, I was in a state of extreme poverty.

Around this time one of my counterpart trainee correspondents (posted to the New York bureau) collapsed on the street and was taken to Bellevue Hospital, where an intern phoned the New York Reuters office, asking to speak to the chief correspondent. 'We have one of your men here,' he said, 'with evident signs of malnutrition.'

'Good Lord,' the New York bureau chief replied, 'we thought he had friends here.'

My case was not quite as extreme (it is difficult really to starve in Paris) but led me to develop an expert knowledge of the seamier Paris hotels. For a considerable time I was compelled to stay at the Hôtel Stella, a Left Bank establishment frequented mostly by Conservatoire music students and impoverished musicians and then one of the cheapest hotels in the world.

There was an excellent reason for this: The hotel was owned, and run, by three villainous sisters, all in various stages of deafness. One of them had a husband, a shell-shocked First World War veteran, subject to occasional fits when he would charge the stairs with a broom shouting, 'We'll get them!' There were also various professionals of the night of both sexes, who would rise at 5:00 P.M. and haunt the *toilettes* in seedy dressing gowns.

For all their deafness, the sisters had a sixth sense which enabled them to keep their creditors in line. Anything went at the Hôtel Stella, as long as the bills were paid. But woe betide the young man whose rent was in arrears and who was rash enough to bring a girl back to his room. Donning her hearing aid, the least deaf sister would keep close watch, lurking on the culprit's floor. Then, when unmistakable noise of sexual congress emerged from behind the door, she would burst in, waving the bill and threatening to call the police.

The sisters, who could have served as models for Daumier's cartoons, were not easily shocked and based their appreciation of their guests solely on the regularity with which the weekly bills were paid. One early dawn the ex-policeman driver of Reuters came to fetch me in the Reuters office car, a black Citroën of the kind used by the police, to drive me north to report on a large strike in progress there. The sisters—up and about as usual at 5:00 A.M.—watched me go with much 'I told you so' movements of the arms, shaking of the heads, and shrugging of shoulders. I returned late that evening. As I walked up the stairs past their loge, one of the sisters cried out, 'They kept asking you questions all day? But finally, they let you go?' Angrily I attempted to explain that I had not been arrested by the police. 'Forget it, I haven't said a word,' said the least villainous of the three. 'In any case, it's none of my business.'

I must stress that conditions at Reuters have changed

considerably since the days I describe and that Reuters' correspondents in Paris no longer have fo live at the Hôtel Stella. But our poverty then was compounded by a strict house rule forbidding any Reuters correspondent from working for anyone else. This rule I occasionally broke, and have no compunction in announcing the fact nearly thirty years later.

One successful French pocket-sized monthly was a *Reader's Digest* type of magazine called *Constellation*, whose editor was the late André Labarthe, a talented scientific journalist. The feature editor, however, the person most responsible for each issue, was a forbidding lady, called Madame Lecoutre, who with scarcely any prompting would embark on the oft-told story of how, as a visiting German Young Communist, she had been sent on a mission to Moscow and been seduced by Stalin.

True or not, the event had a marked influence on the kinds of features she wished to see in *Constellation*. A surefire formula, she was fond of saying in her staggeringly accented French, was *sexual ou stratégique*; the ideal story was the one which combined the two. Encouraged by her above-average fees and her somewhat tolerant attitude toward journalistic reality and license, a host of impoverished French journalists among my acquaintances—some of whom have since become so well known that I will name no names—set about fulfilling her somewhat unusual needs. I joined the group.

Many of the articles for *Constellation* were based on partial truths. Others were total inventions, but so plausible that they sounded right, fleshed out as they were be a certain amount of painstaking research. I helped get some facts right for other people's stories, earning a small slice of their fees. The only piece I can remember writing from beginning to end was a so-called autobiographical article entitled 'I Was King Ibn Seoud's Harem Doctor.'

Needless to say, the article was a fabrication, but it read plausibly, because rather than indulge in an Arabian Nights erotic fantasy, I emphasized the boredom, the emptiness, and the frustrations of harem life and researched my subject fairly thoroughly.

Madame Lecoutre never appeared to show any surprise that her stable of writers was able to produce the most amazing people to write for *Constellation*. But after a while she did insist that she meet the alleged authors. Thus, in the case of the harem doctor, an Italian was duly produced, and there was a considerable difficulty when, later, one of our small *Constellation* circle wrote an article entitled 'I Was Mao Tse-tung's Private Secretary.' A Chinese resident in Paris was duly found and suitably briefed. The personal encounter went off well. Somewhat overplaying his hand, the French journalist who had been responsible for 'I Was Mao Tse-tung's Private Secretary' went one better still and wrote a further piece, entitled 'I Was Secretary to Ho Chi Minh.' The same Chinese contact was called upon to meet Madame Lecoutre. 'She'll never tell the difference,' said the real author. She did, but handled herself with immense tongue-in-cheek aplomb. 'You were the secretary to the great Ho Chi Minh?' said Madame Lecoutre. Our Chinese friend admitted this was so. 'But you also worked for the great Mao Tse-tung?' The Chinese 'front' muttered that this had indeed been the case. 'Young man, young man, what an interesting life you must have had,' said Madame Lecoutre, handing over her check.

But perhaps the most lasting autobiographical fake ever to be published in *Constellation* was 'I Was Stalin's Nanny.' The putative author, a certain Boudou Zvanidze, was not to be found among our somewhat limited range of corrupt acquaintances who would impersonate the author in return for a small percentage of the fee. Indeed, the fluent Russian-speaking Madame Lecoutre would have seen through such an impersonation, even if the venerable nanny had survived that long (she would have had to be nearly a hundred years old at the time). Prodigies of eloquence were needed to persuade the *Constellation* editors that a Russian émigré of our acquaintance, remotely related to the Zvanidze family, had come across certain 'family papers'—including a diary kept by Stalin's nanny during his earliest years.

Needless to say, Boudou Zvanidze depicted her charge as a monster—smashing his toys, torturing animals, pulling the wings off flies, and providing other early evidence of inhuman behavior. After Stalin's death and the 20th Congress of the Communist Party of the USSR, at which Stalin's crimes were posthumously revealed, the article on Boudou Zvanidze assumed considerable importance. One rumor was that Khrushchev himself had referred to it in his famous speech attacking Stalin, as an example of Stalin's cruelty, and it has since been included in the endless biographical data concerning Stalin, not only in the West but, I am told, also in the Soviet Union itself.

My knowledge of the way *Constellation* was put together left me with a lasting distrust of sensational 'as told to' or directly autobiographical 'revelations.' Not long ago the editor of a well-known European magazine phoned me to offer to sell to *Newsweek* an exclusive story, 'culled from an impeccable East European source,' proving beyond doubt that Stalin, at the time of his death, was planning a third world war. Remembering Boudou Zvanidze, I turned him down.

It also left me with 'a healthy distrust of sensational photo-journalism. At the height of the Congo troubles in the sixties, a French free-lance photo-journalist called on *Life* magazine in Paris to offer, at a huge price, exclusive pictures of a Belgian woman allegedly being raped by Congolese troops. The pictures supposedly taken by one of the soldiers involved (the unexposed roll of film, the story went, had been conveniently found on a dead body), did indeed show a young woman being forcibly undressed after a struggle, held down, and raped by a succession of black soldiers. The pictures struck us all as phony, but mainly because the story of the film's discovery was so improbable.

We had a collective brainwave. 'I'll consider buying the pictures,' said *Life*'s bureau chief, Milton Orshefsky, 'if you'll show me the contact sheet.' It was duly produced. The last few frames showed the whole group posing in the equivalent of a school group photograph, the semi-nude Belgian girl with her arms around her rapists, and everyone grinning broadly.

It was while I was in the Reuters bureau that France was shaken by the 'Drummond murders.' Sir Jack Drummond, his wife, and their small daughter were bivouacking by the roadside in southern France one night when they were gunned down, and after an incredibly bungled investigation, an aged farmer, Gaston Dominici, was arrested and eventually tried. Because Sir Jack Drummond had been the British government's chief nutrition adviser during the war, the French press—encouraged by the police investigators—hinted darkly at a secret wartime *réglement de comptes* with Sir Jack Drummond in the role of a secret intelligence agent.

The case was never really solved. Gaston Dominici, thought by many to have been set up to 'take the rap' simply because he was the oldest of the clan, maintained he was innocent to the last. And the trial, a mixture of drama and high comedy, which a later film starring Jean Gabin in the role of Gaston Dominici failed to convey, was chiefly memorable for its end. As in all major trials in France, the jury was empowered to submit questions at the end of the proceedings. The president of the court reminded the jury of this and sat back, obviously expecting a host of questions to clarify what had been a muddled, confused trial. There was much whispering among the jury. Finally, the head juryman rose. '*Monsieur le Président*, we do have a question,' he said. The judge looked at him expectantly. 'Yes, it is this: How do we get reimbursed for our lunch expenses?'

It took me nearly four years to find out that I was not cut out for a Reuters career. Harold King had made this obvious from the start. Subject to fits of drooling rage almost indistinguishable from epileptic fits, this capricious martinet was not unlike the big man in *City Lights* who bullies Chaplin when sober and acts affectionate when drunk.

Reuters' Paris office was then a row of minuscule offices, overlooking the Place de la Bourse, of such squalor and filth that even my most bohemian friends were appalled when they visited me there. One distinguishing feature of the place, apart from its reform-school trestle tables and airless stench, was the fact that there were never sufficient typewriters to go around. Like rats in some Pavlov experiment, we waited to pounce on a vacant typewriter as soon as its previous user had his back turned. And sometimes, late at night, a typewriter would be immobilized; Harold King, in the middle of writing his editorial for the now-defunct *Continental Daily Mail*, would collapse over it in a snoring stupor. I would then take hold of his collar, lift him up, slide the typewriter away from him, and let his face slump forward onto the trestle table.

An ardent Gaullist, Harold King was the only foreign correspondent whom De Gaulle addressed using the intimate *tu* form of speech, and King habitually referred to De Gaulle in his stories as 'General de Gaulle, Savior of France,' in much the same manner that today East German officials refer to East Berlin as 'Berlin, capital of the DDR.' Harold King also stretched the competitive limits of Reuters to occasional unacceptable lengths. He prided himself on his intimate knowledge of the voting habits of the notoriously fickle deputies of the Fourth Republic. Since the fall of governments was determined, on an almost monthly basis, by the way the deputies voted in the National Assembly, the collapse— or momentary survival— of a Fourth Republic government was inevitably a cliff-hanging, suspenseful affair.

After haunting the lobbies of the National Assembly on a crucial vote-of-no-confidence night, Harold King would phone in a totally premature bulletin, announcing the government's fall or survival, on the basis of his own intuitive sense. He was often right, but he was wrong not an inconsiderable part of the time, with elaborate 'rowbacks,' including the somewhat shop-soiled phrase 'A later recount showed that the government had survived by a narrow margin.' King, on the nights he guessed accurately, thus scored appreciable 'beats' over his rivals. When he was wrong, Reuters turned a blind eye.

I inevitably fell afoul of Harold King and as punishment was sent back to London to act as night editor of the Latin American desk, than which there was no worse fate. It was grim, boring work, starting at 6:00 P.M. and ending at 4:00 A.M., made worse by the fact that the man I had replaced was dying of cancer—and I was the obvious choice as successor. I started looking in earnest for another job and in 1954, quite coincidentally, was approached by a friend on the staff of Jean Monnet, then president of the High Authority of the European Coal and Steel Community, who needed a public affairs officer.

'You can't leave Reuters,' I was told. 'You owe us too much money.' (I did indeed owe some. Accumulating a debt in Reuters in those days was as easy to do as it is for a Bihari peasant today to fall into the clutches of a moneylender.) I bought my freedom with a loan from my family. But only months after joining the ECSC, Jean Monnet himself was removed from his post, and I was faced with the prospect of looking for another job or going back to Reuters.

I chose to free-lance in Algeria (of which more later), and after a year I became a *Time-Life* correspondent. Suddenly for the first time in my life, I was living a life of relative affluence. *Time* sent me to New York to 'learn to write.' Assigned to a junior writer's cubicle in *Time*'s old Rockefeller Center offices (the Time-Life building was not yet completed), I left my desk one day for a lunchtime beer and sandwich. When I got back to my tiny windowless rabbit hutch, there was someone in my chair: an elderly man with a lined craftsman's face, in a suit *Time* would have described as 'rumpled' and of shocking, electric blue. He was typing away at my typewriter, and at first I thought he was a mechanic sent to repair and clean my somewhat defective machine. I waited for him to put away his tools. I then noticed he hadn't any. 'Hey, you can't stay here,' I said. 'This is my typewriter.' He looked up, mumbled something, grabbed some papers, and left. I had just kicked Henry Luce out of my office.

In my seven years with Time Inc., this was the only moment we actually came face to face. Subsequently, on his visits to Paris, I contrived to be sent out of town on improbable reporting assignments.

Not that Henry Luce, or 'Harry,' as he liked to be called, was the ogre he has been portrayed. As in all cases of extremely biased biography, Luce may well be in for at least partial rehabilitation. He was Victorian in his sense of mission, his belief in the superiority of his native land over all others, his indifference to good food and drink, and his belief in hard work as a cathartic experience. He was, of course, abominably prejudiced in some respects, with a black-and-white vision of the world and a belief that it was divided into 'good guys' and 'bad guys.' There was a tendency on his part to equate action with movement, and his endless globe-trotting and mingling with the great and near great appeared to stem from a fear of loneliness as much as from a snobbish craving for distinguished company. But he had immense charm and that other indefinable quality: an instinctive ability to inspire loyalty in others, even those dramatically opposed to his political views. In his later years the worst *Time* excesses were caused by subordinates who tried to prove their zeal by exaggerating the prejudices entertained by Luce himself. Had Luce not died in 1967, it is almost certain that some subsequent management errors (hasty investment in MGM and software stock and the purchase of *Saturday Evening*

Post subscriber lists, which increased *Life's* already top-heavy circulation) would not have occurred, for Luce was a shrewd and cautious businessman, for all his innovations.

Though autocratic, ill-mannered, and direct to the point of rudeness, Luce could also display himself in singularly humble colors, determined to show that riches had not divorced him from the fraternity of newsmen. In a crisis Luce would delight in being 'one of the boys,' holding phones, running errands, and even volunteering to do some legwork himself. In this respect he reminded me of another newspaper tycoon, *France-Soir* editor Pierre Lazareff. Both had a genuine passion for the craft of journalism, and both, I suspect, attempted to recapture their youth whenever they played at being reporters again. These days such a passion may appear suspect to an increasingly suspicious generation that regards any single-minded search for facts as a manifestation of mere prurient curiosity, unless it is accompanied by a politically motivated crusade against the political Establishment.

It was a passion for facts which set *Time* and *Life* aside from other publications. Never was there a more thorough outward search for factual accuracy. Teams of researchers checked every sentence, and indeed every word, in every story appearing in print in both magazines, marking each checked word with a penciled dot. At the same time it was often said in those days that one's acceptance of a *Time* story was in inverse proportion to one's knowledge of the facts involved. This was due not only to recognizable *Time* (and *Life*) prejudices but to the need to compress, to refine, to encapsulate, which often resulted in gross distortions creeping into the final story despite the search for factual accuracy.

For *Time* and *Life* correspondents in the field, the net result was like being on the receiving end of questions from an outrageously querulous, eccentric millionaire, demanding instant replies.

The rapid-fire question was also a Luce technique, used

to deflate self-important correspondents, and the result was that before Luce's arrival in any foreign capital, Time Inc. staffers would be seen feverishly swotting up facts of every description about the countries in which they operated, ranging from the sexual proclivities of leading politicians (for Luce was an inveterate gossip) to the number of Communists in the armed forces in their area. And such was the Luce gift for asking odd questions that these attempts at instant expertise were usually doomed to failure and served no useful purpose. Luce's examination almost invariably took one by surprise.

But if Luce's stream of questions was both original and ingenuous, the stream of queries from both *Time* and *Life* editors defied description. One I vividly remember concerned the well-known French cabaret and musical comedy star Mistinguett, who had just died at a ripe old age.

The cable read: 'Our information is that she had no pubic hair. Please check soonest and advise.' It was like a game: Find, within the space of two hours, someone who knew what Mistinguett's cunt looked like. It's a tribute to the kind of resourcefulness journalists develop, useful only in reporters, criminals, detectives, and secret agents, that between 7:00 and 9:00 A.M. we managed to track down a surviving French roué with firsthand experience of Mistinguett's androgynous, delectable body—and apparent total recall. 'She had some, but very little,' he said with more than a hint of slobbering nostalgia, coupled with amazement that anyone would want to know.

Needless to say, the presence or absence of Mistinguett's pubic hair was never featured in the published story about her. Indeed, most *Time* and *Life* queries of such an arcane, intimate nature seemed designed to satisfy a private rather than a public curiosity: hardly ever were the facts, sometimes obtained at considerable trouble, delay, and expense, embodied in the finished article. *Time* and *Life*, after all, were 'family' magazines. This was the time when

The New York Times, in its color magazine ads, brushed out navels.

Sometimes, however, *Life*, which, even more than *Time*, assumed its unique status with a good deal of hubris, let fly with such uninhibited arrogance and brashness that one was tempted to reply to some cables in the same fashion as the legendary *Time-Life* bureau chief in London during the Second World War: 'This one I frame.' The story was that during the war *Life* noted that because of severe fuel shortages, the British government was appealing to the British people to take their baths in not more than five inches of hot water. This struck someone in New York as a fine *Life* photo opportunity. A cable duly went out to London. 'Want to photograph King George Sixth in his bath,' it read, adding, with unusual reticence, 'Back view will do.'

I myself, about to embark on a lengthy and authoritative story in text and pictures of the Algerian War, was somewhat concerned to note that among the pictures photographer Howard Sochurek and I were expected to bring back was one showing 'Algerian FLN rebels carrying out a successful attack on a French *pied-noir* farm.' At the risk of appearing a sissy, I felt it my duty to point out, in a self-deprecatory memo, that should we indeed be privy to such pictures, they would doubtless make a terrific *Life* spread—but would also require *Life* to hire an entirely fresh reporting team, since statistically speaking, all such attacks on French farms in Algeria ended in the gory deaths of all those who stayed to watch.

Not surprisingly, *Life* photographers, around whom *Life* was built, exhibited egos more in keeping with coloratura sopranos from the Metropolitan Opera than journalists. 'Tell them we're from *Life* magazine' was the rejoinder of the irritated photographer who felt that his lowly reporter was not making sufficient progress or displaying sufficient 'chutzpah,' or when the subjects approached by him failed to react positively to *Life*'s wish to photograph them in the nude, or jumping up and down, or up to their necks in water.

It was necessary, on such occasions, to deal firmly with prima donna photographers. 'You tell them yourself' was one ploy. (Few *Life* photographers spoke foreign languages, and when they did, their English was usually incomprehensible.) 'We tell them we're from *Life* and they'll cut our little throats' was another possible rejoinder, not altogether fanciful in places like Algeria and the Congo, where threats of violent death were bandied about with considerable freedom. It is difficult, now that *Life* has been dead for so long, to imagine the awe a really distinguished *Life* photographer inspired in junior reporters and researchers.

Their bulky equipment invariably required the services of hordes of porters, and they themselves delighted in the directorial tantrums I have seen exhibited on Cinecitta sets only by Fellini and Visconti.

The late Margaret Bourke-White made an Indian refugee family, at partition time in 1947, bury and rebury its dead several times before extracting sufficient pathos from the scene. A *Life* photographer, it's said, obtained a compelling picture of a small weeping Chinese child in Indonesia by the simple expedient of cuffing the unfortunate boy across the head when no one was looking. The dedication of star *Life* photographers to their craft, their finicky passion for perfection, drove otherwise sane reporters into a shaky determination to seek out some other way of making a living. And since most of them were thick-skinned and egotistical beyond belief, they never realized how impossible they were.

I only twice knowingly scored off *Life* photographers. In one instance, as *Time-Life* New Delhi bureau chief, I received the visit of Alfred Eisenstaedt, the dean of *Life* photographers, who appeared on the Indian scene with an assistant, a woman anthropologist from Australia, in tow. This was the era of endless animal stories, and Eisenstaedt was on an assignment to do a huge *Life* spread on 'the social life of monkeys,' an essay that was to take him not only to India but to Malaysia as well.

After unsuccessfully attempting to interest Eisenstaedt in a bunch of monkeys that habitually boarded Indian trains near Calcutta to ride out to feeding grounds and lush sugar plantations—riding back to their native habitat on the 'down' train in the evening like worthy commuters—I was brash enough to dare to discuss photography techniques with him.

'You know, Eisie,' I said, with all the self-confidence of a Roman Catholic convert discussing points of doctrine with the Pope, 'I've discovered that the light here in India is so intense that it's sometimes even brighter than what's recorded on light meters.' Eisenstaedt looked at me, speechless. He was a guest at my house, so he didn't say, 'Look, buster, you stick to your side of things, and I'll stick to mine,' but he made it clear to me that I had committed an extraordinary faux pas.

Weeks later, after Eisenstaedt had expedited more than 100 rolls of color film back to New York, I received the following cable from *Life*'s senior photo editor. 'Break the news gently to Eisie,' it said, 'but some film badly overexposed. It will need reshooting.' Mindful of the earlier snub, I simply handed the cable over to him and said, 'Read this.'

The other occasion involved the late Eliot Elisofon, perhaps the most egotistical of all *Life* photographers—and one of the most accomplished photographers of any generation. *Time-Life*, when I worked for it, occupied palatial premises overlooking the Place de la Concorde in Paris. I happened to be inside the elevator when Elisofon appeared with several metal suitcases then favored by *Life* photographers for storing their gear. From my appearance, he immediately assumed I was the elevator operator. 'Here, boy,' he said, 'take these up to the second floor, *compris?*' I complied and pocketed a tip, assuming he would be duly mortified, in due course, to discover who I really was. But Eliot Elisofon never realized that I *wasn't* a liftboy.

My revenge came a few years later, in 1963. Having left Time Inc., I was making a TV movie about avant-garde New York artists in the West Village. In a studio where the poet Allen Ginsberg was holding forth, I suddenly spotted Elisofon, shooting away. 'Get that punk out of here,' I said, in mock outrage. 'How can I possibly work with that creep clicking away?' He was duly ejected.

The cost of *Life*'s editorial operation must have been staggering, for not only did *Life* teams roam the world at huge expense, but editors invariably ordered up more stories than they could possibly publish. I never understood why, though one possible reason was that they wished to foment, and maintain, an element of competition between *Life* staffers, elevating tension to an art form. No one likes to go month after month without seeing himself in print, and some *Life* photographers and staffers were driven to desperation, and to extremes, by their failure to get their stories into the magazine. This egged them on to ever greater efforts.

Another consequence of this tendency to over-order stories for which there was no space was that on occasion *Life* teams left considerable ill will in their wake. Aggrieved parties, who had gone to immense trouble and inconvenience in baring their private lives and opening their homes to *Life* teams, would wait, often for months and sometimes forever, for stories about them to appear. Bitter recriminations invariably followed.

I was perhaps more fortunate than most in that nearly all the stories I worked on ran. But it's worthwhile giving a detailed account of the tribulations of one that didn't. In 1960-61, with photographer Pierre Boulat, I spent nearly two months, first in Algeria, then in Chad and Niger, working on a definitive color story about the Sahara. After flying to Fort-Lamy, as it was then still called, the capital of

Chad, we found every single bed in town requisitioned by a Berliet truck expedition crossing the Sahara from south to north and had to sleep in an aircraft hangar on camp beds provided by the local airline representative. Our intention was to attach ourselves to this desert convoy for a few days, which eventually we did. (On New Year's Eve, by some incredible logistics feat, the Berliet organizers even provided for the trucking teams a *reveillon* of lobster and champagne.)

We flew back to Algiers, then back to Niger and Chad, hiring small planes by the day. One was a French government four-seater, lent by the cooperative governor of Chad, Daniel Doustin. The crew was provided by the French Air Force, and the captain, a Corsican, had only one theme of conversation: how he had been unfairly passed over in his bid to begin jet fighter training.

We soon understood why. Whenever he landed, he barely made it, submitting our small plane to groaning, crunchy stresses, accompanied by copious smells of burning rubber from the complaining tires. On one flight, when we seemed to have been in the air for more than the prescribed time, I got a little nervous. I consulted with the pilot. 'Can't find the damned oasis,' he said. A look at the map revealed there were two oases side by side. Knowing the pilot, I was virtually certain that he had flown wide of the mark and was, in fact, flying away from them.

'How much fuel do you have left?' I asked.

'We're OK,' he said. 'We have at least enough for twenty minutes.'

We were flying over some of the most barren desert in the world, and only a week previously, the local Algiers papers had featured the story of the discovery of this very area of the remains of a British Blenheim bomber, which a nomad caravan had just stumbled on. The bomber had been missing since 1941.

I consulted briefly with Boulat. 'Turn back, turn back,' we both screamed hysterically. We landed at the oasis with enough fuel to keep a Zippo lighter going for a few seconds.

This oasis, called Oulanga Kebir, consisted of a stretch of water that was spectacularly beautiful to look at, but was salty and brackish and hot to the touch. A French NCO from the colonial infantry ruled over the area with thirty somewhat mutinous militiamen. The NCO told us that he had volunteered for this, the worst hardship post in the French Army, because time counted triple here. A few more years and he would retire at the age of thirty-five. He had bought himself a young local 'wife' (whom he refused to introduce) and in our honor made us a huge omelet out of an ostrich egg she had just given him. I asked him how he passed the time. 'A camel convoy comes once a month and delivers mail and *Constellation*,' he said.

'Surely you must get rather bored?'

'I'm a slow reader,' he said.

A few days later we set out with a Camel Corps patrol, still French-officered, across some of the most inhospitable country in the world. The officer in charge, a captain, was extolling the extraordinary sense of direction of his nomad militiamen. 'They can spot who owns a camel simply by looking at its spoor in the sand,' he was saying when his NCO came up to him, saluted smartly, and said, '*Mon capitaine*, we're lost.'

Our Saharan adventure included a hair-raising drive from Algiers to Tamanrasset and back. This was 1960, the height of the Algerian War, and there were few signposts to guide us on our way, but there were numerous tracks of oil exploration convoys which petered out into blank desert. Boulat was crazy about cars, and claimed that a certain type of Renault he had been lent in Algiers was just the kind of vehicle needed for such a trip. We mended thirty-eight punctures, and it was some time before I was on speaking terms with Boulat again. We got lost so many times, spent so much time digging ourselves out of sandy ruts, that the original purpose of the experience—to try to take pictures of desert mirages, of which there were plenty—was all but forgotten in a frantic struggle for survival.

When we finally returned to Paris, however, we had enough material to put the *National Geographic* to shame. But we were victims of a typical *Life* syndrome. By the time we returned *Life* editors had lost interest in the story. The net result was that for all our crisscrossing of the Sahara and Boulat's spectacular pictures of Toubou and Touareg tribesmen, French oil fields, and skulls of victims of inter-tribal warfare piled up in the desert, moonlike surfaces, and bustling oasis markets, only three photographs of his were even published by *Life*, in its later book on the desert. Each one, I reckoned, must have cost more than $20,000 to take.

This was par for the course. At Pamplona once a celebrated *Life* photographer insisted that an archway be built across the main street, the better to photograph, from a height, the rush of oncoming bulls. The edifice, costing $10,000, was never used, and the photographer himself, knocked over by a bull early on in the day, never took a single picture.

In France at least, many *Life* assignments were carried out in conditions that bore no relationship to journalism as I had previously practiced it. *Life* teams at work on a French story would proceed at a leisurely pace from three-star restaurant to three-star restaurant. A typical *Life* team included a researcher, or a girlfriend, cronies to play poker or gin rummy with in the evenings. A favorite on such trips was Peppi Martis, an ex-Foreign Legion NCO, fluent in at least six languages, who would invariably skin everyone at cards.

Another feature of the *Life* bureau in Paris was a personal friend of Henry Luce's, who looked like a typical 'man of distinction' in the old Hathaway shirt ads. He had numerous elevated social connections, an extremely rich wife, a Rolls-Royce, a private mansion in Neuilly, and an immaculate wardrobe, and only rarely did any reporting or writing.

Not surprisingly the French socialists he mingled with assumed that he was the overall boss in Paris of both *Time* and *Life*—an assumption he never openly endorsed but did little to dispel. So, on numerous occasions throughout the years, both *Time* and *Life* bureau chiefs (who, like most working reporters, socialized little and spent most of their spare time with colleagues) would meet prominent Paris figures, both French and American, who would say, casually, with a trace of condescension, 'By the way, I met your boss at a party last night.'

His Rolls-Royce figures in a number of *Time-Life* stories. Thus, in 1952, when the British diplomats Guy Burgess and Donald Maclean defected to the Soviet Union, *Life*, in common with all the news media in Paris, tried to seek them out and followed wild leads and tip-offs, since the rumor was that they had gone to ground in France. A number of such leads, all, it turned out, baseless, kept the press corps busy for weeks, on mushrooming expense accounts. One such lead had an element of fact to it: Maclean's wife, Melinda, was indeed found vacationing near St. Tropez, and hundreds of reporters of all nationalities gathered around her rented villa, making her life miserable.

Life received a different tip-off. Burgess and Maclean, according to this information, were not in the Soviet Union but had romantically 'eloped' together, to a château in the South of France. The usual *Life* expedition was mounted, consisting of a photographer, reporter, and researcher in Luce's friend's chauffeured Rolls. After the ritual mandatory stops at three-star restaurants along the way, the Rolls two days later glided into a stately château driveway. Rather the worse for wear, a reporter emerged and rang the front doorbell. A liveried valet opened the door. 'Excuse me,' said the reporter, 'are Messieurs Burgess and Maclean staying here?'

'*Non*, monsieur,' said the dignified servant.

'Well, thanks a lot,' said the reporter, and the Rolls

headed back to Paris.

Life's affluence in the fifties was in sharp contrast with the ill-paid, struggling French press, which, except for the *Figaro* and *Paris-Match*, operated on the proverbial shoestring. But *Life* was nothing if not hospitable. During the events of May–June 1958, when General de Gaulle returned to power, the French left organized a huge protest march through the streets of Paris. *Life*, to cover the event, not only deployed its own and contract photographers on the streets but also hired a suite in a hotel overlooking the Place de la République. There, in between taking pictures of the procession below, *Life* staffers and their guests drank whiskey and champagne served by white-coated waiters. The suite became a press bar. A number of French reporters, in between drinks, commented on *Life*'s 'going to a party' in somewhat derogatory terms.

Perhaps the hallmark of *Time-Life* in the halcyon sixties was a mixture of immense sophistication and abysmal ignorance. Art Buchwald, then writing his column in Paris, was a frequent visitor, who regularly played gin rummy for hours at a time on Fridays. His columns told one more about France than most reports did. But one *Life* bureau chief, newly arrived in Paris and summoning stringers and local correspondents in his area to meet him, staggered our Geneva stringer by asking, 'Do you speak Swiss?'

Encouraged by Buchwald, I played a practical joke on one of my more senior colleagues which undoubtedly caused a serious blight on my *Time-Life* career. One of *Life*'s senior editors had, after De Gaulle's accession to power in 1958, been awarded the Legion of Honor by Jacques Soustelle, then still De Gaulle's faithful aide. The years went by, and as it became clear that De Gaulle was intent on granting Algeria independence, Soustelle and De Gaulle fell out. Eventually Soustelle found it necessary to go into exile, to escape possible arrest. Inevitably rumors floated that he was connected with the counterterrorist 'Keep Algeria French' OAS (Organisation Armée Secrète)

100

movement.

During one of those gin rummy games with Art, I suggested playing a cruel joke on our *Life* senior editor. Why not, I suggested, send him a letter, purporting to come from Jacques Soustelle, asking him to show his support and friendship by sending back his medal to De Gaulle, as many prominent Frenchmen protesting against De Gaulle's Algerian policy had already done?

The drinking that accompanied the gin rummy games probably explained my irresponsible behavior. It so happened that I had once received a letter from Jacques Soustelle and therefore had his signature in my possession.

My own 'Soustelle' letter, in excellent but obviously somewhat Frenchified English, was perused by Buchwald and other gin players with approval. It recalled the award of the Legion of Honor 'in happier times.' It went on to say that a number of personalities had sent their medals back. It appealed to our senior editor to do the same. And it ended with a veiled threat that should such action not be forthcoming, the OAS in New York might just blow up the new Time-Life building. (The letter was mailed in West Germany, where Soustelle then was.)

This last bit, inserted to show that this senseless and vulgar prank was indeed a farce, was my undoing, for the recipient of the letter took it very seriously. The first thing he did was to send it to the French Embassy in Washington, asking whether this was indeed Soustelle's signature. The reply came back that it was.

Then our senior editor canceled a scheduled trip to Europe. Finally, he showed the letter to some equally senior executives, who decided to hire Pinkerton guards for an indefinite period, and at considerable cost, to watch over the Time-Life building.

I was appalled to find my admittedly tasteless prank had been taken seriously. After a week I decided to admit all. I phoned a senior colleague in New York and explained that I was the originator of the threatening letter, that I took full responsibility for it and wished to apologize. But the colleague in question was no friend of our senior editor. 'Let's make him sweat it out,' he said. So for some weeks an elaborate and expensive comedy was played out in the Time-Life building, until the butt of my joke learned, at long last, that there had been no OAS threat on either his life or on *Life* itself. He was understandably furious and may have been responsible for my next posting. For after a successful few years covering the Algerian War, I had been told that I would probably be able to pick my next assignment. I timidly ventured to ask whether I could become *Time*'s junior movie critic. Instead, I was sent to India, just in time to witness the brief, humiliating India-China War of October 1962.

The war, which should perhaps be described as a 'war,' began with mutual recriminations at alleged frontier violations by both Chinese and Indian troops on the India-China border at Ladakh and in India's North-East Frontier Agency (NEFA). It escalated into a series of skirmishes, all at 16,000 feet and over, in a lunar landscape so arid and inhospitable that it was difficult to imagine at first why either side wanted any of the countryside involved. At first there was considerable Indian self-congratulation at what looked like a series of successful mini-battles, enabling Indian troops to wrest control of some border points occupied by the Chinese. But the battles escalated, and I went to investigate.

The headquarters of the Indian Army corps waging the skirmishes was in the Assamese town of Tezpur, a tea-growing area which had once before seen an invasion of reporters, for the Dalai Lama had come this way after fleeing from Tibet in 1959. Our first night in Tezpur was a nightmare: a hotel room with wooden boards for beds, bugs of every kind, and a washbasin and toilet, both unconnected to any plumbing, and, needless to say, no water.

The second day *Life* photographer Larry Burrows and I

102

thought we had found a marvelous billet. Old soldiers both by this time at the game of making oneself comfortable under adverse conditions, we sought out a local American mission hospital and were grudgingly offered a room for as long as we needed it. But our host, a Baptist missionary of the strictest, most fundamentalist kind, obviously regarded us with considerable suspicion and was torn between his Christian duty to help fellow travelers in need and his own religious principles. A deeply conservative Republican who spent an unbelievable proportion of his working day rehearsing the local Christian population in hymn singing, our host regarded *Time* as a dangerously liberal organ. What's more, he had the impression that reporters, even in Tezpur, spent their time drinking and whoring. 'If you have any liquor, be sure and keep it locked up. I don't want any drinking here, even in private and behind locked doors' was his initial warning to us on showing us to our quarters.

Alas, our sanctuary didn't last long. During my first week in Tezpur, unable to go to the 'front' (Evelyn Waugh's classic *Scoop* contains some archetypal situations which keep repeating themselves generation after generation), I wrote a piece about Tezpur: the sudden army activity, the muted alarm among the townspeople, the calm of the tea planters, and the fact that while the Baptist missionaries had sent their families to Calcutta for safety and were themselves making contingency plans to leave town, the Catholic missionaries had expressed the determination to stay on at all costs.

With the country in a quasi-state of war, disrupted communications, and India's naturally slow postal system, it seemed to me unlikely that our reluctant and prickly host would receive his subscription copy of *Time* during our stay. I knew that if he did, he would be angered by my reference to his mission. Though he had complained to me that copies were reaching him as much as a month late, the issue with my story in it arrived, by some freak of the Indian postal system, that very week. Larry Burrows and I were

103

taking furtive nips from a bottle of scotch we kept concealed in his camera case when our missionary burst in on us in a furious temper. 'That does it,' he said. 'Out.'

We packed, under his sullen eye, making sotto voce remarks about the limits of Christian charity. I had had the foresight to rent a taxi full time, and we drove back to our woodenboard hotel. Fearing—rightly as it turned out—that some transport might be requisitioned should events turn sour, I had hired a car—and a driver—that no army in its senses, even in the midst of a Caporetto-like retreat, would ever think of requisitioning. Its flanks were an interesting pattern of intricate shades of rust and successive paint layers, half Jackson Pollock, half Jean Dubuffet. The engine had to be hand-cranked to start. As it shakily progressed on its way, it emitted a black smoke screen of burning oil. I first came across it in the company of a young Canadian reporter who had arrived with me from Calcutta. 'Take me to military HQ,' I told the driver. He got out, waving a starting handle. Then, remembering something, he bent underneath the car and dragged out an aged beggar who had been sheltering there, a latter-day Diogenes. The beggar was obviously very sick, and I remonstrated with the driver, urging him to take the beggar to hospital instead of—as he appeared set on doing—dragging him to the nearest ditch and leaving him there to die. Overcoming the driver's protests, we loaded the beggar into the car and drove off to the hospital, which is how I discovered the American Baptist mission in the first place.

As we proceeded, my Canadian companion was wrapped in thought. 'Ask the driver,' he said, 'how long the old man has been underneath the car.'

'He says two days.'

'My God, how about that! D'ya mean to say he hasn't had a fare in two days?'

The overall commander of the NEFA front was Lieutenant General Brij Mohan 'Tikki' Kaul, who had been a major on the staff of the brigade of which my own Garhwali battalion had been part. With an increasing number of Indian and foreign correspondents arriving on the scene, he promised to arrange for us to visit the front, which at this time was still, apart from minor skirmishing, largely static.

With time on our hands, we became honorary members of the Tezpur Club (mainly frequented by tea planters, now almost all Indian, but still clinging to the trappings of quintessentially British tea planters' routines, with tennis, snooker, squash, and bridge to while away the days). The district commissioner, whom we called on, assured us of his willingness to help 'in any way I can.' (When I next saw him, he was in the front seat of a truck with his not inconsiderable family and belongings packed behind, heading for the Brahmaputra ferry and the safety of West Bengal. The town's police force followed in their own transport, similarly burdened.)

Eventually the kindly Tezpur Club committeemen allowed the ever-growing band of reporters to use not only the few club bedrooms but also the club grounds. General Kaul provided some army tents, latrines were built, and we settled into a frustratingly empty routine, causing the club's liquor supplies to reach unprecedentedly low depths. And one day General Kaul made good his promise: A convoy of several army jeeps, packed with correspondents, left for the NEFA front.

It was a fascinating ride—like suddenly becoming a fly on the rim of some huge crater. At one point, we peered over the knife-edge ravine to watch, several thousand feet below, a Dakota plane unloading supplies by parachute in the narrow valley below us. Statuesque NEFA tribesmen, almost naked and carrying spears and bows and arrows, watched our convoy in silence, understandably failing to respond to our officer's cry of '*Jai Hind.*' A few tea-stall owners and small shopkeepers along the way did wave back, returning the ritual cry. Rumor, later, held them to

105

be fifth columnists in the pay of the Chinese.

After forty-eight hours we reached Sela Pass, the point where the Indians and Chinese were eyeball to eyeball. By a strange coincidence, a battalion of my former regiment held this crucial part of the border, at over 16,500 feet. I found a few old friends, including B. M. Bhattacharjia, the battalion commander, who had been my contemporary in Sumatra.

I couldn't help noticing how ill-equipped this battalion was for mountain warfare; the Garhwalis had no winter clothing, only pullovers and greatcoats. I gave my battalion commander friend my gloves and a scarf. We spent the night at Sela Pass. Some my colleagues were overcome by the altitude. Its effect on me was one of exhilaration. Larry Burrows took picture after picture of Second World War vintage artillery being hauled into position.

I had planned to stay with the battalion but was refused permission to do so. The following morning, at dawn, we began the long, hair-raising trek downward, toward the steaming Assam plain. We left the Garhwal battalion still expecting a Chinese attack, but with high morale, considering the climate, their equipment, and obviously out-of-date weapons.

The trip back was uneventful, but when we reached Tezpur, the town was half deserted, police and local administration were fleeing, and anyone with any transport was leaving for Bengal.

For moments after our departure from Sela Pass, the Chinese had launched a massive attack. Not only that, but having infiltrated the mountain road to Sela Pass days before, they attacked at points along it in a well-coordinated, sophisticated operation, cutting the road, and somehow, almost miraculously, we had slipped through the same road just ahead of the Chinese attackers, leaving carnage and confusion in our wake.

To stay or not to stay? One veteran British correspondent said, with commendable *J'y suis, j'y reste* bulldog pluck, 'I'm not leaving without my laundry.' Needless to say, he never did get it back, but most of us stayed anyway. Tezpur had the beleaguered air of a city about to fall to the barbarians, but there was a carnival air about it, too. Inexplicably, before leaving for the relative safety of the Brahmaputra ferry (which kept functioning throughout this period), local authorities had not only released prisoners from the local jail and patients from the local mental hospital but had also ordered that all rupee note stocks in Tezpur banks be burned. Huge bonfires were started, and hundreds of townspeople, too poor to leave, fought each other for half-charred notes. Harmless lunatics roamed the streets. Prisoners mingled with the crowds but apparently did no one any harm. The overall impression was of a burlesque *Désert des Tartares*, in an Indian setting. But the Chinese never came. With incredible self-restraint, the advance unit of the Chinese ambushing party stopped short some twenty miles of Tezpur itself. Then they about-turned and walked back to Tibet.

While all this was taking place, a far more momentous drama was being played out elsewhere: The 1962 Cuban missile crisis was in full swing. This enabled me to confirm the golden rule of journalism, never officially admitted but everwhere tacitly observed: A conflict or calamity in the 'developed' world has precedence over a similar event in the 'developing' world. Its corollary is equally pertinent; as with Gresham's law, so with conflicts: New wars drive out old wars. In May 1958, for instance, news media all over the world were reporting news of a nasty little civil war in Indonesia, being waged mainly in Sumatra. Then came the Beirut crisis of 1958 and the events of May 1958 in Algeria and France—and I defy anyone to find out, from reading the papers, even of 'record,' what subsequently happened in Sumatra or how the civil war ended there in 1958.

In short, our India-China War story, which in normal times would have made the front page all over the world and brought a certain amount of ephemeral fame to those reporting it, went almost unnoticed not only in the United States but also in the rest of the world. The press was not the only body to rue the coincidence of this mini-war and President Kennedy's confrontation with Khrushchev. Professor J. K. Galbraith, then American ambassador in New Delhi, was equally frustrated. Never averse to the limelight and having masterminded a delicate arms lift to India, he found himself upstaged by events elsewhere and referred to the fact, in restricted company, with his inimitable wit, which would have sounded callous to outsiders but was in fact a humorous safety valve to relieve his considerable tensions.

After my return to Delhi from Tezpur, I may have reinforced Galbraith's belief in the evils of nuclear proliferation, for I mentioned to him a conversation I had just had in the Indian Parliament with a senior Congress figure. 'We are a peace-loving, Gandhian nation,' the politician had told me. 'But if we had the H-bomb, we would have dropped it on those bastards.'

Our Tezpur trip was not entirely in vain. Both *Time* and *Life* gave the story considerable space, though our troubles with the army censor assumed a tragicomic intensity. It was required that all pictures of our trip to Sela Pass be submitted to the Indian government. After the collapse of the whole NEFA front, such orders no longer made sense, and many of us relied on cooperative airline crews to smuggle pictures out of the country. Some of the *Life* film, however, was handed in to the authorities for processing, with the result that pictures taken by Larry Burrows several weeks previously of Indian troops manhandling guns around Sela Pass were 'censored.' 'They give away our positions and our equipment,' said a Defense Ministry spokesman.

'But the whole area is in the hands of the Chinese, the guns have been captured, and the men in the picture are either captured or dead!' I argued.

'That makes no difference,' said the spokesman.

I was reminded of this when, years later, on a TV assignment in Calcutta in 1966, I had to resort to a camera concealed inside a golf bag to film Howrah Bridge. Because the bridge was a potential 'military objective,' government notices at both ends of the bridge—built at the turn of the century—warned that photography was strictly forbidden. It was, however, presumably all right for putative spies to buy picture postcards of the same Howrah Bridge, on display all over Calcutta.

Though I wasn't present at the editor's conference in New York when Larry Burrows's pictures of the India-China War were selected for a *Life* layout, I had watched the process so many times that I imagined the scene easily. The editor, a huge cigar in his clenched fist, looked down on a table. Researchers aligned their own picture selections from among the hundreds of pictures Burrows had taken, reciting the while, like a litany, the summary of their contents. The editor scattered ash, fingered picture after picture, rejected those he didn't like, dropping them on the floor, where they were trampled by the small crowd that invariably, like students watching a master surgeon operate, congregated to watch.

Eventually, and not always happily, pictures were matched, text was decided on, space allocated. Huge folders of unwanted photographs were consigned to oblivion, and a fresh team of researchers, like African women bearing their native produce for white traders to haggle over, offering derisory sums, trooped in to replace those offering the Behr-Burrows story. Few people in New York cared about, or were even aware of, the circumstances in which the pictures had been obtained: Throughout our trip to Sela Pass, Burrows had scrambled about from one vantage point to another, oblivious of the pain that resulted from a badly infected case of athlete's foot which would have confined most people to their beds. The prodigies of deception I had to go through to persuade 'pigeons' (as they're known in the trade) to carry the film back to New York had led to nervous exhaustion, for past a certain deadline, I knew, the pictures and story were valueless, and our trip all in vain. Had Burrows—who was killed in Vietnam in 1971—known that the magazine he cherished and worked so hard for would no longer exist a year after his death, would he, then and subsequently, have taken such risks and pushed himself to the limits of physical endurance?

My guess is that he would. Like many of the truly great photographers, Larry Burrows simply failed to notice what went on around him when he was engrossed in a major story. So, in Vietnam, he went on one dangerous military operation after another, simply to seek out the ultimate, perfectly composed picture that would both illustrate the horror of the war he deplored and satisfy him as an artist. Unlike some photographers, who confessed to an inexplicable exhilaration in moments of danger, an exhilaration I found myself at times sharing, Larry Burrows was a quiet, reflective, if sometimes inarticulate man, for whom the outside world simply faded away when he concentrated his talents on one assignment, much in the same way as a truly great painter isolates himself from everything that is inessential during the act of creation.

I wish I had some kind of film record of Larry Burrows in action, to show to all the embryo photographers who think that it's a glamorous, easy profession. One of the hallmarks of Larry Burrows's work was that regardless of the circumstances, it was almost invariably technically perfect.

The profusion of would-be professional photographers, ever on the increase in Europe and America, is a source of considerable irritation to those well-established ones who find the field already sufficiently crowded. One well-known war photographer, in Vietnam, was infuriated by the presence of other reporters and photographers, spoiling his picture composition by getting into his own field of fire. 'Move over, you bastard,' he would shout in the most harrowing moments, muttering that 'the best picture in the

110

world is spoiled when you get stuck with someone with a camera around his neck, gaping in the background.'

But perhaps the most spectacular instance of reporters getting in one another's way came with the India-Pakistan War of 1971, which I covered on the Indian side, on the Jammu-Kashmir front. With a CBS team, I went to the forward lines in the Jammu sector, held by a Gurkha battalion, well dug in, and peering across the bed of a river called the Munnawa Tawi at the Pakistani front line, similarly ensconced on the other side of the river.

The occasional shell plopped down in the middle distance, but things were so quiet that the CBS reporter thought that this was an ideal occasion to do an on-camera piece. He stood up and began his spiel thus: 'Here I am, on the south bank of the Mannawa River, behind me, which is the furthest forward position of the Indian Army. The Pakistanis are a mere four hundred yards away, across the banks of this dry river. . . . ' He was about to continue when a clump of shells, very much closer, drove us into the safety of the bunkers.

After a few minutes he got up, and the cameraman positioned himself, and he started again. This time he had barely begun his first sentence when another clump of shells, ominously near this time, interrupted the proceedings again.

Considerably shaken, he tried a third time, and the same thing happened. By this time there was a certain amount of tension in the air, and by common accord, the CBS team decided to call it a day. We dispersed and ran back to our vehicles, with shells landing—it seemed—just behind us.

The war ended just before Christmas, and on Boxing Day I was in Rawalpindi, on the Pakistan side, reporting on the wake of Pakistan's defeat. I came across some CBS staffers I knew. We began exchanging our war experiences. 'And where were you on December seventeenth?' I asked, remembering the misfortune of the CBS team on the Indian side.

111

'Funny you should ask that' was the reply. 'We went up to the front, very near a dried-up riverbed. The Paks wouldn't let us visit the very front line, so we asked the Pak artillery to fire away at anything they saw on the other side, so that the trip wasn't entirely a waste of time.' In effect, through this insistence on filming the Pakistani guns and mortars, one CBS team had almost annihilated another CBS team.

War, insurrection, and civil strife can also show the media at their callous worst. One of the best-known photographers in Vietnam, now in charge of his agency's photo unit, was in Portugal in 1975, when, in small northern towns, angry anti-Communist mobs started attacking local Communist headquarters buildings. The riots that ensued were the invariable consequence of the presence of the media, including TV teams with hand-held arc lights to illuminate the scene. For how could anyone, especially after an evening's drinking, fail to satisfy the media requirements of such a large body of journalists from all over the world? The Communists, from within their party HQ, would keep the mobs at bay, occasionally loosing off with shotguns. Miraculously, casualties were few.

One young and inexperienced free-lance photographer got too close on one occasion and was badly wounded by a shotgun blast. Someone rushed up to the agency photo director, a well-known Vietnam veteran, and shouted, 'A Frenchman has been shot in the stomach.'

The answer, in heavily accented English, was memorable: 'Who gares? Zere are too many fucking French free-lance photographers around anyvey!'

Though he would not have approved of such callousness, Larry Burrows, like most great photographers, was a loner, who usually contrived to be where other photographers were not. Before his own death he also began having doubts about the future of photo-journalism, as expressed in *Life*.

My own doubts had come much earlier. I was in New

York when espionage history was made by the exchange of Soviet spy Rudolf Abel for U-2 pilot Francis Gary Powers in 1962. The events occurred shortly before *Life* went to press, and there were frantic conferences and last-minute layout changes to include the exchange in that week's *Life* issue.

For obvious reasons, the Abel-Powers swap had occurred secretly, without benefit of photographers. And the *Life* layout simply reproduced pictures already run elsewhere, showing Powers's trial and Abel's arrest. I argued unsuccessfully that we had just time enough to ask Ian Fleming, then in New York, to write a special piece for us on the implications of this new spy mart. I was turned down. Later, in my hotel room, watching news on TV, I saw the animated news clips from which the photo stills had been made—which would not come out in *Life* for another five days. There and then I realized that this particular form of photo-journalism was doomed.

IV. THE TRAIN
TO AÏN-SEFRA

ALGIERS IS a city built on hills, like Rome, but unlike Rome, these hills run straight down into the Mediterranean. Curiously, it is a town which turns its back on the sea. In the city itself there are no sweeping seafront boulevards and nothing of the Mediterranean quality of Nice or even Genoa. Rather, in its gray drabness, and despite its name, *Alger-la-blanche* ('Algiers the white'), it resembles Marseilles, and indeed, when I first went there on a visit, in 1953, and then later during the Algerian War, Algiers and Marseilles were complementary. After the Indochina War came to an end for the French, in 1954, Marseilles-based French shipping firms found that most of their business was with Algerian ports. Subsidized freight rates enabled French shopkeepers in Algeria to make a killing on almost everything imported they sold, for markups were high, despite the absence of import duties and the fiction that *L'Algérie, c'est la France.* Later on in the war, when the French Algerian settlers began leaving Algeria, many of them, especially the shopkeepers, did so with considerable fortunes, which probably explains why the French economy, in the 1963-65 years, was able to absorb some 1 million French settlers from Algeria without turning a hair. It was the farmers, especially the small farmers, who fared worst when the exodus came. Fourteen years after Algerian independence, landowners and property holders from Algeria were still engaged in litigation with the French government to obtain adequate compensation, and their bitterness at French government indifference has become, in France itself, a political factor of some importance.

But when I went to Algiers, complete with car and personal belongings, in 1957, to free-lance for *Time, Life*, the BBC, and the London *Observer*, Algeria was in the midst of a wartime boom, and most of the French population and the Algerian middle class had never experienced such prosperity.

I had chosen Algiers after much atlas thumbing. Saigon I had considered and rejected, simply because I was not, then, familiar with Indochina. Algiers I already knew. My choice was a good one. For though the war had begun on a small scale, in November 1954, by 1957 it had escalated to a pitch of urban terrorism and large-scale conventional operations in the countryside which were pinning down some 400,000 French troops. Despite this situation, when I arrived in Algiers, the only non-French reporter on the spot was Tom Brady of *The New York Times*, whose home was in Rabat. Between us, for some months, and until the large-scale influx of correspondents into Algiers from all over the world began, Brady and I literally had the North African story to ourselves.

My Algerian trip began in Marseilles on an inauspicious note: I was standing in line to board a ship to Algiers, having spent several hours consigning my car for shipment at the docks under the eyes of suspicious French gendarmes. Another line, leading to a parallel gangway, consisted of a unit of the French Foreign Legion, complete with fierce Alsatian dogs, also on its way to Algiers. One of these animals suddenly broke loose and made straight for me with a growl. Before its Teutonic master resumed control of it, with much raucous German swearing and some kicking and cuffing, so that the animal eventually was led, whimpering, back to the line, my left trouser leg was in tatters and I had a deep scratch on my hand. These dogs, I noted, were obviously trained to make straight for the groin, for only by using my portable typewriter as a shield had I escaped, quite literally, having my balls chewed off.

The French Foreign Legion troopers, their close-cropped skulls emphasizing their ethnic origin, laughed uproariously during and after the unprovoked attack, slapping one another on the back and uttering wild, incomprehensible German cries. An obviously German Foreign Legion NCO looked me over, inspected the damage, and said, '*Il fous a bris bour un fell*' ('He took you for a "fell"'). He said so inquisitorially, almost threateningly, as though about to let his dog loose once more to confirm such suspicions. 'Fell,' the French equivalent of the later 'cong,' was short for 'fellagha' or 'fellouze' meaning 'rebel.'

As in all colonial circumstances, language reflected the contempt of the colonizers for the colonized. 'Fellagha,' 'fellouze,' 'fell' were not strictly speaking derogatory terms. But there were others—'bic,' 'bicot,' 'bougnoule,' 'melon,' 'crouille'—and the French use of this series of derogatory terms to refer to the Algerian Moslems was part of the overall schizophrenia affecting the entire French population of Algeria. Officially Algeria *was* French and had been so ever since 1847. There were departments, prefects, subprefects, and overall supervision of Algerian affairs from the relevant French ministries. In practice, of course, the situation was completely different, as was inevitable in a country whose population was only a little more than one-tenth French, with 9 million Algerians, of whom only a small proportion lived in a French type of economy.

The terms used by most French Algerians when referring to the Algerian Moslem majority reflected the contempt of the educated and civilized for the poor and primitive, but despite the obvious ethnic, linguistic, economic, and social differences of all kinds between the European minority and Moslem majority, the overwhelming majority of all French settlers sincerely believed in Algeria's 'Frenchness,' ignoring the glaring disparities between the two communities and the obviously non-French majority in their midst. It wasn't enough for the French settlers to have the Algerian Moslems accept their Frenchness. The fiction that the Algerian Moslems loved France was also propagated among them. I sat once with some correspondents in a tiny hole-in-the-wall restaurant in Bab el Oued, where most of Algier's poorer French settlers lived, and heard the owner expatiate on this at some considerable length. 'I tell you they love us,' he said. And turning to his cook, expertly broiling lamb cutlets on a charcoal stove and using a hair dryer to activate the flames, he said, 'Go on, tell them you love us, Ahmed, you S.O.B.'

The myth of a 'French Algeria' was to reach a hysterical pitch with the May 1958 'putsch' which overthrew the faltering Fourth Republic and eased General de Gaulle into power. In primary schools all over the country, tiny Algerian tots were taught to get up and scan, as part of their French lessons, 'I am one hundred percent French.' In geography lessons, France extended from Dunkirk to Tamanrasset. On at least one occasion the literalness of French teachers' instructions led to a ludicrous incident. On one visit to a southern Algerian town by De Gaulle, shortly after his Fifth Republic had begun, I heard a French teacher say to his small infants' class, drawn up to greet De Gaulle, each tiny schoolchild clasping a French flag, 'You must shout "Long live De Gaulle" from the bottom of your lungs.' De Gaulle appeared, and the children chanted, 'Long live De Gaulle from the bottom of our lungs. Long live De Gaulle from the bottom of our lungs. VIVE DI GOL A PLEIN POUMON!'

It was difficult not to break into racist fun at the Algerians' handling of the French language. It was almost as difficult to refrain from some snide imitations of the handling of the French language by the French settlers themselves. For the *pied-noir* accent, rich and unmistakable, was itself a proof of the difference that

117

existed between the French 'from the *métropole*' and the others. Many of the French settlers were of Italian or Spanish descent and spoke French execrably. '*Je souis aussi Froncé que vous*,' I heard an elderly Frenchman from Oran say to a French reporter from Paris. It was significant that only a tiny majority of French Algerian settlers spoke more than a few words of Arabic. To an outsider, with no sentimental or jingoist ax to grind, the Moslem and the French communities were—even without a war—almost completely segregated, even if such segregation officially did not exist. Unlike the situation in South Africa, the Moslems did not need to have special permits to enter the 'white' areas, and those who lived in the French style were totally 'assimilated.' But since, economically, most of them were unable to afford 'white' rentals, the great majority of Algiers' Moslems lived in the hideously overcrowded Casbah or in all-Algerian cheap housing suburbs. These last, though also overcrowded, owed much to the initiative and dedication of the French Mayor of Algiers, Jacques Chevallier, who was immensely respected by the Algerian population but hated by most diehard French settlers. In 1957, Chevallier, a humanist and a Christian liberal, was—alas—among a tiny minority of French residents of Algeria who felt that the French domination of Algeria was inevitably coming to an end. Many such Frenchmen died during the Algerian War, some at the hands of the extremist OAS, which had pledged itself to keep Algeria French at all costs, some at the hands of the Algerian rebels, the FLN (National Liberation Front), once the war had entered its decisive stage, for in order to strike terror in the French ranks and emphasize that no racial collaboration was possible, the FLN struck at liberals as well as diehard conservatives.

It's easy, from the distance of some twenty years, to make fun of the French Algerian predicament. The French Algerian settlers were in many respects admirable people. The farmers had created the country's all-important narrow coastal strip of lush vineyards and orange groves.

I had come to Algiers in 1957 prepared for the worst. The bustling prosperity of Algiers and its outward normality, in the French districts at least, surprised me. Things were very different in the Casbah, entirely segregated by a barbed-wire fence, and in the poorer suburbs. Here French paratroopers were very much in evidence, and the expressions on the Algerians' faces were eloquent. In the last two decades we have become so inured to violence we no longer consider the body search at airline terminals and the ritual inspection of handbags in the lobbies of London hotels at all unusual. Algeria was the first place where these routine security precautions were adopted on a large scale. Veiled Algerian women, entering or leaving the Casbah, were searched by French soldiers, using unwieldy metal detectors known as frying pans. All cars in Algiers were compelled to carry large stickers numbered from one to five, showing the home district of its owner. Any car left in an unlikely part of town for any length of time was regarded as suspect. And to try to end the wave of bombings and grenade throwing in Algiers itself, the paratroopers, under the orders of the Algiers district commander, General Jacques Massu, engaged in torture on a wide scale. As in occupied Paris, when some houses were taken over by the Gestapo as interrogation centers, so several villas in Algiers came to have a deservedly sinister reputation. How many people died under torture will never be known, but the figure was certainly in the thousands, perhaps in the tens of thousands if one includes those 'shot while trying to escape' after the torture sessions.

If the United States had its My Lai in Vietnam which, more than anything else perhaps, brought home the unacceptable, dehumanizing nature of the Vietnam War, France had dozens, and perhaps hundreds, of My Lais in Algeria. The difference was that few French soldiers came forward to denounce their comrades, and the press, under few restraints in Vietnam, was almost completely

119

hamstrung in its efforts to report the war from the field during the Algerian War.

The dominant mood among the French Algerian settlers, then and throughout the war, was one of total support for strong-arm methods—and General Massu became the most popular figure in Algeria in French eyes. How mob rule came to influence official French policy in Algeria can best be shown by the fate of a parliamentary committee, set up by ex-Premier Pierre Mendès-France and consisting of four MPs from his own Radical party, whom he wished to dispatch to Algeria in April 1957 to investigate alleged army atrocities.

The then governor-general of Algeria, Robert Lacoste, a veteran socialist who had become a firm supporter of army methods in Algeria, wrote the leader of the committee that 'to ensure your own safety, I shall most certainly have to use thousands of men, at a time when police and troops are permanently engaged in highly important operations.' Denying them permission to come, he admitted that this decision had been the consequence of threats from French settler organizations. As he put it: 'The population of Algiers will not be able to control its feelings.' The French settlers had made their point: They intended to prevent the MPs from landing at the airport. Local civil servants announced they would refuse to answer the MPs' questions, and restaurateurs and hotelkeepers said they would refuse to have anything to do with them. Probably the most tragic aspect of the situation was that most French people in Algeria at the time felt such behavior, and the government's response, were perfectly normal.

There were honorable exceptions to the conspiracy of silence about Algeria in 1957: Pierre-Henri Simon, a distinguished Catholic intellectual, wrote *Against Torture*, a factual account based on survivors' accounts; Jean-Jacques Servan-Schreiber, who had served as a reservist officer in Algeria in 1956, wrote *Lieutenant in Algeria* and in barely disguised fictional form both confirmed the extent of summary executions in Algeria and the total inability of the French Army there to distinguish between friend and foe, terrorist and victim. The French Catholic hierarchy exposed the prevalence of torture. *Le Monde*, defying possible prosecution, published an unabridged and hitherto-unpublished government report on torture and army excesses. I myself, in *Time*, referred again and again to the substantiated reports of torture. Gisèle Halimi, the French lawyer (and later the well-known campaigner for women's rights in France), was a frequent visitor to Algeria to defend those accused of terrorism and sentenced by military courts. After initial suspicion had been overcome—for to her, as to many French left-wing intellectuals, *Time* was a mouthpiece of American imperialism, and she couldn't at first bring herself to believe that the American press would write anything to impair Franco-American relations—she became a precious source of information. Almost without exception, her clients, some of whom received life terms, had been tortured, and the kind of evidence she produced (mostly in the form of doctors' reports) was incontrovertible.

Indeed, my first awareness of the untenable nature of the French commitment came in 1957, after I attended a series of trials of Algerians before special French military courts. One young FLN accused stood, manacled, before a French colonel with the bureaucrat's pallid complexion, in what might have been an austere and characterless schoolroom. I was the only reporter present. The accused had been captured in a French Army operation in Kabylia, and French intelligence had linked him with a bomb-making gang in Algiers which had split up a few months earlier.

The Algerian, speaking in quiet, almost detached tones, admitted in court that he had made a number of bombs which had been used in FLN bomb outrages in Algeria. 'I have never killed anyone,' he said, 'and I was tortured to make me admit my role in the FLN. I fled to the maquis because the civilian casualties made me sick and I didn't want to make bombs anymore.' The court sentenced him to death, and the Fourth Republic's ministers were so lacking in moral courage that all attempts on the part of his lawyer to get the sentence commuted failed; he was guillotined, even though it had been proved, at the trial, that had he refused to make bombs the FLN would have executed him.

This case, exceptional even for the times, convinced me that it was only a matter of time before an unusually passive and indolent French public reacted to the war on moral grounds alone—as indeed happened, with increasingly publicized cases of torture and summary executions.

Perhaps the most appalling aspect of the war was the French troops' habit of picking up civilians at random, questioning them, torturing them, and then letting them go. It wasn't difficult, as a result, to talk to Algerians who had actually been tortured. Shortly after my own arrival in Algiers, Homer Bigart, the famed World War II and Korean War correspondent, arrived in Algeria to write a series of pieces for *The New York Times*, which he had recently joined after years at the *Herald Tribune*.

Bigart, wall-eyed, unemotional to the point of caricature, and speaking not one word of French, was assisted by Marvine Howe, now a *New York Times* staffer herself, then a *New York Times* stringer. Bigart's directness appalled her. 'Bring me someone who's been tortured,' he ordered. 'I wanna talk to an Algerian who's been tortured *recently*.' There was, alas, no shortage of candidates, and the following day Marvine Howe showed up in the Aletti Hotel with a mild-mannered, bespectacled Algerian. He had been submitted, a few weeks previously, to the water treatment, or what in French Army slang was known as *la baignoire* (the bath). Marvine Howe almost broke down as she translated the man's account of how he had been stripped, plunged into a bathful of water, and kept underwater repeatedly until he almost drowned. I was eavesdropping unashamedly. 'Hey, waidaminit,' said Bigart, ponderously making notes. 'Ask him: Wassa wader hot or cold?'

Equally bizarre was the behavior of a *Life* correspondent, later on in the war, who, during a demonstration of veiled Algerian women, which had been photographed by a *Life* photographer, went up to one of them and said, 'Ma'am, what's your surname, first name, and where do you live?'

Even the admirable Tom Brady, whose anguish at the excesses and brutalities he was compelled to write about was very real, was not immune from this almost caricatural concern for minor facts. I was with him when, one weekend night, FLN terrorists placed a huge explosive charge under a popular jazz bandstand, blowing the dance hall, the Casino de la Corniche, to bits, killing 16 Europeans and wounding 150 more. We went inside shortly after the bomb had gone off. Many teenage French girls there had had their legs blown off. All that was left of the orchestra were bits of bodies, including, I remember, some outsize black shoes with feet in them. The walls were splashed with fast-congealing blood. Brady took one look at the Rorschach-like stains, and turning to a gendarme, he said, in his fluent but strongly accented French, 'Is that blood?' 'It's not red wine, monsieur,' said the gendarme gravely. At which, incredibly, Brady touched the spot, looked at his bloodstained finger—and licked it.

FLN violence was not always directed against the French. I had only been in Algiers a short while when I got the news that the village of Melouza had been raided by the FLN, and all its inhabitants murdered. I managed to hitch a ride on a French Army helicopter, and in the village of Kasbah Mechta, near Melouza, where the villagers had been herded and then butchered, I witnessed a scene I had hoped I would never see again, after Peshawar. In all, the French Army counted 302 corpses. Some had already been summarily buried by the Army, for the weather was warm and the stench unendurable. The FLN, from its Tunis headquarters, at the time denied that it had been responsible for the killings. Many years after Algerian independence some high-ranking erstwhile FLN leaders, who had since fallen out with the postwar Algerian regime and were living in exile, did indeed confirm that the FLN had ordered and carried out the massacre of Melouza. Its inhabitants, after supporting the FLN in somewhat lukewarm fashion, had decided to switch sides and support the rival, much smaller MNA nationalist movement, which many Algerians believed to be French-manipulated. The mass murder was punishment for such betrayal.

I was first on the scene at Melouza but was soon joined by other French reporters who had arrived by road, including Jean Lartéguy, the ex-officer who was writing, at that time, the manuscript of his best-selling *Centurions* and was then working for *Paris-Presse*. Lartéguy, who habitually drove at high speed along dangerous Algerian roads with grenades rattling in the glove compartment, which terrified me every time I shared a ride with him, eventually settled in the shade, after making copious notes, opened a haversack, and produced a bottle of red wine, some bread, and a can of sardines. He began eating with relish, and despite the surroundings and the sights we had just witnessed, I began eating, too. We both were ravenous. Lartéguy paused in the act of making himself a huge sardine sandwich, took a long slug of wine, wiped his mouth, and said, 'Atrocities always make me peckish.'

John Gale had not been with me at the Casino de la Corniche. But he did witness another bomb outrage. FLN terrorists, masquerading as municipal workers, filled the bases of seven streetlamps in a central Algiers street with explosives, timed to explode at peak traffic hour. They went off as planned, and the carnage was spectacular.

The French reaction was predictable. The day the French victims were buried, Frenchmen fanned out into the streets, killing and beating senseless any Moslems who happened to be in the vicinity of the funeral procession. The sight of Moslems being beaten to death with meat hooks taken from nearby butchers' shops apparently gave the mob some satisfaction, and there was precious little interference from either French troops or police, though individual French officers did attempt, quite ineffectively, to get them to stop.

Shortly afterward, in 1957, Gale and I took a trip together to Tlemcen, on Algeria's eastern border. The train was full of hard-faced French civilians with guns in enormous shoulder holsters. At the hotel the Algerian servant cleaning my room was so used to seeing Europeans with guns he rushed after me, shouting, 'M'sieur, m'sieur, don't forget your gun.' What I had left on my bed was, in fact, a metal stapler.

It was in Tlemcen that Gale and I experienced at first hand the full folly of the Algerian War. We were walking the streets when, somewhere nearby, a bomb was thrown. Almost immediately black troops from a Senegalese colonial infantry regiment appeared as if by magic, in trucks driven at high speed, shooting wildly at anything they saw. At first we couldn't believe it. Then, whinnying with panic, we threw ourselves to the ground, crawling to the inadequate cover of a mangy sycamore tree. We huddled together, each attempting to edge the other away a little to take fuller advantage of the illusory tree-trunk protection until the absurdity of our craven cowardice caused us to burst into hysterical laughter.

The firing continued for what seemed like hours but was probably about thirty minutes. When it died down, we both made a dash for more secure protection. We found ourselves, after a brief run, inside a garage. Here, huddled together as though waiting for a bad storm to end, were Algerians and French men and women. For once their predicament was common enough to lead to some halting, commiserating conversation.

Later still that day a somewhat disgusted gendarmerie captain, who, only three weeks before, had commanded the crack cavalry squadron of the French president's troop in Paris, confirmed that the Senegalese had fired off some 30,000 rounds. 'You know,' he said, as though this were an adequate explanation, 'how they like to loose off their ammunition.'

John Gale and I returned to Algiers, where his behavior became mildly eccentric. He drank a great deal, talked vaguely of joining the FLN, and became wildly excited, engaging complete strangers in long, rambling conversations. Much of our drinking was done in a small café misnamed Le Bar de la Presse. The thin, peroxide-blond barmaid there had part of one finger missing. On the basis of this one fact, John invented a lurid past for her. She was an ex-prostitute, he claimed, and the bar owner was a pimp who had punished her by chopping off part of her little finger, forcing her to become the unwilling member of a gang in league with the local police, whose role was to spy on foreign correspondents.

Perhaps my mistake was to enter John's fantasy. Partly to humor him, partly because he made it all sound hilarious, I supplied other, equally improbable details about her past. Needless to say, I didn't at the time realize that John was not just indulging in undergraduate whimsy and that our game, not after all so very different from the fantasies indulged in by Isherwood and his friends and described in his autobiography, *Lions and Shadows*, was, in fact, the first clear manifestation of an impending mental breakdown. For shortly after leaving Algeria, John displayed alarming symptoms of paranoid schizophrenia. He believed the *Observer* staff in Paris was trying to poison his tea. He thought he was being followed by the French secret police. He himself, with considerable candor and skill, later described these events in a book, *One Clean Englishman*, which should by rights have become a classic but failed to achieve the popular success it deserved. Much later, after years of apparently successful treatment, John resumed his career on the *Observer*. Then, only a few weeks after a memorably hilarious evening together in

1974, he killed himself.

It's entirely possible that John Gale's breakdown might have come in an entirely different form; but his brief Algerian experience, at the height of FLN terrorism and French repression, was the catalyst, and in a sense he was as much a victim of the Algerian War as the maimed survivors of both French torture and FLN terrorism.

My own Algerian reporting took on a breathless quality with the arrival of a *Life* team to do a full-scale essay on the war. Together with a burly ex-Korean War veteran photographer, Howard Sochurek, we crisscrossed the country. We spent many nights in isolated, fortified French farmhouses, accompanying the swashbuckling Colonel Marcel Bigeard, the hero of Dien Bien Phu, and his paratroopers on an operation—almost the only time a non-French reporting team was allowed anywhere near the war. It was a somewhat disappointing exercise. A grinding night march, followed by a sweep across some low hills, yielded no action, except some shelling of an already much shelled and deserted village. There were no casualties on either side, though several of Bigeard's men—during a rest break—were treated for gonorrhea, which they had contracted that week. 'Can you remember where you caught it?' said a medic, after giving a huge paratrooper a jab.

'Difficult' was the reply. 'I went to six houses last night.'

Our search for a photogenic fortified French farm took us to Bône and a farmhouse, whose owner, scanning the hilly horizon with binoculars, could make out, as a tiny dot on the landscape, an FLN lookout permanently at his post. It was while we were driving back in my by now battered Opel that we had the scare of our lives.

Halfway between Bône and Algiers is the town of Sétif, birthplace of the Algerian nationalist leader Ferhat Abbas. Our journey, until we reached the outskirts of Sétif, had been uneventful, for French military police refused to allow us into the town, where a large army search was obviously taking place. Instead, we were waved on and directed along a country road. There were posters saying, 'The French army is vigilant,' but the soldiers' assurances that we would be directed around the town by a whole series of French Army traffic NCOs proved, to say the least, illusory. There was no one around, and as we headed farther and farther away from the town, we came to open countryside and our first farm. It was blazing fiercely. There were no signs of life. Unwilling to slow down in order to turn back, I pressed on. Other French farms, dotted over the empty fields on both left and right, were all in flames. Thick columns of smoke from these oversize bonfires streaked the sky. There was no wind, and all we could hear was the crackle of the flames. Finally, we came to a village. It, too, was deserted, but I recognized the local gendarmerie building, built on the same pattern as other gendarmerie barracks throughout Algeria. Both Sochurek and I had been too tense even to talk to each other since spotting the first fires—a sure indication that the FLN was in extremely close proximity. Now I jumped from the car and began hammering on the closed armored barracks door. I saw that gendarmerie troopers, in full battle order, crouched behind windows, their guns at the ready. 'You can't come in,' said a voice from the inside.

'But the whole countryside's on fire!' I shouted back, with what I hoped was only a restrained note of hysteria.

'We know that,' said the voice. 'They may attack this place any minute. Get going.'

It seemed fruitless to protest, so we resumed our drive. Eventually we did find a road taking us to the western outskirts of Sétif. At an army checkpoint I described what I had seen and added that French Army traffic arrangements left a great deal to be desired. 'You're all right now,' said an NCO. 'There's an army convoy leaving in a few minutes for Algiers. You can travel the rest of the way with them.'

We did indeed follow a large army convoy of trucks, jeeps, and armored cars, for a few miles, on the Sétif-

Algiers road, but so slow was their pace that we realized that if we stuck with them, we would not reach Algiers till well after dark. I passed the convoy and drove on fast.

Nothing untoward happened, though at one point I thought I saw some Algerian *barkis* (pro-French Moslem militiamen) waving us down. But I didn't let up until I came upon a major army roadblock near the point where the Sétif-Algiers road forks off to Tizi-Ouzou. There we stopped and showed our press credentials, but instead of waving us on, an NCO said, 'Wait a minute. The major wants to talk to you.'

An officer looked at us and said, 'You're lucky.' I know, I said, we had a bad time earlier on, and I began telling him about the French farms on fire and the FLN, presumably swarming in the area. 'That's not what I meant,' the major said. 'You drove through an ambush. They let you go by, presumably because they were after bigger things.' The convoy behind us, which we should have traveled with, had been attacked, and six French soldiers killed.

Many years later, driving from Saigon to the Cambodian border in 1971, I was not at all surprised when *Newsweek*'s stringer, tipster and local philosopher, Cao Giao, urged me on. 'Overtake the American convoy ahead,' he said. 'It's always better never to travel with army convoys.' It was a lesson I had already learned.

Another memorable trip, also with Sochurek and *Life*'s Tim Foote, was by train from the French base of Colomb-Béchar, on the edge of the Sahara, to Aïn-Sefra, 170 miles to the north. Though I had been assured by the French authorities in Algiers that a Colomb-Béchar train ran regularly and on schedule from Colomb-Béchar all the way to Oran, I had also heard hair-raising reports of ambushes, bombings, and general FLN derring-do. We decided to see for ourselves.

In Colomb-Béchar, which we reached by plane, the local French officials were singularly evasive. Of course there was a train; it ran at least once a week, 'normally.' Then

perhaps there would be no problem about getting tickets
and boarding it?

'Ah, there is a problem.'

'What kind of a problem?'

'The train does not take passengers, only freight.'

'Then perhaps we can travel in the freight
compartment?'

'That, unfortunately, will not be possible.'

Having left a mutinous Foote and Sochurek at the hotel,
I drove out to the station and hung around the tracks. Some
French conscripts on guard duty were a good deal more
forthcoming. The train, they said, did indeed leave
Colomb-Béchar at irregular intervals. It carried neither
passengers nor freight. It ran, at least as far as Aïn-Sefra,
solely so that the French authorities in Algiers could say to
people like myself that the train ran. But it wasn't really a
train at all. It consisted of a few freight cars, heavily
ballasted with sandbags, veritable bunkers on wheels,
interspersed with open platforms completely loaded with
sandbags. A dummy 'dolly' wagon was pushed ahead of the
train to explode possible mines, of which there were great
numbers. And thousands of Foreign Legionnaires went out
on patrol, with their 'frying pan' detectors, before the train
was due, inspecting most portions of the track.

It sounded too good to miss, but a certain amount of low
cunning was needed, to avoid attracting too much attention
from the perennially suspicious French. I let it be known, in
loud, disgruntled terms, that we were very disappointed
and were taking a plane straight back to Algiers. We
packed up and left the hotel with every characteristic of
people about to board planes. On the way I made certain
our taxi driver was Algerian and tipped him handsomely. I
explained what was required, and he entered the spirit of
the thing. We didn't, of course, drive to the station; on my
first visit I had noticed some military police looking
inquiringly in my direction. Instead, we drove along a road
which ran parallel to the railroad tracks in a sandy

wasteland outside the town itself. The train appeared, moving, as I had been told it would, at comfortable walking pace. Poised for the transfer, we waited till the sandbagged freight cars were level and scrambled aboard. French conscripts gave us a helping hand.

We soon found out that reports of widespread sabotage of the tracks were true. The track had been torn up and repaired so many times, and so many trains had been blown up, that at times the two sides of the track looked like scrap heaps. The FLN rebels had blown up the small bridges between Colomb-Béchar and Aïn-Sefra no less than 116 times, one French engineer sergeant told me. The train was now solely a prestige-and-patrol run, for the real freight trains out of Colomb-Béchar, carrying Algerian coal from the nearby coal mines, crossed into Moroccan territory a few miles north of Colomb-Béchar and re-entered Algeria hundreds of miles to the north.

Traveling at some five to seven miles per hour, we made it into Aïn-Sefra the following evening, around 6:30 P.M. Hot, filthy, and badly in need of creature comforts, we said goodbye to our French Army train crew and hitched a ride into town on an army truck. We had asked to be taken to the local officers' mess, and what we saw brought tears to our eyes. Here, in a superb terrace setting, a French Foreign Legion mess was impeccably set up for a grand meal, with solid silver table settings, dark-red carafes of wine, buckets of ice, and mineral-water bottles. A small string orchestra of the French Foreign Legion was rehearsing some schmaltzy tunes in a corner. The scene was straight out of central casting, including the squashed-faced Hungarian legionnaire who barred the entry. 'You'll have to report to the colonel first,' he said, adding, more in sorrow than anger, 'but I don't think you'll be allowed in.'

We were indeed an odd-looking trio, but I had hoped that an ingratiating explanation of our predicament would enable us to sample the traditional, much vaunted French Foreign Legion hospitality.

'*Mon colonel*,' I said, 'we have just traveled by train from Colomb-Béchar and we wondered . . . '

'You are Americans?'

'*Oui, mon colonel*, from *Life* magazine.'

A pained rictus flickered over his pinched, brutish features. '*Life* magazine, eh? *Eh bien*, messieurs, I advise you to move fast. Curfew is at seven P.M., and my men have a habit of shooting on sight. *Bonsoir*.'

Emerging in a daze from his office, we noticed the town was dead, shuttered, ominously still. Carrying our gear, we entered the town center. Everything was closed. There was not a hotel in sight in the tiny French quarter.

Bowed down with gear, we hobbled down some narrower streets in what was quite obviously the Algerian quarter. Here a welcome 'hotel' sign, in French and Arabic, beckoned. Just in time, as 7:00 P.M. struck, we found ourselves inside an adobe rooming house, built around a patio, and for a ridiculously small sum we were given a room with a double bed and a mattress on the floor. It was an airless, dusty, strange-smelling room, with no running water, but at least we were out of the Foreign Legion's field of fire, and judging from the comments of the Algerian hotelkeeper, the Legion did indeed shoot on sight. But as we chatted with him and with other transients, all Algerian, in the hotel, it was clear that we had arrived at a particularly inauspicious moment. Earlier that day the FLN had raided the town, shooting up some army sentinel posts and blasting some French-owned shops. The Legion had retaliated with incredible ferocity, and indeed the pockmarked walls of some buildings had a simple explanation. To hear the Algerians talk, the colonel we had just seen was mad, an advocate of electrode torture and summary execution. We had stumbled across an Algerian 'heart of darkness' situation.

Much later I was curious enough to inquire into the colonel's behavior toward us, which was odd—even taking prevalent French attitudes toward the American press into

132

account. I soon found an explanation: By an ill-fated coincidence, this same colonel had been a press officer in Hanoi at the time that David Douglas Duncan, of *Life*, had published his memorable photo essay on the Indochina War in 1953, predicting French defeat, and showing, among other things, deserted French HQ offices, the long Asian siestas and *dolce vita* indulged in by staff officers, while the troops suffered in the jungles. Only an FLN visiting card would have made us less welcome still, for the colonel's career had suffered as a result of the *Life* article, and ever since then he had vented his rage on everything American, especially American journalists.

But it was concern lest we find out in more detail the extent of FLN activities in the area—and the extent of Foreign Legion excesses—which commanded our immediate expulsion from the colonel's area. Somehow, through the grapevine, he must have found out where we had spent the night, for early next morning, a Foreign Legion sergeant, Italian this time and armed to the teeth, motioned us out and ordered us into his jeep. By now none of us would have been surprised if we had ended up in front of a firing squad, so it was with some relief that we found ourselves on the edge of a small military airstrip and ordered to board a small French Air Force transport plane.

There was, however, a hitch. The colonel's writ didn't run as far as the French Air Force, especially since this particular plane was already full of troops and freight. 'The colonel says you're to take these three individuals,' said the sergeant.

'You can tell the colonel to stuff it,' said the pilot. Caught up in this interservice quarrel, we waited like sheep.

'*Allez, montez*,' The Foreign Legion sergeant said, urging us onto the plane with a wave of his submachine gun. We boarded the plane. The pilot remained motionless. then, slowly, with infinite care, he taxied along the airstrip, and turned the plane, perhaps a shade deliberately, into some sand and rocks, where it stalled. The undercarriage seemed to have given way. With scarcely concealed glee, the air force pilot inspected the damage. 'I believe,' he said to the sergeant, 'this could prove quite expensive.'

'Sorry,' he then said, turning to us. 'It's the Legion's fault, as usual.'

A by now fuming Foreign Legion sergeant drove us back to the hotel we had left an hour previously. After a second night there we were ready to beg the colonel to get us out of Aïn-Sefra. In twenty-four hours I had learned a great deal about the war in that part of southern Algeria, but on our second night the patio of the hotel, in the middle of which was an open-air privy, had been the theater of some violent arguments, followed by what to our ears, in the pitch-darkness, appeared to have been a homosexual gang rape. Perhaps the colonel intended our stay in Aïn-Sefra to be permanent or entertained other, even more Machiavellian plans?

I had a brainwave. We had taken the train to Aïn-Sefra. Surely we could hitch a ride back to Colomb-Béchar. We found a train waiting to leave. It was exactly the same kind of armored train we had ridden up on, but it would be some hours, we were told, before we left. The FLN had blown up the tracks a few miles south, and these were now being repaired.

Finally, the repairs were complete, but by this time it was nearly dark. 'I'm not supposed to leave after dark,' the young French conscript in charge said, with the air of a Paris taxi driver who is about to return to his Levallois garage at the end of a busy day.

We explained our predicament. I exaggerated it a little, saying that the colonel was after us and that another night in Aïn-Sefra might be fatal. 'In that case . . . ' the soldier said. And off we went.

I never thought we would be glad to see Colomb-Béchar again, but the luxury of the hotel swimming pool and the chance to clean up and rest compelled us to stay yet another night. Eventually we flew back to Algiers by commercial

Air Algérie flight. I attended a routine press briefing the following day at the Gouvernement Général headquarters. With deliberate, casual innocence, I asked the briefing officer whether the trains still ran from Colomb-Béchar north to Aïn-Sefra. 'Of course, *normalement*,' he replied.

V.   ANYONE HERE BEEN RAPED AND SPEAKS ENGLISH?

THE SUN was blazing hot outside, and even under the relative shelter of the aircraft hangars the humidity was intense. Packed resignedly inside, thousands of Belgian civilians, mostly women and children, waited their turn to be airlifted out of the newly independent ex-Belgian Congo, out of Africa and to new lives in Belgium. Some had been driven out of remote, upcountry towns by the excesses of Congolese soldiers and rebels on the rampage. Others had succumbed to an understandable fear psychosis and had fled mostly imaginary terrors, leaving everything behind save their pathetic bundles.

Into the middle of this crowd strode an unmistakably British TV reporter, leading his cameraman and sundry technicians like a platoon commander through hostile territory. At intervals he paused and shouted, in a stentorian but genteel BBC voice, 'Anyone here been raped and speaks English?'

This was my first vision of the Congo, that huge land which straddles the center of Africa and was later to be renamed Zaire by President Joseph Mobutu, who realized that the word 'Congo' had, owing to the chaos of the postindependence days, become an adjective rather than a proper name. Zaire and its capital, Kinshasa, formerly Léopoldville, still bear the traces of Belgian colonization, and some of the more marked excesses of the immediate postindependence period have vanished. But Zaire, for all of President Mobutu's efforts, is still today a predatory, arbitrary state, where, at almost every level, self-serving and brutal officials terrorize their underlings and where the police and Army ransom those they are paid to protect. On my last visit to Zaire in 1975, three riverboat officials were being tried for gouging out the eyes, and then murdering, a passenger who had traveled in a first-class berth with a third-class ticket. They were acquitted.

To many people, Kinshasa is the place where in 1974 the Muhammad Ali-George Foreman fight occurred and where the rival boxing camps lived in considerable luxury before the fight took place. Reporters covering the fight will almost certainly remember the bemused account of one of the members of Muhammad Ali's entourage, describing his night in the company of an attractive Zairoise (for, as in *The Thousand and One Nights*, distinguished guests of President Mobutu often found themselves provided with feminine company, some of whom were recruited from his Women's Army Corps). 'There we were, in bed,' said the Muhammad Ali man, 'and a butterfly came into the room and landed on the bed. And what do you think happened? She ate the fucking butterfly!'

On my first visit to the Congo in 1960, the BBC reporter's callous cry summed up for me the tragic, yet wildly surrealist nature of the country itself, where several rival ethnic groups, some of them in areas as big as France and all totally unprepared for independence, were placed on a collision course with the United Nations bureaucrats attempting to impose order on chaos. The UN's linguistic and racial mix—involving Indian diplomats and Ghanaian, Nigerian, Tunisian, Moroccan, Irish, and Gurkha troops—turned UN headquarters in Léopoldville into a Tower of Babel.

Confusion caused by the UN's multinational bureaucracy meant that even at the peak of unpleasantness, it was impossible not to experience the feeling that one was a character in the middle of a Third

137

World farce. A *Life* photographer, threatened with instant execution on countless occasions by Congolese troops of various warring factions ('*On va vous fusiller*,' 'We're going to shoot you'), talked his way out of trouble every time by producing a Polaroid camera and snapping his would-be firing squad, to their delight. His only trouble was that he was compelled to load himself down with huge quantities of Polaroid film, because every soldier wanted a picture.

I accompanied an Irish battalion which had become part of the United Nations force in the Congo and had arrived, complete with First World War uniforms and puttees, to patrol a remote area of the Congo, including what was then known as the King Albert Memorial Park, one of Africa's best-stocked game reserves. The Irish troops took it in their stride. Elephants, leopards, lions, yawning hippopotamuses—this was their collective schoolbook vision of Africa before they left Dublin, and it was reassuring to find that the image corresponded to reality. It was tempting to tell them that this was not the real Africa, but it would have been cruel to do so. They were to find out soon enough.

The padre spent most of his time blessing planes about to take off. 'Everyone here's a volunteer except for meself,' said the CO. I asked him how he felt the Irish and the Congolese soldiers would get on in their proposed mixed patrolling of the town of Bukavu. 'Splendidly!' he said in a great brogue. 'Haven't we both been colonized ourselves once?'

The honeymoon, alas, was short-lived. An Irish soldier was killed by some Baluba tribesmen, leading to the probably apocryphal story, which nevertheless went the rounds of the bars wherever correspondents gathered in the Congo, that on being told that her son had been strung up by the Balubas, his aged mother had replied, 'They shouldn't have done that. There was no call to hang him up by the balubas.' And the Congolese looted, and drank, an entire cargo of Guinness sent out especially for the Irish contingent by the Guinness brewery, which laid a permanent pall, for the duration of the troops' involvement, on Irish-Congolese relations.

I went deep into the bush with two young Irish doctors fresh out of Dublin, whose first tropical experience this was. They were part of an extremely praiseworthy effort on the part of a World Health Organization team in the Congo to try to palliate the exodus of the Belgian doctors and nurses from the Congo.

We drove deep into the jungle by jeep to a model bush hospital whose entire white staff had, without warning a few days earlier, upped and left in a motorcade that ended up in nearby Uganda, then still a British colony. The Belgians had left the Congo totally unprepared for independence, with only a few university graduates and not a single doctor. They were, however, in the habit of training semi-educated Congolese to perform one single function with robotlike efficiency. The senior Congolese male nurse in the hospital had been trained to reduce fractures and put patients in plaster. He had taken charge of the hospital until the Irish arrival. We were surprised, on entering the first ward, to find the whole place so still. The Irish doctors then discovered why: Each seriously ill patient was encased in plaster, from the neck downward.

One desperately ill patient was a Pygmy tribesman, in a room by himself. He too had been encased in plaster, and the doctors believed that this might well have saved his life. He had suffered a terrible festering wound, which had ripped his body from anus to navel. It was impossible at first to find out how this had happened. Finally, a four-man translation team managed to communicate with him, from Pygmy dialect to Swahili to French, with me translating on the last leg from French to English. He had been out hunting and had been attacked by a wild boar. My confidence in the doctors' competence was slightly shaken when one of them said, 'Dear, dear, we thought it was bad case of hernia.'

In many respects the Belgians may have been admirable colonizers, especially in exploiting the Congo's natural resources for their own ends. But their colonial administration had chiefly inspired fear, and it was odd, in the days following the reopening of the hospital, to watch Congolese stand in line for treatment, who, our Congolese interpreters told us, would never have dared show up before independence. They feared, we were told, that if they had allowed themselves to be caught up in the white man's system, they would have been punished by being heavily taxed.

Among those seeking treatment were several lepers, and this surprised the Irish team a great deal. Leprosy, in the Congo, was supposed to be well under control, but here were leper patients, suffering from hideous and disfiguring stigmata of the disease, who had obviously never been treated in their lives. With commendable initiative, the two Irish doctors followed up an initial hunch. The lepers, they discovered, all came from the same village, whose very existence had been kept secret from the Belgian colonial administration. It took several hours' drive by jeep and a long subsequent trek on foot to reach this village, and when we got there, we came across an unforgettable sight. Apart from the children, every villager bore some trace of the disease, either in the form of missing fingers or toes or barely describable facial deformities.

We had been taken there by one of the hospital outpatients, reassured that no one would be taxed or penalized for obtaining treatment, and it was odd to see the Irish doctors, only a week out of Dublin, solemnly shaking hands with lepers without the trace of either shyness or other qualms. I too shook hands with the villagers, forewarned by the doctors that leprosy, contrary to popular superstition, was not thus superficially transmissible. In a small guesthouse a few miles away, where the doctors had set up a temporary headquarters, I nevertheless scrubbed my hands over and over again, until distracted by

140

extraordinary long and hairy caterpillars which seemed to have turned my bathroom into a village conclave. To those who—to this day—regard the United Nations mission to the Congo as an expensive, useless farce, I can testify that thanks to two Irish doctors from Dublin, a Pygmy hunter recovered from his near-fatal wound and that leprosy in the secret leper village was brought under control.

Back in Léopoldville, the main problem was to get one's story out. Overworked telex technicians kept a twenty-four-hour vigil in the post office, but the telex lines broke down again and again. The best way was to find a 'pigeon' to carry it out, but this was not often possible. Perhaps the most handicapped of all the foreign correspondents were the Japanese.

This became obvious on a weekend across the Congo River, in Congo-Brazzaville, then a newly independent country still very much dominated by French influence. Correspondents would use Congo-Brazzaville, its well-ordered town and countless dance halls, as a weekend R and R (rest and recreation) center, and one Sunday, while I was there, the French military garrison paraded through its main streets to the delight of the Brazzaville population, to commemorate either a French holiday or, perhaps, Congo-Brazzaville national day. We were sipping Pernod and watching the scene, so different from the chaotic mess across the river, when our attention was drawn to a Japanese TV team, filming the parade and the smiling black faces with grim determination. The team spotted us. Its leader, recognizing fellow journalists, paused. 'Excuse, please,' he said quietly, but interrogatively, 'no tlubbel in Congo?' We explained, as best we could, without hurting his feelings, that he and his team were in the wrong country and gently led him to the ferryboat terminal, where the town of Léopoldville was just visible on the other side of the Congo River.

A few days later I was in Elisabethville, now Lubumbashi, and caught sight of the same team, carrying its TV equipment out of the lobby and into a taxi.

'How are you doing?' I asked.

'Very good. Today we had an interview with President Tshombe.'

'Excellent. What did he tell you?'

The Japanese TV reporter burst into spasmodic, near-hysterical laughter. 'We no unnerstand,' he said.

Eighteen months later, during the time the French counter-terrorist OAS movement almost brought the French administration in Algeria to a state of collapse, I remember asking another Japanese reporter how he managed to file his stories. 'I send many by post,' he said. 'Mine are not urgent news stories.' As he talked, he pointed to a letterbox outside the Aletti Hotel, which, he told me, he always used. A sticker, in French, on the box, read: 'Do not post letters here. Owing to the circumstances, collections have been discontinued since February 12.' We were in May.

Shortly after I arrived in the Congo in 1962, Patrice Lumumba was put under house arrest, and his house guarded by Congolese troops. Lumumba's undeniable gifts were marred by fits of eccentricity. There was no saying when sudden, irrational anger might flare up. His arrest did not prevent him from making an occasional foray into the city. One afternoon a convoy of large American cars defied the guards outside and toured Léopoldville. I followed. Lumumba was in one of them. There were also a number of large Congolese ladies, dressed to the nines. Some nursed bottles of Grand Marnier, and I soon understood why. The Lumumba 'cortege' would stop at a dance hall. Here Lumumba would order beer for his party. All glasses were heavily spiked with Grand Marnier by one of the ladies present. Dreamily Lumumba would then dance with one of the ladies in attendance. He would also make a little speech, between dances, to the attentive but puzzled audience. This ritual continued throughout the afternoon, and by the time evening came everyone was ill-tempered and drunk. I had followed Lumumba into the Hôtel Regina, his last port of call, with no objection from the Congolese guards, and found myself in a bar, with yet more beer and Grand Marnier, in the presence of several Lumumba followers and a middle-aged Indian journalist from Beirut, obviously unused to liquor. Lumumba insisted on making, to me, the only Westerner present, the same speech he had been making in the dance halls. 'The imperialists will be defeated,' he said, 'the imperialists who are responsible for the crushing of the revolution, whether in Africa or Asia. Take India,' he continued somewhat inconsequentially. 'The white men crushed the revolution in India. The white men killed Gandhi.'

This infuriated the Indian journalist present. 'The whites didn't kill Gandhiji,' he screamed. 'You bloody fool, *we* killed Gandhiji.' There was almost a riot, and a Lumumba bodyguard drew an enormous revolver.

I did my best to restrain my Indian friend, irate beyond words at this perversion of history. Lumumba himself put an end to the controversy. 'I am going out tonight to die like Gandhi,' he said, somewhat unsteady on his feet but in the full flower of the famous spellbinding Lumumba oratory. And in prophetic words, he added, 'If I die, it will be because the whites have paid a black man to kill me. . . . Fetch Kasavubu [then President of the Congo], fetch Mobutu; tell them Lumumba challenges them to a duel. Tomorrow,' he added as he staggered to his car, 'I will die with the people. I will be the people's hostage.'

The same air of unreality, I recalled, hung over Léopoldville in 1961 as over Beirut in 1958, when, to put an end to the threat of civil war, President Eisenhower ordered the U.S. Marines into Lebanon.

It was then still difficult for Jewish correspondents to obtain visas for Arab countries, but so many had lied about their origins in order to cover the crisis that Stanley

Karnow, arriving somewhat late on the scene and surveying the crowded bar area of the St. Georges Hotel, in Beirut, said, 'Any more of us here and they'll be able to open a liberal synagogue.' I spent most of my time during the Beirut crisis in Amman, Jordan, but returned to Beirut in time to be invited to a dinner party by one of Beirut's long-established diplomats. This ambassador, straight out of a Graham Greene novel, lived with his mother and a prized lapdog on a secluded hill, but not far from one of the most turbulent suburbs. The dinner party was not a success. Several of the foreign correspondents among the guests got noisily and abusively drunk. Someone trod heavily on the ambassador's Pekinese. Both of them were visibly glad to be rid of us, all the envoy's suspicions of boorish reporters confirmed. We had expected to be given a lift back to town in his limousine, but though his driver was standing by, the ambassador was obviously determined to make us pay dearly for our behavior. 'If you turn left,' he said, 'and keep going down the hill, you stand a ninety-percent chance of survival. Good night.' We made it, past ominously close crackling gunfire.

A later visit to Beirut, in different circumstances, was equally fraught with hazard. Standing in for the *Time* bureau chief there in 1961, I had recently arrived in Beirut when Egypt and Syria formally broke their union, for the first, but certainly not the last, time. In a cable *Time* told me to expect a *Life* photographer, Charles Bonnay, and to get to Damascus with him as soon as he arrived. I knew Bonnay well. A dare-devil ex-French paratrooper, he had made quite a name for himself in Indochina and by parachuting recently over the SS *Santa Maria* for *Paris-Match* after it had been hijacked by Captain Henrique Galvão in January that year as a protest again Salazar's regime and Portugal's Angola policy.

The problem was that after arresting Nasser's man in Damascus, the new Syrian ruling junta had closed the border between Lebanon and Syria, and not even phone

144

communication was possible. 'No problem,' Bonnay said to me mysteriously in the taxi from the airport. I noticed that even for a *Life* photographer, Bonnay appeared to have an immense amount of luggage, including a soft, shapeless, and surprisingly weightless package which looked rather like a small gift-wrapped bedding roll. In the security of my hotel room, he unfolded his master plan. 'In there,' he said, pointing to the package, 'I have two parachutes. You have jumped before, no? What we do is book ourselves on a flight that overflies Syria. Then we simply open the door of the plane and jump out.'

It was some hours before I managed to talk him out of it. I pointed out that by strapping ourselves into our harness, we were bound to arouse the curiosity of even the most jaded stewardess. Besides, opening the door of an airliner would probably do terrible things to the passengers inside the pressurized cabin, and this in turn might make us, and *Time-Life*, liable to criminal procedures later on. 'Think of it, Charles,' I said. 'We might be banned from all commercial flights anywhere!' Finally, and by this time he must have detected a note of desperation in my voice, I pointed out that the Syrians were notoriously spy-conscious, nay, spy-obsessed. Two civilians parachuted out of the skies and landed without visas on Syrian territory would immediately be shot as spies.

Bonnay looked as crestfallen as a child denied a favorite outing. I promised to find some alternative, and the following morning, on the doubtful premise that the frontier between Jordan and Syria might not be quite so hermetically sealed, we flew to Amman.

So much invariably goes wrong in capers of this kind that one must note the few times when—inexplicably—luck takes over. From Amman, without much hope, I put through a call to the new interior minister. Amazingly, I was soon speaking in French to a courteous, indeed courtly, minister, who promised to phone the Syrian customs post at Der'a on the Jordanian border and to warn the local authorities there to issue us visas and facilitate our arrival. Another phone call—to a Damascus taxi service—enabled us to order a Syrian car on the Syrian side of the frontier, for the minister told us that our Jordanian driver would not be allowed to cross. Still, things looked promising, and we set out at dawn the following morning imbued with the sense of adolescent glee and expectation that comes over reporters only when they steal a march over their colleagues. The car duly took us to within a few hundred yards of the Der'a checkpoint. We unloaded our gear, the driver turned around and left with immediate visible relief, ignoring our request to wait a moment in case the trip turned out to be abortive, and we trudged the sandy no-man's-land between the Jordanian and the Syrian checkpoint.

Inside the Syrian 'gendarmerie' post we bitterly regretted having come. For no one had phoned, and it was impossible to convince the local commander to phone the new interior minister. Did we not realize, said a villainous-looking sergeant in a mixture of French, English, and Arabic, that we were now illegally inside Syrian territory? With regal gestures, he ordered us incarcerated. Bonnay's cameras were impounded, together with our luggage, passports, and wallets. It looked as if it would be a long stay.

I asked Bonnay if he knew of Der'a's reputation. He did not. I explained this was probably the very spot where T. E. Lawrence, disguised as an Arab, had been whipped and then buggered by an assortment of Turkish gendarmes. (This was before Lawrence's self-created myth had been exploded by historians.) 'I'm sure the tradition has remained even if the Turks have gone,' I told Bonnay. 'They're bound to prefer a handsome French photographer to me. If Lawrence could stand it, you can.' He was not amused.

What seemed like days, and was probably not more than a couple of hours, passed, and from our cell we heard the sound of a phone ringing and then conversation ending on

146

an unusually deferential note. Minutes later our cell was unlocked. The minister, unaccountably, had phoned after all. The same sergeant was now painstakingly writing down my name particulars in a huge book. I stopped him just in time from writing down my name as 'Colorofeyes Brown.' But our troubles were not yet over. A curfew was in force from 6:00 P.M. onward, and it was now 5:00 P.M. Each visa took what seemed like hours to prepare. Finally, having almost completed each of our passport entries, the sergeant demanded some Syrian pounds for government stamps to be affixed. Perhaps Jordanian money would do? Lebanese pounds? Dollars? No, they would not. Not only that, but the exact amount was to be tendered.

A small boy now took over the proceedings, spoke roughly to the sergeant, demanded dollars, and disappeared, emerging a short while later with the requisite amount. Foiled of his prey, the sergeant grudgingly affixed the stamps with imbecile slowness. He then opened one drawer after another, searching for his rubber stamp and purple ink pad to complete entry proceedings. It was nowhere to be found, and when found, it proved to be dry.

Again the small boy came to our rescue, using his saliva to produce a smear of purple. Our luggage was restored to us. All that was left for us to do was to cross the checkpoint, where our car, miraculously, still waited. I tipped the small boy handsomely. All seemed set. But the sergeant thought otherwise. Rushing to the opposite end of the customs post, he now behaved as though he were seeing us for the first time. As we passed, he snapped his fingers, and shouted, 'Passports.' He then painstakingly read each passport page by page. He studied the visas he himself had issued with mild surprise. Then he motioned us to open our luggage. Finally, he handed the passports back to us. We bowed and smiled with what composure we could muster, and I endeavored to cover Bonnay's loud 'I'll bash the fucker's face in.' Two hours later we were in Damascus. The rest of the press did not arrive for another two days. Bonnay got

147

some fairly good pictures of Syrian tanks in Damascus streets (taken from his hotel window, for all photography on the street was forbidden), which *Life* did not publish.

Nevertheless, our two-day advance on the rest of the press was invaluable—many correspondents followed our example and transited via Amman later that week—and Bonnay left with his parachutes unused.

In Beirut at the time the net was slowly closing around 'Kim' Philby, the 'third man' in the Maclean-Burgess defection affair, and his dramatic escape (probably by East European tanker) from Beirut, on being unmasked as the most successful double agent of all time, was to cause a huge stir a year later. It would be nice to be able to recall moments with Philby that might, with hindsight, have thrown light on his astonishing career. As resident Beirut correspondent for the London *Economist* and the *Observer*, Philby was well known to the whole press corps and on the whole well liked. He drank a lot. There were occasional, embarrassing rows between him and his latest wife. He was a pillar of the St. Georges Hotel bar, where he held court and where the barman acted as unpaid secretary, accumulating phone messages and mail for him. To me he was kindness itself, on the few occasions I asked his advice on arcane points of Middle Eastern policy, and never once did I detect in his behavior either any outward strain or a bias toward the Soviet Union. I must confess that my last meeting with him was banality itself. We were on a plane together, Cairo-bound, and Philby talked of the the comparative cost of living in Beirut and Cairo. 'It's so *cheap* here,' he said as we alighted. I noted with some envy that Philby's diplomatic connections then were such that while I battled for a taxi to take me to my hotel, Philby was met by a British Embassy car; for the duration of the trip, he was the honored guest of a high embassy official.

A few months after my Beirut stay I went to Albania for

Life. A small West German travel firm, specializing in East European holiday package tours, had organized a two-week visit to Albania, in conjunction with Albturist, the Albanian Government Tourist Board. The tour plan was not a success and was abruptly canceled after two trips.

It's unlikely that bona fide tourists would have rushed to sample Albania's tourist delights, but in any case very few of them were allowed to do so, for understandably, they were in a minority. Most of those who took advantage of the organized tour of Albania were, of course, reporters and photographers, masquerading as tourists, and perhaps a few spies as well. In my group the only incontrovertible tourist was an elderly German lady, visiting a lifelong friend who had married an Albanian and had been denied the possibility to leave the country to see her German friends and relatives, even for a brief visit. Otherwise, the most prominent members of my own group were Dominique Berretty (on assignment for *Life*) and a delightful man from *Asahi Shimbun*.

The journey began badly. My visa came through just as I was recovering from a severely infected foot, and I was forced to leave for West Germany (whence we were to depart for Tirana) on crutches. The visas were actually issued by the Albanian Embassy in East Berlin, but mercifully Berretty was able to take my passport across the border for me, while I rested from an overdose of antibiotics in a West Berlin hotel room. Then, in Budapest, between planes, my suitcase was off-loaded by mistake. On arrival in Tirana I owned a pair of crutches and a typewriter and little else. Berretty lent me a shirt and trousers about two sizes too big. As I soon found out, Tirana's shops were so bare that any plan I had for stocking up on Albanian clothing had to be abandoned. Even the razor I managed to find turned out to be unusable.

Our guide was a slight, sad-faced man who immediately realized the calamity we represented. No, he said in beautiful, sad French, we could not spend more than the allotted time in Tirana. Yes, we were compelled to spend ten days in Durres (formerly Durazzo), the seaside resort about one hour's drive from Tirana. Yes, we could visit castles and 'places of historical interest' while in Durres, but all visits to any coastal area, apart from Durres, were out of the question, as was any trip north to the Yugoslav and south to the Greek borders. No, Enver Hoxha would not be available. 'Remember,' he said, eyeing my typewriter with loathing, 'here you are tourists only.'

Albania was at the time, even to a superficial observer, in the middle of an economic crisis of truly disastrous proportions. With no shops to speak of, no restaurants (apart from a few street booths still serving kebabs), little traffic on the streets, Tirana was a grim place indeed—the more so since our Japanese friend insisted on coming with us on my fruitless quest for a spare shirt or two. In shop after shop we looked at what was available—none of it my size and all of it appalling quality. 'How much this shirt?' said the man from *Asahi Shimbun*. He was told. 'How much you earn in one month?' he asked the salesperson. He was told another sum, in *lek*, the Albanian currency. 'Ah, so, very interesting,' he would say. 'Three months— one shirt.' This sort of thing did not endear us either to our guide or to the locals, and soon a small crowd of rather obvious plainclothed police dogged our every step. Albania is known to its own people as Republika Popullore e Shqipërië, and our *Asahi Shimbun* friend seized on this to coin his own phrase. 'These people,' he said, 'very skippy people.'

Before we left the capitalist world, our German travel agency had given us each a brochure published by Albturist describing the touristic delights of Albania. I wish I had it still. One showed a svelte, bikinied water skier as she was towed along by an expensive-looking motor launch. Others showed happy bathers playing in the water, or reclining on beaches, or playing volleyball. This was Durres, and reality was somewhat at variance with the illustrations. I recall, from notes and a diary kept at the time, there was indeed a beach at Durres, all right, with a promenade area behind it, a little like Deauville. But the beach itself was closed off at one end by army pillboxes and barbed wire, for beyond it on the right began the harbor proper which was, naturally, out of bounds. And to the left there was a solid barbed-wire fence, too, separating the public beach from a secluded zone, where, we eventually learned, party bigwigs had their seaside dachas.

For some reason, a zone of trees immediately behind the beach area was also out of bounds ('Unexploded mines from the Second World War,' said our guide cryptically), but perhaps the most curious travesty centered on the sleek motor launch with its putative water skiers. Of the latter there were none, but recognizably the identical motor launch, manned by uniformed guards, swept incessantly to and fro beyond the bathers—but at a distance which seemed to me to be dangerously close to them. I asked our guide about this boat. He was at first embarrassed and unable to tell us more than that it was there 'to make sure nobody drowned.' Eventually, however, I learned the truth. I swam beyond the ritual 200 yards. Immediately the motor launch came cruising up, and unmistakably, in sign language, I was ordered back. The boat was there to keep the bathers from swimming beyond the 200-yard limit, not to protect them from misadventure, but to make sure that none was tempted to swim out to a passing merchant ship as it left the harbor to our right and ask for asylum aboard.

Maybe things have changed since; some carefully censored TV programs can be captured from the Italian coast not so far away, I am told, and on the night of the Ali-Foreman fight, televised live, crowds of young Albanians descended on Durres and demanded, in the middle of the night, to watch it.

In our Durres hotel, French windows gave on to a common terrace, and by possible accident, but more likely by design, each 'tourist' had been allocated a room

151

sandwiched between those of Chinese technical advisers. They were clearly on orders to have nothing to do with us and stared ahead when we nodded or said hello. They all had radios in their room and would listen to Radio Peking in the small hours of the morning. After a night of this (for they turned the sound full on) we met at breakfast to devise some peaceful counteroffensive. Our Japanese friend said that he would convey a written message to our Chinese neighbors. In his underpants and undershirt, and carrying a bottle of black ink and a small brush, he strode out onto the terrace and with his brush penned a series of vertical signs on the Chinese-occupied windows, bowed again, and passed on to the next. I asked him what he had written. 'I say, "Please make big noise small,"' he answered. Alas, the following night, and indeed every successive night till our departure, Radio Peking came on stronger and stronger.

In Tirana we had barely had time to find our bearings when we had been whisked away to Durres, and I pleaded with our guide to return—on the pretext that we had not had time to visit the famous Museum of the Revolution. Our wish was granted, and we spent several hours in the company of a formidable lady partisan who lectured us on the military genius of Enver Hoxha and the bloody defeats inflicted on both Italian and German occupying forces. To hear her talk, the beloved leader Enver Hoxha had not only booted out the Italian Fascists and the Nazis but had also been largely responsible for liberating most of Yugoslavia as well, and only Albanian courage and revolutionary ardor had succeeded in propping up the flagging, spent Tito partisans. Since, at war's end, Enver Hoxha had pleaded with Tito to incorporate Albania into Yugoslavia's federal system (Tito wisely refused), such claims seemed a little farfetched. What also seemed designed to cast some doubt on the claims—repetitively intoned by the lady partisan—that Enver Hoxha had shared all the dangers of his partisans, sleeping in the rough and tirelessly leading them on to ever greater heroic feats, was the nature of the

152

photographs of this period, all inevitably featuring Enver Hoxha in various poses, uniforms, and martial stances. Often he was photographed alone. But some pictures showed him with his partisans, and here the contrast was noteworthy. Enver Hoxha, even as a relatively young man, was not what one could call slim. Any reporter versed in Timese would refer to him as 'sleek' (always supposing one rejected the word 'plump'). His well-tailored uniform failed to conceal the fact that he had both a tummy and a double chin. In contrast, his partisans were lean to the point of emaciation, in ill-fitting frayed and ragged uniforms.

Needless to say, my attempts to call on Enver Hoxha never came to fruition. Even the decision to write to him from Tirana, explaining my presence and our innocent deception in making the trip as tourists, caused our unhappy guide so much obvious torment (at one point, when I explained I had written a letter asking for an interview, he burst into tears) that I desisted. With face-saving grace, I explained that no one had been willing to sell me a stamp and that, therefore, I was entrusting my letter to him. Could he perhaps forward it? He did so with such alacrity that I knew he had wisely torn it up and flushed its contents away.

The European diplomatic community in Tirana was restricted to French, Italian, Turkish and Yugoslav representation. We called on the Yugoslav chargé d'affaires, who insisted we lunch with him in his home. He had just had a somewhat unusual experience for a diplomat and wanted to tell us about it. Yugoslavia and Albania were then in the process of exchanging protest notes on alleged frontier violations.

Tirana's ministries, he explained to us, were in a 'forbidden quarter' restricted to permit holders and high Albanian officials. Delivering Yugoslavia's latest note to the Foreign Affairs Ministry, he had failed to stop with sufficient alacrity at the entrance to the forbidden zone—and security guards had promptly riddled his car with bullets. He and his driver had miraculously escaped, but his car (we saw it) was a colander. Not the least of his problems was that this singularly undiplomatic assault on one of the most important resident diplomats had led, inevitably, to his government's penning yet another protest note. 'I don't know when I'll deliver it,' he said. Throughout our stay in his house various servants with ill-defined status hovered nearby. 'Spies, all of them,' the diplomat hissed at us when their backs were turned.

Our guide himself symphathized with our predicament when, cutting short our stay by four days, we decided to return to Paris. We waited for some time at the airport for a Yugoslav plane which was late. 'Never mind,' he said, with obvious relief at our impending departure. 'All good things come to him who waits.'

But no trip could compare in sheer madness with my ill-advised decision to accompany General de Gaulle on a visit to Djibouti (then still capital of French Somaliland), the Malagasy Republic, and the island of Réunion in the summer of 1961. I made it largely at the instigation of Tom Brady, who had been detailed by *The New York Times* to cover the visit in full and who wanted company. Having arrived in Djibouti after a hellishly long trip aboard a propeller-driven plane, we were installed in a specially furnished naval barracks. Djibouti, lacking sufficient hotels, could not easily cope with the huge numbers that a de Gaulle visit generated. That evening the French governor of Djibouti threw a small party for the press in his residence. Inevitably conversation veered away from the topic of de Gaulle (who was arriving the following day) to the leafy drug *kat*, chewed by so many Djibouti inhabitants. This 'social affliction' (*fléau social*), known to the locals as *la salade*, from its green resemblance to watercress, was imported daily by plane from Ethiopia and freely sold throughout Djibouti immediately after the plane's arrival. From 10:00 A.M. onward, hundreds of Djiboutians could be seen, contentedly chewing *kat*. 'It has to be consumed while still fresh,' said the governor, explaining that attempts to ban the drug in Aden had merely led to gang warfare and inflated black-market prices caused by smuggling.

It was inevitable that Tom Brady, the following morning, should insist on sampling some. To indulge him, I acquired a bundle, looking rather like watercress, and he sat, in our hired car, ostentatiously chewing the bitter green leaves. I started chewing, too. Having never sniffed cocaine, I can't vouch for the effect. All I can say is that, in the dreadful morning heat, we gradually became not only at ease with the world but in full control of our immensely enhanced faculties. Brady was the first to react to our new sense of euphoria. 'What do they mean,' he asked, 'putting us up in a naval barracks? Let's find a decent place to stay before de Gaulle arrives.'

Usually I was Sancho Panza to Brady's Don Quixote, with a negative, dissenting view. On this occasion my inhibitions were gone. 'Driver!' I said. 'First we will pack. Then you will take us to the residential quarter.'

In Djibouti's residential quarter it was some time before we came across a house we liked. Then, ordering our driver to stand by, we walked in, carrying our suitcases. The house was empty, save for an elderly houseboy. We opened door after door, eventually selecting two air-conditioned bedrooms to our taste. We unpacked, and so self-possessed were we that the servant assumed we had indeed been foisted on his master and asked whether we had had breakfast and whether we required lunch.

The rest of the Djibouti visit is something of a blur. More *kat* was consumed on the way to the airport, and when de Gaulle arrived and began shaking hands with a long line of native tribesmen, the scene, to us at least, seemed so comic that we could not understand why others around us were not having, as we were, to suppress their mirth. For de Gaulle and the Somali desert chieftains, mostly aged and wrinkled, some with wives, servants, slaves, and herds of goats, some with goiters and unmistakable signs of other advanced tropical diseases, appeared to us as freakish as the madmen in the second act of Ibsen's *Peer Gynt*. De Gaulle, however, addressed them as formally as if they had been papal nuncios. '*Bonjour, emir*,' he said in his deep vibrant voice, or, '*Enchanté de vous voir, sultan*,' or, '*Ravi, altesse*,' as he went down the line shaking hands with these ragged, wild old men.

Later de Gaulle was due to address the local Parliament, and again we found ourselves in a minority of two, overcome by the spectacle of hysterical comedy as starched admirals and generals, their places neatly labeled, were pushed aside by the same emirs and sultans who had greeted de Gaulle at the airport, while above the jostling din the President of the local Assembly made a welcoming speech in mostly unintelligible Armenian-accented French.

Both Brady and I sent what we privately felt were the funniest pieces we had ever written to our respective papers. My story never appeared. 'It wasn't exactly gibberish,' someone in New York commented later, 'but we all assumed you'd had a touch of the sun.'

The Malagasy Republic—formerly Madagascar—was chiefly memorable for its rococo palaces, de Gaulle absently shaking my hand at an official reception and muttering, '*Bonjour, princesse*,' and a British envoy who surprised me by saying, over the phone, in this sleepiest of capitals, 'Won't be able to fit you in today, old boy. You can imagine how busy we are.'

'How about the afternoon?' I asked.

'Never come in in the afternoons.'

When I did finally call on him, I was somewhat surprised to discover that the British Consulate General, soon to become a full-fledged embassy, was housed in the same building as the local Communist bookshop—and said so. On the ground floor were the standard works of Marx, Lenin, and Engels, huge posters commemorating Gagarin and Sputnik, and French translations of *And Quiet Flows*

156

the Don, 'Communist, old boy? Are you sure? I never noticed.'

It was on the island of Réunion, our next stop, that Brady was to goad the French authorities into impotent fury. He had taken to wearing an Algerian dark-blue woolen djellaba, regardless of the weather, and native Tunisian yellow slippers, which were constantly slipping from his plump feet. In order to irritate Jacques Soustelle, who accompanied de Gaulle on this trip, he would ask, in a loud voice, whenever Soustelle was within earshot, 'Are there any nationalists here?'

The island of Réunion is the remotest of French departments and boasts a large Communist minority. There had been elections shortly before the de Gaulle visit, and the Communists maintained they had been rigged. The night of our arrival, angry Communists burned cars and scattered large nails, puncturing tires and causing traffic jams. There were gendarmes everywhere, and the atmosphere was tense. The prefect, a sad-looking man with a wispy mustache, should have been in bed. His arm was in a sling. Rumor had it that *Madame la préfète* had come across him in compromising circumstances and shot him with a revolver. She was nowhere to be seen.

The main event here was a de Gaulle speech at the sports stadium, and we were told to come early and to be sure to exhibit our press credentials, as well as our special local passes. Brady, as usual, arrived late. Gendarmes, nervously awaiting the imminent arrival of de Gaulle and expecting trouble at the stadium itself, brusquely asked him for his press card. Brady searched his pockets interminably and in vain. Then his face broke into a grin. He had found, or thought he had found, what he was looking for—a scrap of paper of the kind issued us at the prefecture. But this was yellow, and as he unfolded it, like a magician, it grew and grew, until finally it was the size of a wall poster. It was a poster, of the kind stuck up all over the island by the Communists, and it read: 'Down with rigged elections.' A

157

French official rescued Brady as he was being frog-marched away, an obvious *agent provocateur* in his flowing robes.

Tom Brady's dark-blue djellaba was known all over North Africa, for he was the uncontested dean of that small, incestuous group of correspondents known, in part envy and part derision, as the Maghreb Circus. Headquarters of this group, not so much a club as a cartel, was located for most of the Algerian War in Tunis, but later the circus became a movable feast, especially after the French cease-fire which preceded Algerian independence by several months.

Members of the Maghreb Circus hunted as a pack, swapping information and helping one another out. Though some of its members were better placed than others, one essential criterion for admission was that one had to be able, on occasion, to add to a common pool of knowledge. Hangers-on with no special skills to contribute were not encouraged and found themselves excluded in a number of ways.

It is difficult to explain just what qualities in a reporter were necessary for membership, since the terms were never defined. One criterion was an understanding of the historical background to the events then taking place in North Africa and a familiarity with the large, and confusing, cast of characters involved. Apart from Brady and myself, most of the Maghreb Circus members were French, and Jean Daniel, now editor of the *Nouvel Observateur* and then a special correspondent for *L'Express*, was its co-chairman.

Not that the Maghreb Circus was solely a work-oriented organization. Its members also played together, and one of the venues of the club was a small restaurant in the old part of Tunis specializing in a typically Tunisian, and outwardly somewhat revolting, dish much beloved by Tom Brady, consisting of an entire sheep's head, split in two and baked in a primitive charcoal-fired oven. Nor was membership exclusively male. Indeed, one of the attractions of the

Maghreb Circus was the floating population of girlfriends, groupies, FLN sympathizers, and comely Algerian exiles gravitating around it, and its sexual aura was certainly one of the main reasons why so many visiting correspondents sought to become members in good standing.

Tom Brady's family lived in Rabat, but he was in Tunis a great deal of the time. What attracted Brady was not simply the availability of attractive and intelligent young women, but the atmosphere they created. Seldom unfaithful, he nevertheless enjoyed their constant presence much as an old-fashioned patriarch might enjoy that of palace houris he was too old to bed himself. The young women gravitating around Tom Brady adored him, too. Retrospectively, it may seem strange that neither the FLN nor the French Secret Service ever bothered to infiltrate the Maghreb Circus with agents of their own.

Not all personal relationships within the Maghreb Circus were platonic or trouble-free, and a number of friendships and marriages foundered as a result of the ebb and flow of passion. There was something about the jasmine-scented nights in the tiny village of Sidi-Bou-Saïd or Hammamet that made even the staidest, most work-oriented reporter lose his head momentarily, and it was presumably to try to recapture the flavor of those days that Tom Brady, many years later, resigned from *The New York Times* (which had—after posting him to Delhi and Beirut—brought him back to New York to write obituaries and cover the local New York scene) and took up a post with the United Nations Mission in Tunis. There, in 1971, he died, probably in a manner he would himself have chosen; after a Tunisian couscous luncheon with Hedi Nouira, the Tunisian premier, he had a heart attack, keeled over, and never recovered consciousness. He had been, as many French correspondents were to acknowledge, a more effective American ambassador than any diplomat ever posted to the Maghreb. And even if some French officials felt that Brady was worth several FLN divisions, he had never allowed his own personal sentiments to affect his writing, though he did, of course, enormously contribute to American understanding of what the FLN and the Algerian independence movement were about.

Many ex-members of the Maghreb Circus remember Tom Brady vividly, and it's curious how alive he still seems to me. I saw a great deal of him in the post-Algerian-independence period, when we were both Delhi-based correspondents, for he shared my house for several weeks there, a lovable, irritating, eccentric, beaming bear of a man who would never pass a beggar without giving him money or say no to a snake charmer peddling his act or resist the dubious delights of a roadside sweetmeat or curd stall. He was, of course, light-years away from the image *New York Times* executives sought to project for their correspondents abroad. He was never 'the gentleman from the *Times*,' adept at embassy cocktail-party-circuit chatter, at ease at formal Establishment dinner parties where well-bred small talk and banal generalities were exchanged. Tom's perceptions of a country were different; a populist *avant la lettre*, he identified with the simple people, the poor, the under-privileged, preferring their company to that of their rulers.

This did not endear him to his *New York Times* hierarchical superiors, for whom he was incorrigibly bohemian and unconventional in a pre-Watergate age far more straitlaced and intolerant than now. Many of Tom's colleagues felt then that his qualities were not fully perceived at the time. Any foreign correspondent who returns to his home base after years in the field experiences, as Tom did, a period of maladjustment. But Tom's return to Tunis with the UN at the end of his life was the fulfillment of an old dream. While a reporter with *The New York Times*, he had bought a house at Sidi-Bou-Saïd. His heart was in the Maghreb. He was at home in the souks of Tunis and the Algiers Casbah, not in the Times Square jungle.

I have often wondered how Brady would have reacted to

the intolerance of the regimes whose independence birthpangs he witnessed. Would he, I wonder, have come to believe that the FLN's Algerian struggle was futile and that 'happiness,' as Henry Luce might have defined it, lay in a continuing dependence on France?

The Algerian example is an extreme one, for no sooner was independence achieved than a protracted struggle for power within the FLN movement itself quickly led to the physical liquidation of many of the original leaders of the Algerian revolution. The comradeship of the years in the resistance and Algerian underground seemed forgotten overnight, and today nearly all the 'historic' leaders of the Algerian Liberation Movement are either dead, liquidated, or forgotten, while the most colorful of them all, Ahmed Ben Bella, has been under house arrest for the last thirteen years.

On my frequent postindependence assignments to Algeria, I have been constantly reminded of the brutality and the merciless quality of the independence struggle. Here, at a street corner, I remember watching a young Algerian, blown to pieces by his own bomb, lie dying, half hidden underneath a car, being surveyed with unmistakable glee by an elderly French lady of obvious means. She bent and scooped up a severed finger, which she slipped into her handbag as a souvenir. Here, strung up on the tramlines of Bab el Oued, I once saw the corpse of a French anti-OAS informer. I expected, naïvely, that Algerians would recall the war in the same vivid way. Perhaps the trauma was simply too enormous, or perhaps the new generations coming to adulthood after independence simply never experienced the war as we reporters did, for though I found lip service paid to the revolution, I found few Algerians willing even to talk about their experiences.

More depressing still was the realization that in many cases the new regimes, and especially the new Algerian regime, no sooner found themselves in power than they began to take a leaf out of their former colonizer's book, vying in brutality and arbitrariness with the paras and legionnaires of the past and in some cases surpassing them. It is unfashionable to attack 'developing countries' of the Third World for the arbitrary police-state ruthlessness which liberals find it possible to denounce in East European countries. The existence of a one-party state, of a rigidly controlled press, and of political police with limitless powers is now the rule rather than the exception in most of the former colonies in Africa. Periodically liberals wring their hands over this situation, comment on the waning of individual liberties, and plead for the release of some of the 700,000 political prisoners believed to be held in jails around the world. But this hardly prevents the freedom-loving Western world from trading with these countries, and I know of no Third World country, save possibly Uganda, which has been submitted to effective sanctions as a result of its behavior.

During the course of the Algerian War (1952-62), I had probably done more than most reporters to try to explain why the Algerian National Liberation Front had been compelled to engage in a cruel struggle for independence, using terrorism as a weapon. I was on one occasion threatened with expulsion from France, for 'pro-FLN bias,' and a cover story I had written for *Time* in 1961 on the counterterrorist French OAS was one of the few U.S. magazine issues seized by the government of General de Gaulle, which eventually allowed it to be distributed in France, but with a blacked-out cover where ex-General Raoul Salan's picture had been (Salan was the 'Scarlet Pimpernel' of the OAS, on the run in Algeria but finding considerable sympathy for his cause with elements of the French Army officer corps there).

In the course of reporting the war, I struck up what I had believed to be real friendships with FLN spokesmen who later became prominent figures of the independent Algerian government Establishment. How I later became persona non grata in Algeria is instructive because it shows how an independence movement rapidly transformed itself into an authoritarian, bureaucratic state, unable to stomach any criticism and intent on allowing into the country only reporters who would further a favorable propaganda image.

In 1974 a British doctor, Ian Young, wrote a book called *The Private Life of Islam* which told of his earlier experiences as an intern in the gynecology ward of Tizi Ouzou Hospital in Algerian Kabylia. It was an exceptionally well-written, convincing story, based on his daily diaries, of bureaucratic mismanagement and inept and sadistic behavior by two resident Bulgarian doctors, who terrified their patients into submission, to the utter indifference of city-educated Algerian nurses and midwives, themselves highly contemptuous of their Kabyle peasant charges.

The book was also a reflection on the appalling condition of Algerian women in newly independent Algeria, some of them forcibly married in their teens to men three times their age and subsequently brought to the hospital with lacerated vaginas. 'This dark side of Algeria has already been the subject of books,' I wrote in a review of the book in *Newsweek International* in November 1974, 'some of them by Algerian women like Fadela M'Rabet who recalls how, after independence and despite the active role of women in the FLN during the Algerian War, they eventually lost out to traditionalists.

But there has never been a book as stark and as factual as Young's. 'I hope,' I rather naïvely concluded, 'that Algerian President Houari Boumedienne has time to read this authentic account. Alas, far more likely is an outright Algerian ban on the book and its dismissal as the work of an "agent provocateur" intent on sabotaging the image of the "new" Algeria.'

The Algerian government's reactions to the book went far beyond my apprehensions. A few months later, in 1975,

163

I took a plane to Algiers to report for *Newsweek* on Algeria's bid for leadership of the Arab world and was held at the airport, made to remain in the transit lounge, and put on the first plane out of the country. In vain I begged to know the reason for such treatment. I had been blacklisted, I later found out, because of my book review.

Needless to say, I protested, privately, to my old FLN friends—and was assured the whole thing had been an 'unfortunate misunderstanding.' So it was without any apprehension that, four years later, in February 1978, I flew to Algeria to take part in a BBC-TV documentary film on Algeria. Reda Malek, a former FLN spokesman and now information minister, had assured the BBC that I would be 'specially welcome' there.

I arrived in Oran, where I was scheduled to interview some Algerian technocrats. To my horror the whole expulsion scenario repeated itself. 'You cannot enter Algeria,' said a plainclothes inspector. I asked why. 'We are unable to say,' he replied. 'We are just obeying orders.'

I spent the night in the cold, stretched out on a couple of chairs in the airport lounge, hoping that word would come that it was all 'an unfortunate misunderstanding.' No word came, despite my plea to phone officials in Algiers—which was denied—and none of the phones in the airport lounge was in working order, a familiar state of affairs for Algeria. As I watched the Oranais coastline recede, I had the feeling that the wheel had come full circle—and I was glad Tom Brady was no longer around. I also recalled that here was another instance of caricature imitating life. For all foreign correspondents know of the hoary cliché situation, involving their arrival in some Arab country, to the accompaniment of the police inspector's greeting: 'Welcome. Welcome to my country. Why do you tell untrue facts about my country? You will please wait at airport. Welcome.'

VI.   ALGERIA II

IT'S TIME to get back to the Algerian War, which I continued to cover, on an almost permanent basis, from 1958 onwards until the very end. So much has been written about the events which succeeded each other with a kind of implacable Greek-tragedy fatality—the Gaullist and *pied-noir*-inspired uprising of May 13, 1958; their despair at the discovery that General de Gaulle, the man they first believed to be the savior of *L'Algérie française*, was in fact edging his way toward a recognition of Algerian independence; the successive army rebellions culminating in the April 1961 putsch, which ended in ignominious failure; the subsequent OAS counterterrorist campaign of *pied-noir* diehards and army deserters; and the final French exodus in the wake of Algerian independence in July 1962—that I prefer to provide instead a record of my more personal experiences, the funny and the less funny, and such glimpses of the behind-the-scenes raw material of history as came my way and which I never reported at the time, partly because *Time* somewhat discouraged any personal touch in its correspondents' files.

Like Fabrizio del Dongo in Stendhal's *Charterhouse of Parma*, who took part in what he later discovered had been the Battle of Waterloo without realizing that he was witnessing an event of truly cosmic proportions, I frequently, during this Algerian period, found myself taking part in events whose significance I failed to grasp in their entirety until afterward.

It was so with May 13, 1958, the day an Algiers demonstration of war veterans and *pied-noir* organizations escalated into an act of defiance against the French government which was to lead, a few days later, to the collapse of the Fourth Republic and the return to power of General de Gaulle. This was the prejet age, and French commercial planes to Algiers included the sturdy but hideously uncomfortable *Breguet deux-ponts*, whose seats, in the lower tier, were the equivalent of steerage and considerably cheaper than the upper level.

Europeans usually insisted on traveling on the top part, the lower tier being full of poor Algerian workers, but I was happy to get the last seat in the lower deck. My presence on this plane was not entirely fortuitous. On May 12 I had received two phone calls. One was from a French Algerian source, a prosperous Jewish businessman who was very close to a number of *pied-noir* activists. 'If I were you,' he said, 'I'd make every effort to get down here by tomorrow at the latest. The balloon is going up.' A local correspondent in Algiers, Robert Soulé, who worked for *France-Soir* and was among the best-informed of French Algerian journalists, also advised me to get to Algiers as soon as possible. I checked with John Wallis, the veteran London *Daily Telegraph* correspondent in Paris, who also had extensive contacts among Algerian *pied-noirs*. He too had received similar phone calls.

I had little difficulty in persuading *Time* that I had to get to Algiers as soon as possible, and on the morning of May 13 John Wallis and I were in the last *Breguet deux-ponts* that flew into Algiers for some time. We both were present at the demonstration that day in front of the Algiers war memorial, ostensibly staged to protest the execution of three French soldiers recently taken prisoner by the FLN but, in fact, used as a pretext, by the organizers, to storm the Gouvernement Général building, only a few hundred yards away, and bring down the Republic.

Except for aged bemedaled Algerian veterans of the

First World War, most Moslems had wisely decided to stay indoors, but the crowd was, by French Algerian standards, highly disciplined, and there was no 'Ratonnade' (systematic beating up of Africans). It was, however, distinctly anti-American. A young senator called John Kennedy had recently attacked French 'colonial' policy in Algeria, and American journalists were not popular. 'If I were you,' said Daniel Camus, a *Paris-Match* photographer who was himself a veteran paratrooper, and a Dien Bien Phu and Suez expedition veteran, 'I wouldn't let on that you're working for *Time-Life*.' I immediately removed a *Life* sticker label I had foolishly affixed to my camera bag. Among the crowd one middle-class Frenchman, somewhat drunk, was shouting, '*Ni Marocains ni Americains*,' over and over again, obviously fascinated by this poetic alliteration. Luckily my accentless French and overall appearance enabled me to 'pass' as French. (Later that afternoon, in what was subsequently to become an almost ritual act, the French demonstrators sacked the United States Information Service office nearby.)

At this time I knew none of the cast of characters who were to become famous overnight: Jo Ortiz, the Poujadist leader of the middle-class *pied-noirs*; Pierre Lagaillarde, the rabble-rousing student leader; and Jean-Jacques Susini, his henchman. All I saw was a red-bearded young man in a paratrooper's uniform—Lagaillarde—making a speech which I couldn't hear because the pressure of the crowd was such that I couldn't get near enough, and there was no loudspeaker system. Then the crowd surged up the steps and, like a tidal wave, spilled into the Gouvernement Général building at the top, with local police making only token attempts to stop them. I remember watching French paratroopers arriving in a convoy of trucks and my apprehension at a possible showdown. But instead, obviously on orders of local military commanders, paras and demonstrators fraternized. The French troops did nothing to try to evict them from the Gouvernement

167

Général building, but rather lounged about, witnessing the scene with broad smiles. They were kissed and surrounded by attractive French girls. I remember, in the middle of the screaming, yelling mob, turning to Serge Bromberger, of *Figaro*, and saying, 'It's the end of the Fourth Republic.'

'Musn't lose our cool,' he replied.

The demonstration leaders found themselves on the main balcony of the Gouvernement Général building, along with anyone and everyone who had managed to squeeze in behind them, endlessly addressing the crowd below. Official papers were scattered into the square. In what was meant to be a touching example of interracial goodwill, Algerian women joined the predominantly European crowd on the square, but their credibility was somewhat strained by my discovery that some of them were from the Algiers Casbah's many *maisons de tolérance*. Others were in regimented squads with carefully prepared 'integration' banners. Indeed, lurking behind almost every women's contingent was a French 'special affairs' army officer, recognizable by his pale-blue kepi.

I remember going up to a young French artillery captain in Algiers that afternoon, to try to obtain some spontaneous French Army reaction to what had just happened. 'How do you feel about the Army's takeover of Algiers?' I asked him.

He stared at me incredulously. 'You must be joking,' he said, looking around him and seeing thronged streets and crowded café tables. I gave him the briefest account of what I had seen. 'My God,' he said, 'it all happened while I was at the movies.'

Years later I asked the late Georges Pompidou whether he had had any advance notice of the May 13, 1958, events. 'I knew absolutely nothing about it,' he said. 'To tell you the truth, I was watching a movie on the Champs-Elysées at the time.'

May 13 was a Monday, and as invariably happens with stories of this magnitude, my concern shifted to the questions: How do I file? How do I get the pictures out? Phones were working only intermittently, telex lines were unreliable, and all air services were suspended from midday onward. But the overnight Algiers-to-Marseilles passenger and cargo vessels continued to operate, and I managed to get a berth on Tuesday night. I arrived in Marseilles on Wednesday morning. French international airline services had also been disrupted, but *Life* had chartered a small plane for me, and by Wednesday afternoon I was in Paris and had delivered quantities of film—including some on behalf of my *Paris-Match* and *Jours de France* colleagues.

On Thursday morning I was on my way back to Algiers, first to Barcelona, where *Paris-Match* and *Life* had between them chartered yet another plane, piloted by a character straight out of *The Dogs of War*, to fly us back to Algiers. Among the *Paris-Match* team on this return journey was Joel le Tac, a French reservist officer and Second World War resistance hero who had been the press officer with the French paras at the time of the Suez operation. Then there had been rumors that he had indulged in some slight favoritism, dispatching *Paris-Match* film back to Paris but holding the rest of the correspondents' pictures back until deadlines were past. He later became a Gaullist deputy. His impeccable Gaullist credentials guaranteed that we would not be ignominiously expelled. When we landed, thanks to Le Tac, French Army NCOs speedily and efficiently arranged for us to pass through customs, and as I recall it, there were no police formalities whatever. There was a problem with transport, however, and precious minutes were wasted as we looked for a vehicle to take us into town. Eventually we all piled into an Air Algérie bus, like thrifty tourists. One British reporter in our party kept saying, mournfully, 'We should have taken a taxi.' Many days later I read his account of the landing at Algiers Airport with some interest; he made no mention of the prosaic way we arrived at the St. Georges

Hotel, but his description of tense paratroopers ringing the airport and the hint of extreme danger implied in the piece was at considerable variance with reality.

My return to the St. Georges Hotel so soon after leaving it earned me unexpected kudos from the French hotel staff; rumor had it that I had arrived in the same plane as Jacques Soustelle, who had also arrived in Algiers that day. Needless to say, I did nothing to dispel this rumor but, when questioned, endeavored to look archly conspiratorial.

For the rest of 1958 and most of 1959, I commuted among Algiers, Tunis, and Paris and saw a great deal of General de Gaulle on his then-triumphal visits to Algeria. The great man's impassive, Buddha-like calm under all circumstances commanded respect. But he could never conceal his sense of bitter irony and regal disdain for lesser mortals. I was present when he landed in southern Algeria, to be greeted by General Raoul Salan, then still the commander in chief of French forces in Algeria, who was later to become the OAS leader and de Gaulle's most implacable foe. Salan saluted; de Gaulle shook hands and then indulged in the kind of small talk that monarchs affect. He asked about the weather. '*Mon général*, the sun just came out, minutes before your plane landed,' Salan replied.

De Gaulle looked at him with obvious distaste. 'I suppose it came out specially for me?' he said.

De Gaulle's surprise nominee to succeed Robert Lacoste as chief administrative delegate in Algeria was Paul Delouvrier, a highly respected technocrat who had worked, as I had, with Jean Monnet, at the Luxembourg-based European Coal and Steel Community. In the Sahara, on an inspection tour, Delouvrier formally shook hands with a number of correspondents he was meeting for the first time. My turn came, and he said, 'What the hell are you doing here?'

I decided to respond in the same vein. 'I could well ask you the same question,' I said. He grinned.

I visited the newly discovered Hassi Messaoud and Hassi

R'mel oil fields several times, experiencing the deadly mid-August Saharan heat. French oil field workers slept in air-conditioned prefabricated huts, ate like kings, but worked twelve hours at a stretch in the appalling heat, with generous rest and recreation spells in either Algiers or France. On one visit to the Sahara, the French Army press office insisted that I be accompanied by a Regular French Army captain, who proved a pleasant and useful companion. I didn't understand at the time why he had been detailed to travel with me. It was only after the Algerian War was over, when we met by chance on a Paris street, that I learned the real reason. By then he was a civilian, having been forcibly retired from the Army for his involvement in the April 1961 putsch. 'Why did you come with me to the Sahara?' I asked.

'Army intelligence was convinced that you were using the Sahara trip as a pretext for contacting the FLN,' he said. 'I was there to keep an eye on you.'

Alas, in 1958-59 such contacts were extremely rare, though the FLN did hold court in Tunis, where it established a provisional government, even establishing a system of press credentials. The Algerian 'minister of information' was M'hammed Yazid, later to become a prominent figure in the Algerian government and later still Algeria's ambassador in Beirut. Yazid, who came from a family with strong French Army traditions, had met an American girl, Olive Laguardia, whom he subsequently married, while working in New York as an FLN lobbyist. The combination of Italo-American and Algerian life-styles made the Yazid household in Tunis an unusual one. One FLN official told me that when he visited Yazid's house, he never knew whether he was going to be offered couscous, a pizza, or a malted milk shake.

It was thanks to Yazid that I became, in 1960, one of the few correspondents to see action with the FLN. By this time the French Army had built an almost impregnable Challe line (named after the former commander in chief, Air

Force General Maurice Challe, who later went to jail for his part in the 1961 putsch), in addition to the existing Morice line (named after a defense minister of the Fourth Republic, André Morice), to prevent infiltration by FLN troops and supply and arms convoys. On the Tunisian border, in a kind of no-man's-land on the very frontier itself, Algerian FLN units had dug themselves deep cavernous holes in the ground, some of them housing more than 100 men each.

Few FLN units managed to breach the two electrified defense lines, and casualties were appalling. The FLN's 'forces of the interior' were thus hard pressed for replacements and arms. But the highly trained, well-equipped 'regular' FLN army on the Tunisian side, armed with Chinese artillery and mortars, had become extremely adept at harassing French Army bunkers and Maginot-line types of forts on the Challe line itself. With *Life* photographer Hank Walker, I intended to go out on one of these harassing operations.

As usual with the FLN, it was best to arm oneself with endless patience. First we waited for days in Tunis, keeping as low a profile as possible, before setting out for the western Tunisian town of Souk el Arba. Beyond Souk el Arba, we left our car in an FLN compound and continued our journey in an FLN Citroën *deux-chevaux*. Our guide was an irritatingly sententious FLN lieutenant, who spoke solely in basic anti-colonialist clichés. He drove appallingly, changing gear only as the last extremity and constantly using either the brake or the accelerator. This, together with the heat and the peculiar *deux-chevaux* suspension, made us both queasy. We were, I'm afraid, in no mood to listen to his endless chatter, culled exclusively from reading the FLN's official paper, *El Moujahid*. Inevitably the car broke down. 'It's because it's French,' said the lieutenant, kicking a tire.

'It's because you can't drive,' Hank Walker muttered, and proceeded to fix it.

We saw FLN army units in training, we spent an evening in an Algerian refugee camp, and we visited an FLN officers' mess. We found, to our surprise, that most of the FLN officers we met were former Regular officers in the French Army. 'Did you serve in Indochina?' I asked one of them.

'But my dear sir,' said the officer, in exquisitely accentless French, 'we have fought all their wars for them.'

At last we came to the front line, with its deep caves. Here we spent most of the following week, consumed with boredom and fleas. I tuned in to the BBC world service regularly and remember listening to a delightfully incongruous radio version of a Sherlock Holmes story. Hank Walker, unused to Algerian food, lost quite a few pounds. He complained bitterly that all the fleas in the FLN seemed to have concentrated on him.

Came the dawn of our mortar attack on a French fort. Armed with long-lens cameras, we walked for what seemed like a very long time. Despite his Korean War experience and his spell as a U.S. marine in the Second World War, Hank Walker was not in the best of physical conditions, and neither, I suppose, was I. Our Algerian escort ended up carrying Walker's cameras and cursing us for being so slow. 'We are supposed to be in position at seven A.M.,' said our escort. 'Thanks to you, we will be over an hour late.'

Our slow progress caused the death of quite a few Foreign Legion soldiers. For hardly had we collapsed, exhausted, into a bunker near the FLN mortar and rocket emplacements than the FLN officer in charge hissed to his men to hold their fire. Along the road which ran parallel to the Challe line a long line of French Army trucks could be seen heading toward our fort. By some incredible chance, we had arrived just as the unit in the fort was being relieved. No longer did our FLN escort curse us. Quite by accident we had provided them with an ideal target.

The FLN officer held his fire until the trucks had disappeared behind the fort, where the relief force was presumably debusing. Then his squad let loose. From where we were, we could hear the dull crunch of shells landing, followed by columns of smoke. One of the FLN team had a powerful radio and had tuned in to the French Army wavelength. Soon we could hear the fort commander speaking to his headquarters. Despite the French Army jargon, it was clear there had been serious casualties, more than twenty killed and wounded, in fact, and there was a background noise over the radio of confused shouts and cries, as the French officer in the fort asked for an immediate air strike.

Hank Walker's command of French was minimal, so he failed to understand the face I pulled when I heard this. But the FLN officer in charge of the attack was reassuring. 'We'll pull back now,' he said. 'They'll never find us.'

We scampered to another set of bunkers, a bare 200 yards behind our previous position. To my surprise, I discovered a complete underground rabbit warren. 'Except for a direct hit,' said the FLN officer, 'we're completely safe here.'

The strike team had vanished into other holes. From our position, we heard the scream of French jets and saw the napalming begin—several miles away from us. For half an hour we watched a relentless Mirage air strike, never even remotely close. 'Is it always like this?' I asked.

'Almost always,' said the FLN officer.

Later still, back in our cave, Hank Walker was in a pensive mood. 'I've always been on the side of the hardware and the latest technology,' he said. 'Now I've seen the other side at work. These guys aren't doing too badly.'

We slept well that night. Now it was the turn of the FLN to be reluctant to let their mascots go. But we rose before dawn, got our escort officer to drive us to Souk el Arba, picked up our rented car, which we had left parked in an FLN rear-echelon headquarters, and by 10:00 A.M. we were at Tunis airport. Hank Walker returned to Paris, but I got on a plane to Nice and two hours later was on a beach near St. Tropez. There were girls, one of whom was waiting for me, and a few friends and casual acquaintances from Paris. There was the usual St. Tropez chatter: Who was at L'Escale last night? Was it true that gendarmes had begun raiding Pampelonne Beach again and arresting nudists? Who was BB's latest? Wasn't Raoul Levy's party a drag? Someone said to me, 'Where were you last night? I didn't see you at Felix's.' I started to explain and gave up. Suddenly I felt more alone and demoralized than I had been in the FLN cave.

A later Tunisian experience combined the comic and the macabre. In July 1961 the hitherto-moderate Habib Bourguiba unexpectedly sent a letter to De Gaulle demanding the withdrawal of all French troops from the French-leased base at Bizerte, the north Tunisian port. Bourguiba may well have decided that increasing Tunisian anti-French feeling (owing to the slow progress of French-FLN talks) made such a gesture necessary. On the other hand, Bourguiba may also have felt that a vague promise on de Gaulle's part to reopen negotiations over Bizerte, allegedly made when the two met in Rambouillet in 1960, had not been fulfilled. One close adviser to de Gaulle denied this to me at the time: 'Bourguiba talked incessantly during his session with de Gaulle, who was unable to get a word in edgeways. How could he have made such a promise?' At this stage of the Algerian War Bourguiba's position was not at all different from the later predicament of the leader of another small nation, Prince Sihanouk. Like Sihanouk, Bourguiba had perforce to put up with the presence of a powerful revolutionary army on his own doorstep, indeed inside his own sovereign territory, and was a target for both sides. In any event, Bourguiba's method of drawing attention to Bizerte was to order his Neo-Destour party to march on the French air base. The overall French commander, a sophisticated and moderate admiral with a reputation for being somewhat left-wing, had no gendarmes or CRS units at his disposal to keep the crowd at bay. Instead, he was compelled to use his soldiers. When it looked as if the Tunisian crowds might simply overwhelm the base through sheer weight of numbers, de Gaulle ordered 7,000 paras dropped on Bizerte. Bourguiba retaliated by moving his tiny army into Bizerte. The inevitable flashpoint occurred, and for three days a full-scale war raged in the streets and outskirts of Bizerte. It ended in a truce and Tunisian withdrawal, only after 700 Tunisians dead and 1,200 wounded, most of them civilians.

Even before the three-day battle, the French Army claimed a press victim. Jean Daniel, then still working for *L'Express*, was badly wounded when a French soldier opened fire on him near a French Army outpost on the outskirts of Bizerte. Two Tunisian journalist friends with him undoubtedly saved his life, dragging him away under fire. I arrived in Tunis the day after Jean Daniel had been shot, to find the whole town under siege, fully expecting the French paratroopers to come marching down from the north.

I teamed up with a-free-lance photographer, Dominique Berretty, with whom I had frequently worked in Algeria and with whom I had just covered the April 1961 putsch. It was an unpleasant and physically exhausting endurance test. To file our stories, we had to drive back and forth between Tunis and Bizerte (more than seventy miles). Telex lines and telex operators were scarce. The lines kept breaking down. *Time* shared the lease of a telex with a small syndicate, including *France-Soir* and *The New York Times*. The *France-Soir* correspondent, Lucien Bodard, was agonizingly slow in punching his story and working the telex machine, and since *France-Soir* was a daily, he had priority over me. Bodard was expelled by the Tunisians on the second day of the Bizerte siege for writing about the plight of French *colons* still in Tunis. I regretted the Tunisian government's action. Secretly I confess to heaving a sigh of relief, on the ground there would be one less person using the telex. But even without Bodard, I didn't sleep more than three hours a night for the length of the Bizerte 'war.'

On my first day in Tunisia, Berretty and I were stopped about two-thirds of the way to Bizerte at a Tunisian Army checkpoint. We showed our press cards. Courteously the Tunisian lieutenant returned them but, before waving us on, advised us to produce alternative identification if we had it. 'Your card has the tricolor bar across the top,' he said. 'That's not very popular around here right now, and someone who can't read might think you're soldiers in civilian clothes.' We went through our wallets and came up with what we both thought was the ideal identification to show any Tunisian—our FLN press accreditation cards. Soon another army checkpoint came into view. Proudly we flaunted our FLN cards, only to discover they were being scrutinized by a French paratrooper.

With uncommon presence of mind, I managed to snatch both away before he had obtained a complete look at them, substituting my French press card once more. 'You seem to be quite a way south of Bizerte,' I said as chattily as I could.

'Tomorrow,' was the reply, 'we may be in Tunis.'

Street fighting provides the war correspondent with the ultimate challenge. Confusion is such that it's almost impossible to discover who's winning. In the case of Bizerte, the difficulties were compounded by the fact that a stretch of water divided the town in two. Normally a ferry service was in constant operation. Needless to say, it was not functioning now.

On the south side of the stretch of water, a French tank squadron was drawn up, its guns pointing to the center of the town. From time to time rounds would be loosed off, and an armored car would fire bursts of heavy machine-gun fire. We were not made particularly welcome by the French Army. I was with Paul-Marie de la Gorce, a staunch Gaullist who had quit *L'Express* for *L'Observateur* and *L'Observateur* for the Gaullist weekly *Candide*. The officer in charge of the tank squadron asked to see our credentials. He made no comment to me, but to De la Gorce he said, 'Ah! I see you work for that wretched Gaullist rag. Where does the money come from?' It was not a promising beginning, but De la Gorce, as self-assured as though he were in a Paris salon, said, 'I think it simply comes from Franpar.' (Franpar was the big Hachette holding company.) It was an odd conversation, given our circumstances, and I asked the officer what his men were firing at. 'You see that skyscraper in the center of town?' he said. 'Well, on the top floor, there are swine shooting at us.'

I went in search of a small boat, found one, complete with oars, and motioned De la Gorce and Berretty to join me. They jumped in, and I began rowing. 'You learned to row at Oxford?' asked De la Gorce, suddenly impressed.

'No. Cambridge,' I replied, mentally calculating whether by placing Berretty at the rear of the boat, I might not provide better cover for myself. There were pinging noises and other noises of bullets hitting the water, far too close to be healthy. 'Dominique,' I said, as casually as I could, 'if you move to the back of the boat, we're on a more even keel.' He did so, unsuspectingly.

We made it to the other side. I dragged the boat up a shingle path and made sure I knew where I had left it, since it was our only means of getting back. We then set out to find the tall building the French tank squadron had been firing at. All too soon we reached it. The elevators were not functioning, and we emerged onto a small terrace roof eleven storeys up, gasping for breath. Here there were thick smears of blood, and in a corner a wounded French para was lying semiconscious, waiting for an ambulance. We immediately took cover, and not a moment too soon, for there was a burst of heavy machine-gun fire—from the French tanks? from the Tunisians on another roof?—and the French paratroopers on the terrace (there were four of them) started firing back. 'I thought there were Tunisians here,' I said to one of them.

178

'They haven't been in this building all day,' he replied. I asked him if he knew where the fire was coming from. 'All over,' he said. I toyed with the idea of telling him of our encounter with the French tanks earlier in the morning and that the French Army seemed to be doing its best to destroy itself. I decided against it. At best it would lower his morale. At worst he might take me for *agent provocateur*. We skidded on more blood and made a dash for the stairs.

At some point that morning we were joined by Christopher Brasher, the London *Observer* correspondent who had been a long-distance gold medalist in the 1956 Olympic Games. He seemed glad to see us, but disappointed that we were as lost and as confused as he was. Firing was intermittent, always seemingly in the next street, but suddenly there was a horrendous noise that we all took to be a shell landing just behind us. The only cover was provided by an archway about forty yards ahead of us. We all reacted with commendable speed. I hate to admit it, but I easily beat Christopher Brasher to the post. We huddled in the relative security of the doorway and then peered out to see what the damage was. To this day I recall our mixed relief and shame at the discovery that the crash we had heard had, in fact, been caused by Tunisian cars slamming into each other at a crossroads.

We extricated ourselves from a maze of streets and came across a group of Tunisian soldiers, their hands over their heads, being marched away by a squad of French paratroopers. As we crossed an open area, there was more firing close by, and I remember advising a French correspondent, with less experience in these matters, that it was useless to crouch and bend one's head as one crossed an exposed area. What counted was one's turn of speed.

A group of French correspondents had been flown in with the French troops, and we met, off and on, that afternoon and tried to piece the story of the battle together. Gradually the French were gaining the upper hand as time went on. Fighting moved to the poorer, Tunisian quarter of

Bizerte, where continuous French shelling was causing heavy civilian casualties. In one house on the fringe of the Tunisian quarter, a small squad of Tunisian soldiers held out against the firepower of the French paras for several hours with extraordinary fortitude. When they finally surrendered, having run out of ammunition, the house was in ruins. Exhausted and covered in dust and dirt, the Tunisian soldiers stood, dazed but defiant, and the French paratroopers, furious at the casualties the Tunisians had inflicted on their unit during the siege, angrily muttered something about lining them up against a wall and shooting them.

We reporters overheard these remarks. To the everlasting credit of our number, an Italian journalist, whom I had never seen before and have never seen since, quietly walked over to where the Tunisians were standing and stood, hand on hip, in front of them. Dramatically, but without saying a word, he made the point that if the paras executed the Tunisians, they would have to shoot him, too. It was one of the bravest acts I have ever witnessed, all the more so since there was no gallery to play to. An officer arrived, calmed his men down, and the Tunisians were marched away into captivity.

We got back to Tunis the way we had come, by rowing our boat back; but this time there were no bullets, and the mini-war seemed over. I filed part of my story that night, caught a couple of hours' sleep, and was back in Bizerte at dawn the following morning. A cease-fire had just been proclaimed, and Dominique Berretty and I were the first reporters to enter the badly damaged Tunisian part of the town, where the previous day's shelling had been concentrated.

What we saw was yet another spectacle of carnage and death, with the lingering smell of rotting flesh. I stood it for as long as I could, then wandered over to a grassy knoll where corpses were being shoveled into a common grave. The *Time* photographer with me, unused to this kind of

180

story, was overcome by the horror of it all and, rather than take pictures of the mangled bodies, went in search of Bizerte's mayor, whom for some reason he insisted on interviewing. I got hold of Berretty and left him at the site of the mass grave.

Years later, in 1966, I returned to Bizerte to attend a press conference given by Herr Alfred Krupp, who had decided to lease part.of the Bizerte docks to set up a ship-repairing facility. I wandered over to the knoll where I had watched the civilian corpses being buried. There was no commemorative stela, but the grass was unnaturally lush and green. The Krupp press conference was unintentionally farcical. I was with Andrew Borowiec, of AP, who, as a young Pole, had been deported during the war to work as a 'slave' in a Krupp-owned factory in Germany. Krupp himself, a cadaverous, somewhat sinister figure, stood up to answer questions from the group of Tunisian pressmen. There were none. After a long, embarrassing pause Borowiec rose, and the Krupp public relations chief sighed with relief. 'Tell me, Mr. Krupp,' said Borowiec, 'are you wearing an RAF tie by accident or by design?'

I have referred to the various ways enterprising reporters managed to reach Algeria when crises of various kinds interrupted normal travel routes. My most spectacular trip came a couple of months before the Bizerte affair in 1961, when four French generals—Raoul Salan, Maurice Challe, Henri Zeller, and Edmond Jouhaud—seized temporary command in Algeria, interned a number of loyal Gaullist officials, and attempted, for four days, to hold out against De Gaulle's Fifth Republic in an effort to convince themselves, and public opinion, that they could liquidate FLN strength in Algeria and restore 'normal' conditions there.

As with many such sudden, cataclysmic happenings, getting there was half the fun. The morning of the putsch a small group of us met briefly at the Crillon bar to discuss strategy. My own 1958 experience had convinced me that a small group of journalists had a good chance of getting in, either by boat or private plane, and we drove to Orly Airport and caught a plane to Madrid. In Madrid I phoned the pilot in Barcelona who had so successfully carried us across the Mediterranean and to Algiers during the May 13, 1958, events. But he was unable to help us. This time around, he said, he was under close Spanish surveillance.

I had another address up my sleeve—a German smuggler in Palma de Mallorca. Maybe he could ferry us across. I phoned him late that night, and he sounded guarded but promising.

We promptly caught the first available plane to Palma. The smuggler was fearful of the possible consequences of helping us directly. He did, however, offer us sound advice: Why not go to the boat club and shop around for a likely boatowner, who, for a fat fee, might agree to take us across to Algiers? Thanks to him, we found a large motor launch, manned by a somewhat formidable English girl, whom we assumed, wrongly as it turned out, to be either its owner or acting on the owner's behalf. I offered her $1,000 to take us to Algiers. She was interested but wanted $2,000. I finally settled for $1,300, plus the cost of diesel and food.

We were not the only ones looking for passage to Algiers. While in Palma, I came across a tough-looking, shave-skulled Frenchman with a black eyepatch, who introduced himself as André Canal. He was eager to join our party, adding that 'money was no object.' He seemed somewhat distraught. Though he disclaimed membership in the OAS, his constant reference to De Gaulle as 'that bloodthirsty swine' convinced me that he would be an embarrassing traveling companion. (Canal later emerged as one of the leaders of the most extremist wing of the OAS and in 1974 was murdered, almost certainly in a gangland killing over the ultimate destination of missing OAS 'treasure,' itself largely the product of bank and post-office robberies throughout Algeria in 1961-62.)

I had hoped we would set out there and then, but the

ubiquitous Spanish police heard of our endeavor and came nosing around the boat. It lacked the obvious standard safety extras, having neither life raft, nor sufficient life belts, nor flares. A policeman told me we would be allowed to leave only after a formal Lloyds agent's inspection, to ensure that we departed with regulation equipment for an ocean voyage.

My cash resources didn't run to acquiring a life raft (even at 1961 prices, an inflatable life raft for ten people cost at least $14,000), and the boat, belonging, it turned out, to a wealthy Englishman, had obviously been used more for shoreside entertainment purposes than anything else, and judging by the number of skimpy bikinis lying around, it had been a fun ship. But the spirit of the chase was upon us all, and we were determined to get to Algiers. I parlayed a ship's chandler into hiring all the needed equipment for the afternoon—the time required for the visiting Lloyds agent to check the boat. I then enlisted the support of the British consul, begging him to intercede with the local authorities to allow us to leave and saying nothing about our Lloyds subterfuge. Finally, at the very last minute, we staved off a piratical attempt by a CBS-TV crew to take over the boat. For the CBS people, in our absence and after our verbal agreement, had offered our English friend considerably more money to get her to cancel her deal with us and take them instead. Since there were already nine of us, and since our English girl captain announced she would have a crew totaling three, thre was no question of taking an additional three people aboard; we were already dangerously over-loaded.

But the TV crew, confident that money could work miracles, had already loaded vast quantities of camera equipment on board and confidently assumed we would give in quietly, having already, I suspect, heavily bribed our girl captain, who was fast emerging in a singularly venal light. Luckily, the TV crew had made the same mistake that we had originally made: They had gone in search of supplies without leaving any of their number aboard.

When they returned, they found eight determined reporters physically prepared to do battle to stay aboard. My resolution to fight it out if the worse came to the worst had been endorsed by all. A shouting match ensued, with the American TV crew trying to parley us into surrender from the shore and an embarrassed English girl captain wringing her hands at the proof of her duplicity. I probably clinched matters by seizing, in a rare fit of barely controllable rage, brought about by lack of sleep, what I knew to be a box containing the crew's most valuable camera and lenses and holding it over the side of the boat. 'If you don't come and take your equipment off,' I said, 'this goes into the drink.' I kept the box poised over the rail, like a hijacker holding a pistol at a hostage's head, until the last piece of equipment had been removed. It was one of the oddities of journalism that the members of the CBS crew who tried to commandeer the boat and bribe their way aboard and kick us off it were back in Paris, the friendliest and nicest of men. And it's typical of the ambivalent atmosphere of camaraderie and intense competition within the press that none of those involved in the Palma affray ever bore a grudge against me or indeed ever referred to the incident again.

Our captain's unethical behavior made me increasingly anxious to leave at the earliest opportunity, for who knew what takeover bid would prove irresistible to her if we lingered? She assembled her crew, which could be described only as motley. There was a one-eyed Swedish mate, who claimed to be a mechanic, and a bearded English hippie painter, who spent the entire crossing huddled in one of the berths, abysmally seasick. Just before we left the harbor, a taxi drew up at the dockside, and out stepped Angus Deming, of *Newsweek*. *Time* and *Newsweek* were of course archrivals. 'Take me with you,' said Angus.

A more competitive, hard-bitten reporter of the old school would have refused. But I liked Deming and knew how anxious he must be. I wondered how he would have reacted if he had been in charge of the boat and gave him the benefit of any doubt. 'Welcome aboard,' I said. We have been friends ever since.

Such was our haste to get away that we set out without even checking the weather reports, and had we done so, we might not have left. For once we were out at sea, an appalling mistral started blowing. The boat began doing a fair imitation of a scenic railway in action. Our girl captain, who had begun the journey by offering to sell us liquor at duty-free prices, soon became more subdued, then downright haggard, and finally started weeping hysterically as huge wave after wave crashed across the bows, threatening to smash the portholes and sink us all. Between sobs, she admitted all: The boat's owner had no idea of our caper. Now we all were going to drown. Two of our press party saved the situation. The *Daily Express* Madrid correspondent, who had joined our party, had been a merchant seaman, and Dominique Berretty, on assignment with me for *Life*, could, like all Dutchmen, handle a boat well. It is scarcely an exaggeration to say they probably saved our lives, taking turns at the wheel for more than sixteen hours. By some miracle, we remained on course and arrived smack in sight of Algiers the following day, with the wind somewhat abated. But inside the boat a considerable amount of damage had been done by the storm, and our girl captain was, to say the least, downcast.

We had one final hurdle to overcome. The French Navy (which had remained loyal to de Gaulle) was patrolling the approaches to Algiers to prevent any putschists from rallying Algiers, and I feared that we might be forbidden to berth. When a French destroyer came alongside, I explained, as convincingly as I could, that we were entirely harmless. The captain sent us on our way, wishing us good luck and adding that we seemed to have had more than our share already, since we had survived the night's force-ten gale.

We docked at a deserted, unusually silent Algiers harbor on what turned out to be the morning of the last day of the generals' putsch. None of us had slept, except for Boris Kidel, then a correspondent for the now-defunct London *News Chronicle*, who had wisely consumed our entire supply of Dramamine shortly before leaving Palma and snored on throughout the gale, oblivious of our predicament. There was no time for me to shower and change at the Aletti Hotel, and we dispersed throughout Algiers, unshaved and filthy, to find out what was happening. Our only link with the outside world throughout the night had been the ship's radio, but the French news bulletins had been patchy, though it looked as though the movement were collapsing. I told the crew, including our still-despondent girl captain, to take rooms at the Aletti, where I had an account, and to charge everything to me. I went off on foot, for there was not a single taxi to be found, to try to watch the death throes of the insurrection.

So it was that I witnessed the last appearance of the four putschist generals in front of the Gouvernement Général building and the French Foreign Legionnaires of the *Premier Regiment Etranger de Parachutistes* parading for the last time before embusing for their Zéralda headquarters, west of Algiers, where they were to be disarmed and where they deserted en masse to the OAS. The officer rapping out orders was Major Elie Denoix de Saint Marc, one of the most outstanding and the most decorated officers in the French Army and one of the legendary para heroes of the French Indochina War. While still in his teens, he had played a prominent part in the French wartime resistance and had been deported to Buchenwald. I knew him well, for he had briefly been General Massu's press officer. Even at this fatal instant, with his own army career in ruins and his regiment about to be ignominiously dissolved, De Saint Marc handled his men as though on ceremonial parade at the Legion's Sidi-

Bel-Abbès depot. But the visible strain and misery on his face as he rasped out his last orders to them was such that I was inhibited from going up to him and saying hello. I felt I was watching a private tragedy, for De Saint Marc, a moderate, liberal Christian who abhorred torture and was the antithesis of a brutal 'centurion,' had had his private reservations about the putsch from the start, but had gone along with it because loyalty to his regiment came even before loyalty to the Republic. (He was tried and convicted, like other putschist officers, and later became a successful executive for a French computer firm, turning his back on the Army and refusing to meet any of his erstwhile friends from the press.)

Meanwhile, back at the Aletti Hotel, the English girl captain had slept most of the afternoon and was gradually recovering from her emotions and her exhaustion. That evening she ventured downstairs into the restaurant to have dinner. It so happened that the only pitched battle to be fought between putschist units and the gendarmerie loyal to De Gaulle before the utter collapse of the dissident generals took place on the street outside the Aletti Hotel, just as she had begun her meal. Two gendarmes retreated, firing from the hip, into the lobby of the Aletti Hotel, then into the restaurant, and both were seriously wounded in a brief but alarming firefight, as the hotel guests scrambled for cover. This was too much for our captain. She pitched forward in a dead faint, her head in the soup.

I didn't return to the Aletti until after dark and after the battle. Staff and guests were still recovering from its effects, and I myself, by this time, was tottering with fatigue. So I failed to notice that the glass doors of the Aletti main entrance were closed and slammed into them, almost breaking my nose in the process. The noise of my head against the glass was similar enough to a bullet slamming into the door to make all the people in the lobby throw themselves flat on their faces. My nose bled copiously and swelled up painfully, but I received scant sympathy.

The rest was anticlimactic. I knew things were back to normal when, the next day, I saw the Aletti Hotel manager in deep discussion with a local carpet representative. They were measuring the bloodstained portion of the fitted carpet in the lobby and haggling over how many square meters of it needed replacing. Berretty, already a hero in my eyes for his handling of the boat, scored a notable scoop that day. Disguising himself as an Algerian, complete with chéchia (turban), he bribed an Algerian truck driver to take him to the headquarters of the *Premier REP* barracks, and photographed the legionnaires as they emerged from their barracks, singing Piaf's famous song 'Je Ne Regrette Rien.'

With officialdom resuming its tedious role, problems arose over our motor launch. I begged the British consul to intervene to allow our captain and crew, in calmer seas, to return to Palma.

Eventually, after much bureaucratic delay, the boat was allowed to leave. For our girl captain the sequel was an unhappy one. The boat's rightful owner, reading the British papers, was surprised to learn that his boat had been used to ferry correspondents to Algiers in the middle of the putsch. He was not amused and demanded that she hand over her entire fee and make good all the considerable damage caused by the storm. I never learned how the situation was resolved, beyond the fact that he soon acquired a new resident skipper. . . .

The failure of the generals' putsch made it easier for De Gaulle to negotiate with the FLN, but it also led to an intensification of OAS action. Many of those who had sided with the putschists went underground, and the OAS was a logical rallying point. Throughout the latter part of 1961 and right up to independence, in July 1962, the thrust of news stories was now increasingly concerned with the counterterrorism of the increasingly desperate OAS members.

OAS and anti-OAS forces carried on a secret war which was just as merciless and ruthless as that involving the FLN.

The Gaullists brought in some *barbouzes*, French and Vietnamese, to carry out operations against the OAS which no legal police force could condone. They were called *barbouzes* because of their unusually clumsy attempt to disguise their true calling, as though, metaphorically speaking, they were wearing false beards. Most of these agents died violent deaths, blown up in hideaway villas or kidnaped and hideously tortured to death before being strung up on tramway lines for all to see. Inevitably the Corsican community in Algeria which, like Corsican communities everywhere, had its links with the 'milieu' or underworld, played an important part in both OAS and anti-OAS operations. Some of the *barbouzes* recruited by Gaullist parallel police forces were acknowledged members of the underworld, who found it useful to put in a stint as loyal servants of the Gaullist cause for the immunity from the law they hoped it would win them later. Others were recruited straight out of jail. Some of the OAS and counter-OAS terrorism was in fact a straightforward settling of accounts between rival Corsican personalities. One murder of a Corsican major (and head of an anti-OAS squad in Algiers itself) had little to do with ideology but was the culmination of a long-standing rivalry between different groups of Corsican pimps, all intent on controlling high-class prostitution in Algiers. The major was literally blown to smithereens when a bomb attached to the ceiling below his hotel bedroom exploded in the middle of the night. Two full-time prostitutes in the Aletti Hotel promptly went into mourning.

It was difficult, indeed well-nigh impossible, to write about the realities of OAS and anti-OAS terrorism beyond the bald facts of violence—and that portion of the history of the Algerian War has never really been touched on. OAS sympathies spread over a huge cross section of the French Algerian community. It was an open secret, for instance, that in the months that a heavily disguised Raoul Salan, the titular head of the OAS, was on the run, his most secure series of hiding places were, in fact, the network of French Army officers' messes through the country.

So sure of official complicity was Salan that on a spring Sunday in 1962, at the height of the OAS campaign, he appeared in broad daylight, surrounded by a sizable bodyguard, and actually laid a wreath at the foot of the Algiers war memorial. John Rich, of NBC, interviewed him 'somewhere in Algeria' in one of his hiding places. Huge funds were levied from French Algerian shopkeepers, hoteliers and business, and some entrepreneurs complained to me bitterly that those OAS 'impositions' were far higher than those extracted by the FLN. Additionally, OAS gangs raided post offices and banks almost at will. One raid on a nationalized French bank in Oran took several hours to complete, with several lorries standing by to carry the banknotes and gold bullion to hideaways and armed OAS members cordoning off the center of the city with complete impunity.

Reporting events after dark in Algiers became a hazardous occupation, for though reporters had curfew passes, the only other cars out on the streets during the night were the anti-OAS *barbouze* squads—and the OAS themselves. In every major Algerian city the OAS appeared to gain the upper hand. From early 1962 onward the OAS set off fires and bomb explosions with little fear of arrest or detection—and unlike the FLN, the OAS bomb makers, many of them former Foreign Legion or ex-French Army artificers, knew their stuff. After most French government services had been evacuated to a more secure compound called the *Rocher Noir*, some forty kilometers east of Algiers, there was virtually nobody left in Algiers to brief the press, except for a small group of plucky French officials, mostly young graduates of the Ecole Nationale d'Administration, who lived under siege conditions in the heavily guarded Gouvernement Général building. When a particularly huge explosion rocked Algiers during the night, as happened almost every night in the spring of 1962, it made no sense to phone the police to find out what had happened. One simply had to try to locate the explosion oneself.

I particularly remember one night, when a really huge bang—sounding like a large high-explosive bomb—rocked the entire center of Algiers. Somewhat queasily I jumped into my car to try to locate the explosion. After several fruitless attempts, I decided to drive up to the Gouvernement Général building, fully expecting to see it destroyed. I was stopped a hundred yards away by nervous gendarmes behind secure sandbagged bunkers. 'I came to find out about the explosion,' I shouted. 'Did it happen here?' I could hear the sound of rifles being cocked.

'Bugger off,' said a heavily Midi-accented voice behind the sandbags. 'You'll read all about it in tomorrow's papers.' The bomb had, in fact, destroyed the multistorey Air France building near the waterfront.

OAS violence took many forms. As spring turned into summer and as independence neared, it became increasingly indiscriminate and vicious. OAS killer teams made a specialty of gunning down Algerian civilians, especially veiled women on their way to work as domestic servants. A French publisher who later read the manuscript of one minor OAS leader's autobiography in the late sixties described it to me as 'his callous account of how he butchered a series of Algerian cleaning ladies.' There was also indiscriminate OAS shelling of Moslem quarters.

I was standing about 100 yards from the Place du Gouvernement near the Casbah one day when a crunch of mortar shells scattered bystanders in all directions. The crowded square was littered with bodies, some writhing, some dead. The shells had come from a couple of stolen French Army two-inch mortars fired by highly competent OAS men from just beyond the Casbah limits, who dismantled them in seconds and made a successful getaway in equally stolen trucks.

The main casualty clearance hospital in Algiers was the

191

sprawling Hôpital Mustapha, to the east of the town, and I ran back to the Aletti Hotel to collect *Life* photographer Paul Schutzer. (He was killed while riding an Israeli tank in the Sinai Desert in the 1967 Six-day War.) Paul happened to be at the movies at the time; this caused a minor delay because for security reasons patrons were forbidden to leave before the end of any given performance—on the ground that anyone leaving a bomb in a cinema was not likely to stay and watch it go off. After searching his seat thoroughly, in the nearly empty cinema, the attendant allowed him to leave, and we rushed around to the hospital to count the casualties and try to get some pictures.

The hospital was theoretically out of bounds to the press, and most of the French staff made no secret of their OAS sympathies and affiliations; but from long experience, I had found a sure way of getting in. All one had to do, I explained to Schutzer, was to say that we were volunteering to donate blood. This got us inside the compound. Then, ignoring the blood donors' hut, one simply made for the main casualty clearing station.

Unfortunately, on this occasion, things did not quite work out as I had planned; we were actually compelled to give blood. For me this presented no serious problem, but for Schutzer it was catastrophic. As the result of a previous accident, he had had part of his spleen removed; this meant that giving even a pint of blood caused dizziness, nausea, and fainting. Schutzer was too gutsy to tell me this until too late. The orderly in charge simply came to the conclusion that he had had some minor adverse reaction, and Schutzer insisted on carrying on with the assignment after coming out of his fainting fit. Deathly pale and barely able to stand, he accompanied me to the main emergency casualty ward, where dozens of badly wounded Algerians were being prepared for operations.

Schutzer was able to shoot pictures undetected, using me as a convenient screen. Halfway through, a small group of gowned French interns strode into the ward and surveyed the scene. They started talking to one another in low voices, and I was able to hear part of what they were saying.

By this time I was hardened to the brutalities of everyday Algerian existence and not easily shocked. But I confess to mingled surprise and disgust when I realized from their casual remarks that far from taking part in any mercy mission, the doctors were discussing the OAS outrage among themselves as connoisseurs with considerable relish and counting the casualties to evaluate the OAS score. 'Not bad at all,' said one.

'Quite satisfactory, in fact,' said another. 'How many all told?'

I overheard one of the doctors in the ward explaining in great detail to the rest of the group how the mortar attack had been carried out and came to the conclusion, from the precise nature of his description, that he himself had been with the OAS team and possibly even taken an active part in the attack.

But for sheer callousness, it was difficult to beat the French free-lance photographer, with excellent OAS connections, who actually set up the killing of a veiled Algerian woman, accompanying an OAS killer team, choosing the victim, shooting the actual act of gunning down and the woman's death throes on the pavement. The case came to light only because, after a few too many drinks in the Aletti bar, the photographer boasted of what he had done. An *ad hoc* committee of French reporters met to discuss what action should be taken. They decided to report him to the French authorities—but no sanctions were imposed, and the photographer continued to operate with impunity, though he prudently left just before independence was proclaimed.

The Aletti Hotel had traditionally been the meeting ground of most shades of French Algerian opinion. It had also—in its first-floor gambling casino—provided the one real forum where Algerians and French met on equal terms. Between bombs and murders, I spent many hours in

193

the casino, not just to gamble but also to observe the scene. There were tall, turbaned Algerians in flowing robes side by side with prim middle-class French ladies, and at the roulette tables everyone was united by the common passion and will to win. The disputes over *jetons* were perhaps a little more frequent, and considerably more vocal, than elsewhere. 'Monsieur,' one heard the French ladies say, 'that counter on number eight is not yours, it's mine.' 'No, madame, it belongs to me.' The croupiers would do their best to prevent such disputes from holding up play.

Algerian and French gamblers, side by side, seemed completely unaware of the carnage which was a daily feature of their lives beyond the hotel walls. Some, I'm convinced, came to gamble small sums simply to find a relatively secure haven, for never once was the Aletti Hotel the target of OAS violence, after the generals' putsch, and there was no doubt in my mind that the casino operated with the tacit consent of OAS leaders, perhaps as a convenient means of raising revenue.

There came a time, however, when even the most dedicated gamblers, both Algerian and French, were unwilling to venture forth, even at high noon, and the casino closed. Its restaurant continued to function, however; at one point it was perhaps the only restaurant still open—and then only to hotel residents—in the whole of downtown Algiers. Its clientele was distinctly odd; half the rooms in the Aletti Hotel were occupied by reporters and photographers, the other half by OAS killers, with a strong leavening of Corsicans in dark glasses, who would go to work with no attempt to conceal the bulging weapons under their armpits.

The two groups were rigidly segregated and ate on opposite sides of the restaurant. One night a recklessly brave young French radio reporter, deliberately raising his voice so that the killers could hear, called them despicable, cowardly murderers. The killers reached for their shoulder holsters, and there was a deathly hush. The reporters at the tables nearest them sprang back, and I remember grabbing the long, rounded, but razor-sharp knife used at the buffet table for slicing raw ham. We stood, eyeball to eyeball, for a few seconds. Then the maître d'hôtel moved between us, clapping his hands and saying, '*Allons, allons, messieurs*,' as though dealing with naughty children. Muttering to themselves, the killers sat down and resumed their meal. The following day the reporters' tables were moved even farther away from the OAS tables.

It may seem strange that no effort was ever made to bring any of these killers in for questioning. The reason was that the Algiers administration, to all intents and purposes, had ceased to exist, and after the unilateral French Army ceasefire of March 1962, there was not much enthusiasm on the part of French Army personnel to get involved in any anti-OAS activities. This was left to overworked specialized units, especially to loyal gendarmerie units fresh from France. I remember the disgust felt by William Porter, then U.S. consul general in Algiers, at a cold-blooded killing of Algerian civilians inside the U.S. consulate compound. Three Algerians had fled inside the consulate to avoid an OAS killer commando. But the OAS car simply swung into the consulate courtyard, mowed down the unfortunate Algerians on the consulate lawn, and made a getaway. The French Army conscripts on the guard outside the consulate building failed to fire a single shot or do anything to stop the killers. I asked a senior French officer whether the conscripts would be punished. 'Probably not,' he said. 'After the ceasefire they consider that it's not their war anymore. You should read the letters our troops are getting from their folks back home,' he added. '*Mon petit*, it's all over, don't do anything rash, it's not worth it, that type of thing.'

During this period *Time* shared a grubby office on the rue Pasteur with *France-Soir*, *The New York Times*, and the French radio station *Europe Numéro Un*. It was a somewhat narrow street, opposite a modest café where in

195

happier days French and Algerians alike had whiled away the time drinking anisette and talking about the bets they'd made. Above the café, facing us across the street, was an apartment housing a retired couple. They must have been in their seventies, and often, when we both stared out of our respective windows at the same time, we would nod to each other.

This didn't prevent the elderly pensioner from doing his best to murder us one night, at the height of the OAS crisis, by firing shot after shot into our office across the street. Everyone hit the floor, and no one was hurt. The next day the little old couple were puttering around in their apartment as if nothing had happened, but we no longer nodded to each other.

Partly to get away from the stifling OAS atmosphere, I set out on a trip in western Algeria to try to locate some FLN units in the field after the unilateral French ceasefire. With me were Tom Brady and Jules Roy, the well-known French writer and former air force officer, specially commissioned to do a piece for *L'Express*.

It took us a long time to find an FLN unit, and our first contact was hardly auspicious. The FLN company was on a remote plateau, and its commander at first assumed we were spies and almost had us arrested. We convinced him that our intentions were honorable, and he finally let us stay. But Jules Roy, whose liberal convictions were matched only by his humorless sense of self-importance, blew it by insisting on making a formal speech to the assembled FLN troops. 'As an officer of the French Air Force,' he began, 'I want to welcome this moment.' The only French Air Force officers the FLN troops had ever seen had been in hostile skies strafing them and destroying their villages, and an immediate pall settled over the gathering. Jules Roy failed to understand that he had committed a faux pas and was furious when Brady and I hustled him into the car and away from an increasingly hostile FLN crowd.

Just before we left, I came across one of the FLN officers drawing in a notebook a reproduction of the rampant lion which was the trademark of the Peugeot 403. 'What are you doing that for?' Brady asked.

'It's so that we will be able to identify your vehicle again,' the officer said. It seemed hardly the time to explain that the rampant lion was a feature of the hood of every single Peugeot car, of which there were several thousand in Algiers alone.

The last few weeks before independence were marked by a large-scale army onslaught on the eastern Algiers suburb of Bab el Oued, the stronghold of the OAS, and by the gradual transfer of some government responsibilities onto the shoulders of an FLN-recognized 'provisional executive.' But most remaining local town council officials who had not already been driven out by the OAS simply cleared their desks and left, with Algerians coming in to replace them on Independence Day.

Louis Joxe, De Gaulle's minister for Algeria, had wanted to establish a transitional police force, composed of Algerians who had committed themselves neither to the French nor to the FLN side during the war. He did finally raise such a team and dressed them in uniforms which looked like khaki replicas of those of Paris metro employees. The creation of this body of men led to one of de Gaulle's few fully authenticated witticisms. As Joxe tells it, this police force, somewhat comically dubbed 'Part-time Temporary Auxiliary Police' (ATO), had not been provided for in the original, transition-period, special budget for Algeria. This led Joxe to call on de Gaulle and to say, '*Mon général*, we've forgotten to include the ATO.'

De Gaulle gave Joxe his usual heavy-lidded, scornful stare. 'And what, Joxe,' he asked, 'is the ATO?'

'You must remember, *mon général*,' said Joxe, 'the part-time Temporary Auxiliary Police.'

De Gaulle was silent for a few seconds, then gave an unusual bellow of laughter.

'Come, come, Joxe,' he said, 'with a name like that, surely they don't expect to get paid.'

VII. CHINA

I WENT to China in a highly roundabout way. In 1964 I made
a number of TV documentary films for *Cinq Colonnes à la
Une* with Claude Goretta which attracted some attention.
As a result of one, in particular, a short film about *The
American Way of Death*, based on Jessica Mitford's book,
which received a great deal of publicity and won a prize (it
was the first, and probably the last, time a TV team has
filmed inside a mortician's parlor), one of the program's
producers, in France, made me a somewhat rash promise.
'We can't offer you much money,' said Pierre Desgraupes,
'but tell me where you would like to go, and I'll try to see
you get there.' I replied that more than anything else in the
world, I wanted to go to China. Desgraupes was as good as
his word. In September 1964, shortly after the resumption
of Franco-Chinese diplomatic relations and—hardly
coincidentally—during the staging of a French industrial
fair in Peking, I found myself armed with a two-month,
extendable visa, part of a Franco-Swiss TV team assigned
to make at least two films in China.

At the time I was free-lancing for the *Saturday Evening
Post*, and it was, of course, my intention to write a major
piece for that magazine on my return. As a British national
I was not barred from traveling to China (as were
Americans then), and the Chinese themselves were good
enough to turn a blind eye to the fact that this Franco-Swiss
TV team also included a British passport holder. Nor, as it
turned out, were the Chinese unaware of my American

press affiliations. Knowing the Chinese hostility to all things American then, I had omitted any reference to my *Time-Life* past in the visa-application form I had completed. It was only much later, during a farewell dinner in Peking, that my hosts, two officials from the Foreign Affairs Ministry handling visiting Western reporters, obliquely informed me that they knew perfectly well who I was. We were talking about faraway places, and one of the ministry officials mentioned that she had served in the Chinese Embassy in Pakistan in 1962. 'You too, Mr. Behr,' she said, 'know Karachi well, I think. We were there at the same time. You were covering India and Pakistan for *Time* and *Life*, were you not?'

Like many long-awaited treats, this one began badly. Owing to a ticket mixup, we missed our Karachi connection to Shanghai, and during the day we waited there in transit, we had immense difficulty in clearing our TV equipment through customs. Finally, we caught the PIA flight to Shanghai via Dacca. My accompanying Swiss director-producer seemed, to my chagrin, more concerned with his status as leader of the expedition than with any other aspect of our work in China, and Frank Richard, our excellent Swiss cameraman, turned out to be hopelessly allergic to Chinese food. A great beginning.

Before leaving Paris, I had screened everything that had—up to that date—been shown on French TV screens about China and had embarked on my new project determined not to shoot anything that was already familiar to European viewers. Since, in China, there are not only Potemkin villages and communal farms, but also Potemkin factories, Potemkin housing units and even Potemkin people, and since foreign visitors are rarely, if ever, allowed access to anything but a tiny, repetitive, well-worn beaten track, my ambition seemed doomed from the outset.

Indeed, our first contact with ministry officials was not promising. I had come armed with a formidable list of possible films, complete with a brief outline for each. I had asked to be allowed to visit Tibet and Sinkiang, to make a film about the role of sport in Chinese society and about twenty-four hours in the life of an average family. Finally, on the principle of nothing ventured, nothing gained, I had requested an interview with Chairman Mao himself.

Over endless cups of green tea, our hosts patiently tried to steer me back to the beaten track. How about visiting the 'number one machine tool factory' in Peking? I pointed out that I had seen a film about this factory while still in Paris. How about interviewing a 'reformed Shanghai capitalist'? 'I think I know the one you mean,' I said. 'He has a very pretty daughter and a Jaguar car, and he has been interviewed at least three times by French TV alone, once by the BBC and twice by the Germans.'

I realized that one could never have too much of a good thing, I said, but I had promised my producer that we would bring back something different. He was a hard man, a ruthless, competitive capitalist. If we failed, we would be in trouble. Was none of my projects suitable? If not, why not? Our meetings invariably ended with our Foreign Ministry friends saying they would discuss the matter further and would let us know. I got the impression, perhaps mistakenly, that they would have welcomed a departure from the beaten track but were themselves under pressure not to allow us to innovate. Meanwhile, we were provided with a French-speaking interpreter and allowed to film on Peking's streets.

Our first interpreter was not a success. Timid and frightened, he looked about sixteen and was, in fact, twenty-two. Straight out of interpreter's school, he was permanently ill at ease as long as we were filming. He was carsick. He dodged every question that was not to his liking with one of three replies: 'It is not known,' 'It is not convenient,' and 'He does not know—his spirit is confused.' This led to strange exchanges. To every question we asked him to put to passersby, he would shake his head and say, 'He does not know.'

'How do you mean, he doesn't know? You haven't asked him yet.'

'You should not ask such questions. It is not convenient.'

After a few days of this sort of thing we tried, as tactfully as we could, to get him changed. To do so required prodigies of diplomacy. For to complain that his French was inadequate (which was also true) was to impugn the entire Chinese educational system and thus indulge in an 'unfriendly act' by criticizing Chairman Mao himself, responsible for all Chinese achievements. Luckily I was able to use another approach. Our interpreter came from Shanghai and had been in Peking only two weeks. We were always getting lost, I told our Foreign Ministry officials, and I was afraid of involuntarily finding myself outside the authorized city limits.

I had hoped a switch in interpreters could be made without hurt feelings. But that was not the Chinese way. One morning he approached us in the lobby of the Hsien Tchao Hotel. 'On many occasions,' he said, 'you have expressed the desire to have another interpreter. Your request has now been granted. This is Mr. Wuh.' He shook hands solemnly and walked out of our lives.

Mr. Wuh was slightly older, spoke superb French, and, apart from a somewhat irritating habit of referring to himself in self-deprecatory terms (as if to hint at knowledge of cliché Chinamen in comic strips?), was eager to help, even, on occasion, allowing us to glimpse the glimmerings of a keen sense of humor. We taught him slang, and toward the end of our stay he had learned phrases like 'shit,' 'we've had it,' and 'what a balls up.' Our first day's work ended in disaster through my own miserable absentmindedness. Returning to the hotel, I inadvertently slammed a taxi door on Mr. Wuh's hand. He half strangled a cry, turned white, clasped his bleeding fingers, and said, 'Please excuse my clumsiness.' Seldom have I felt as guilty as I did then.

In retrospect, 1964 was a singularly liberal year for the media in China: TV teams from different networks and countries were literally falling over one another in the lobby of the Hsien Tchao Hotel in Peking, getting in one another's way and eyeing one another with suspicion. I myself was on assignment for the French TV's first channel. A rival French team was there for the second channel. It was difficult to explain to Chinese officials that though we both were working for French TV, we were in effect in bitter competition.

The rival team, headed by Claude Otzenberger, who eventually put together a full-length documentary on China, shown commercially and to critical acclaim in cinemas all over Europe, was also filming in Peking streets. One incident illustrated the pitfalls of reporting in the Chinese People's Republic. One afternoon, doing what, in TV jargon, is known as a 'vox pop,' Otzenberger was holding up a mike to passersby and questioning them at random. A middle-aged man on a bicycle came to a stop, and Otzenberger asked him, 'What do you feel about the Vietnam War?' The man paused slightly for thought and then spoke.

The interpreter took over. 'He wants,' said the interpreter, 'to express his profound indignation at the unjustified aggression committed on the Vietnamese peoples by American imperialism.'

Weeks later, back in Paris, Otzenberger brought in a Chinese linguist to vet the interpreter's translation. What the cyclist had, in fact, said was: 'Well, you know, Vietnam's a long way away. We don't really know what's going on there. All we know is what the papers tell us. They don't say very much, and it's always the same thing anyway.'

While we were waiting for the authorities to make up their minds about us, we filmed all the Peking scenes of everyday life we could. This included the tiny Punch and Judy types of puppet theaters, in a small complex of alleys in Peking, whose expert singer-narrator puppeteers were perhaps, by this time, the only entertainers in China to tell stories void of any ideological content. The puppet shows, designed perhaps for children but watched by packed crowds, were about princesses, dragons, and witches who could turn people into animals and back again. Other themes were from traditional Chinese opera, involving emperors, concubines, eunuchs.

Some of the comedy involved was crude, some raucously funny. It was all greeted with peals of delighted laughter from an audience of all ages. Needless to say, the Cultural Revolution of 1966-67 put paid to this last vestige of non-ideological theater. According to experts, this particular Chinese puppeteer art form, thousands of years old, has ceased to exist.

We also spent a night at the opera, and saw something of the new-style Chinese opera, whose chief protagonist, of course, was none other than Chiang Ching, Mao's wife. The performance that night was called *The Miraculous Attack on the White Tiger Regiment*, and it was set in Korea during the 1950-53 Korean War. As I wrote in my diary at the time: 'The curtain rises on a group of Chinese volunteers, somewhere in Korea. They sing. Mr. Wuh whispers, "They are saying that the USA has invaded Korea, and so they must adopt tactics outlined by Chairman Mao to drive them out." The Chinese volunteers meet up with some Korean peasants. A woman sings for several minutes. "She says," says Mr. Wuh, "that the Korean people have been waiting impatiently for the arrival of the Chinese volunteers. Now that they have come she feels a sense of infinite joy."

'The scene shifts to the American camp. U.S. soldiers, their uniforms unbuttoned, all of them drunk and wielding Johnnie Walker whiskey bottles, stride about, ordering South Koreans to attack. Some Korean peasants rush onto the stage. They sing, at length. "They say," says Mr. Wuh, "that the American imperialists have burned a village and rounded up its inhabitants." An old man sings, interminably. "He says," Mr. Wuh goes on, "that from this

204

moment on he is resolved to condemn everything American." He is shot down by an American officer. End of Act One.

'Act Two takes place in a Chinese bunker. There is a huge picture of Mao on the wall and Army maps. Two senior officers sing. "They are outlining their plans for guerrilla warfare," says Mr. Wuh, "in accordance with the military writings of Chairman Mao." A young officer, the hero of the opera, makes his first appearance. "He is volunteering to lead the attack," says Mr. Wuh. Two generals harangue him for twenty minutes, then embrace him and shake him ceremonially by the hand. The young officer's volunteers appear. They sing. "They are vaunting the friendship of the Korean and Chinese peoples," says Mr. Wuh. The squad of Chinese, disguised as Americans, advance over barbed wire, displaying some of the famous acrobatic skill which has made the Peking Opera famous. There is a battle. All the American officers run away, whimpering. An American soldier is captured. He trembles and reveals all, including the password. "He is a coward," whispers Mr. Wuh with satisfaction.'

But it was obvious to me that the Chinese were not completely hooked on such heavy-handed propaganda. With an East European resident correspondent and fluent Chinese speaker, I saw a Chaplinesque comedy, entitled *Are You Satisfied*? about the tribulations of a disgruntled waiter in a state-owned restaurant who hates his job and makes life miserable for his customers. The first twenty minutes were as funny as anything ever made by Mack Sennett or Chaplin. There was a moral, of course: In the end the waiter is reformed and made to see that he too has a part to play, as a good revolutionary, in the new society. But it was obvious that the denouement had been inserted as a sop to orthodoxy and that the director of *Are you Satisfied?* had an original, inventive comic genius.

Also showing in the Peking cinema was perhaps the most controversial film ever made in Communist China:

February and Early Spring. This was a slow-moving, Antonioni-like love story, set in a small Chinese town, in 1938, about the tribulations of a country schoolmaster in love with the headmaster's beautiful young sister, who is herself being courted by a local aristocrat, and it had only a muted revolutionary message. Its obvious concern was not only in the interplay of emotions between the teacher, the girl, and a poor widow he has befriended, but also in the sheer formal beauty of the images themselves. The schoolmaster finds himself calumnied by village gossips and accused of harboring illicit relations with both the sister and the widow. The poor woodcutter family he has befriended suffers a tragedy, and the gifted son of the woodcutter (who has broken a leg in an accident) is compelled to leave home, and school, and go to work to support them. Out of a sense of duty and because she feels responsible for the teacher's troubles, the widow commits suicide. The schoolmaster then flees the village to join the revolutionary armies and 'fling himself into the mainstream of history.'

This film, shot in color with three of China's leading actors, did, of course, have a message: that individuals cannot reform the world on their own, but usefully act only through the framework of a collective organization. But for the first time since 1949, here was a film which dared show a prerevolutionary China not in stock cliché but in adult terms, giving a glimpse of a courtly, civilized, spacious, and vanished age. Many of the older people in the audience were in tears throughout most of the film. Its dialogue was—for 1964 China—remarkably frank. In one scene, three teachers, including the hero, are gathered around a table after dinner. One of them talks about the possibility of revolutionary uprisings in the area. 'Enough of communism, socialism, and all the other isms,' he says. 'Let us drink.' The audience gasped in shocked, incredulous surprise. Needless to say, the film's 'escapism' and 'bourgeois humanitarianism' came in for bitter criticism in the Chinese press, and shortly after I had seen it playing in packed houses, it was withdrawn—and, to my knowledge, has not been seen since.

At last our Foreign Ministry friends agreed to let me film an 'average' Chinese family in Peking, staying close to them for several days, and I also extracted permission to go to Chinese Mongolia to make a short film about a nomad commune, spectacular pictures of which I had seen in the glossy illustrated *China Reconstructs*.

How 'average,' in fact, was Wong Tsen, a lathe operator at the 'number one machine tool factory' (yes, we ended up filming there after all), and his smiling, stocky wife, Tsah, a crane operator in the same workshop? Probably fairly representative of Peking's large and admittedly better-paid factory workers, they had a one-room apartment, and most of the space in the room was taken up with beds. Life for Wong Tsen and Tsah revolved around the model factory to an unimaginable extent. All the people in their apartment houses worked in the same factory, which had both volleyball and basketball courts, a nursery and children's playground, and a cinema, theater, and larger meeting hall. The canteen was well stocked and cheap, and the pace of work slow by Western standards. But after working hours, at least twice a week, Wong Tsen took part in compulsory political discussions with six other workers from the same workshop. The discussions took the form of reading the latest *People's Daily* editorial aloud and commenting on it. This was shortly after the Bay of Tonkin episode, when U.S. warships shelled North Vietnam, and the editorial called on the Chinese to be prepared for further U.S. aggressive acts and to work harder to make China strong. Wong Tsen delivered what appeared to be a set piece: 'I could not repress a feeling of indignation toward the American imperialists on listening to the editorial,' he said. When I had seen him earlier in the week, he had been gentle and soft-spoken. Now, at the meeting, his voice was raucous and hard, like that of a Peking radio commentator. The atmosphere of the meeting, I noted at the time, was not unlike that of a revivalist meeting. Yet when it was all over, Wong Tsen and his fellow workers scampered out with obvious relief, their anger apparently forgotten.

Wong Tsen's responses to my questions were those of a disciplined model worker (no, he said, he was not yet a member of the party) with some views of his own. He obviously adored his children, and when I asked him what he would like them to be when they grew up, he said, 'I would like my son to be a doctor.' But then, remembering this was not the orthodox response, he added, 'Of course, I would be happy to see the party utilize them in the way it thinks best.' He also asked me one highly significant question. 'Tell me,' he said, 'is it true that in Europe workers have cars?'

But it was easy to predict that compared with Wong Tsen, his children would ask no such questions. At their school their reading primer contained no simple 'cat is on the mat' phrases. Instead, as I recall from my notes at the time, the phrases for toddlers learning to read were: 'Chairman Mao watches over his people. During the Long March the soldiers are cold. Chairman Mao takes off his coat and gives it to the soldiers if they are cold during the night.'

In retrospect, it's my conviction that our Chinese friends from the Foreign Affairs Ministry had indeed allowed us to see something of an average Peking family, and in contrast, I recall a recent conversation with one of *Le Monde*'s editors, André Fontaine who, on a visit to North Korea in 1977, had also asked to see the same thing. He was taken to a spacious—by Pyongyang standards—apartment, complete with every conceivable type of household gadget. 'How much did your stove cost?' he asked the housewife living there. 'How much was the refrigerator?'

The lady shrugged. 'I don't know,' she said. . . . The inference—to Fontaine—was that after his departure the decor would simply be removed.

In Peking, in 1964, it was still possible to meet a fairly

wide assortment of Chinese intellectuals, who occasionally were able to accept invitations to small dinner parties in Western diplomats' houses. At the house of a remarkably well-informed and enthusiastic Swiss diplomat, Maurice Hugentobler, I met a famous Chinese painter, then in his fifties, who had spent some years in America and still spoke fondly of American friends he had long since stopped writing to. Together we looked through a glossy album of modern Chinese paintings, including some of his own. Many were highly detailed, naturalistic studies of trees, flowers, and plants, but on one page was a typical example of 'realist' art—Mao Tse-tung shaking hands with some merry peasants. 'Do you do this sort of thing?' I asked.

He gave a wry smile. 'I am a specialist in bamboo,' he said. 'When I am asked to do this'—pointing to the painting—'I always say: "I am much, much better at vegetables."' Many intellectuals, including those employed as translators in various Western embassies, disappeared overnight during the Cultural Revolution and have never been seen again by their employers.

Perhaps the most unusual encounter I had in China was utterly unforeseen. I was traveling, alone, on a night train from Peking to Huhehot, capital of Chinese Mongolia. Exceptionally, I was allowed to do so because our interpreter had gone on in advance with the rest of the TV crew. I found myself in a spotless wagons-lits type of coupé and made my way to an almost empty restaurant car. Here, despite my few halting words of Mandarin and a phrasebook, I found myself unable to order a meal. There had been a small group of Chinese finishing their meal in the rear of the dining car, and one of them had obviously been observing the scene, because the waiter came back from their table carrying a sheet of paper, which he handed to me.

Not only was it in English, but it was penned in the kind of cursive, highly stylized handwriting favored by Old Etonians. 'Dear fellow traveler,' it began, 'you appear to have some difficulty in making yourself understood. If you show the attendant the following few lines, you may get a reasonable meal, assuming, as I must, that you like Chinese food. Please destroy this after use, and have a good journey.' There followed a few vertical lines in Chinese script, and indeed, after showing these to the waiter, I was served a delicious meal, including a bottle of Chinese beer.

I wanted to thank whoever it was who had so elegantly and cryptically helped me out of my impasse, but the party at the other end of the restaurant car was breaking up, and though I caught sight of a possible note writer—a middle-aged man with glasses and a long, sensitive face—I was unable either to catch up with him or to find him later on the train.

I got off the train at dawn the following morning. On Huhehot station, the passengers were doing their inevitable compulsory calisthenics to the inevitable accompaniment of martial music blaring forth from the station loudspeaker (the prevalent tune that year, later banned because it was associated with Liu Shao-chi, was 'Socialism Is Good' and the tune—si si si re si, la sol fa sol la si—was as compelling as any commercial jingle). I scrutinized the passengers lined up on the platform, looking for my ironic, mundane letter writer. I saw the man I thought I had seen the night before. In undershirt and dark-blue underpants, he was indistinguishable from the rest of the passengers, except that, close up, he was older than he had seemed to me earlier. His concentration on calisthenics appeared to be total. What links, I wondered, with faraway Britain enabled him to write so elegantly and in such handwriting? Was he a university professor with an Oxford or Cambridge past? Was he indeed that rarest combination of all: Chinese Old Etonian integrated into the party bureaucracy? I shall never know, but as I stared interrogatively at him, walking as slowly as I could to the station exit, he looked at me in turn, smiled slightly, and, before indulging in an overelaborate swing of arms upward in tune to the music, gave me a brief but unmistakable wink.

Joining up with my cameraman and interpreter in Huhehot, I found that our travels were by no means over. To get to the Chinese Mongol nomad commune we were scheduled to visit, we still had two days' travel to come. Why this particular commune? During our initial waiting period in Peking I had come across an illustrated story in *China Reconstructs* about a commune in Chinese Mongolia whose elected boss was a young woman. The pictures were spectacular, and I had immediately applied to visit it in turn. We were on our way there now.

That day, we caught a DC-3 flight from Huhehot to a small desert garrison town whose name I never did find out. Here, apart from a large barracks, the town's main distinguishing feature was an old and obviously historic disused Buddhist monastery. We were given rooms obviously reserved for visiting VIPs inside the barracks itself and were free to come and go as we pleased. But every time we left our rooms we were discreetly followed by at least one young civilian.

It was the town, rather than the barracks, which interested me, for here, I felt, was the real China most visitors were unable to see. Homes were small, crowded, and cramped, but spotlessly clean. There were few stores, but these sold a basic range of household goods also available in the larger stores in Peking and Huhehot. Everyone looked well fed and happy, with the exception of one or two old men in the vicinity of the monastery, who could have been beggars. At dinner, an unusually lavish banquet, there appeared several unidentified guests, who ate ravenously. They did not introduce themselves, and all our efforts to discover their party rank, or the real nature of their jobs, failed. One was fluent in both Mongol and Mandarin, and acted as interpreter in addition to his other duties. The other was a rotund, bespectacled Cantonese—obviously a party official of some standing.

211

Both were to accompany us to the commune the following day.

We set out early next morning in a packed Russian-made jeep and drove for hours across a plateau. My memory is of an extraordinarily stark and at the same time beautiful expanse of hard ground, savanna, yellowish grass, endless grazing areas. Visible from far away were the neatly aligned circular skin tents, or yurts, which were the commune's mobile homes. Here we were to live for the following week, probably in retrospect, the most exhilarating week of my life.

Obviously, this nomad commune was exceptional, if only because it had been singled out by *China Reconstructs*. But it was by no means the only one in the area, and indeed, we came across traces of other, very similar communes during our stay. Never did I find out exactly where we were, though, from vague answers to our questions, I realized that the border with Soviet-dominated Outer Mongolia was not far away.

The commune looked after 17,000 animals—mostly sheep and horses, with a few hundred camels—and its members nomadized over a 1,000-square-mile area, pulling up stakes every two weeks. September—the month we were there—was the best month of the year. Nights were already cold, and stoves burned in every yurt. But we felt neither the searing dry heat which was a feature of midsummer nor the arctic temperatures of winter, when everything froze for months at a time.

The film, which I called *Mao's Wild West*, was a delight to make; in such a setting, what with the corralling of horses, the landscape, and the cowboy atmosphere, it was impossible to fail. But the film was given another dimension by the personality of the commune's leader, whose name was Pochai. She turned out to be spectacularly beautiful, a small, sturdy figure with a natural elegance which would have inspired Saint Laurent to dress his models in faded cottons and put them all on horseback.

212

What made our Chinese Mongolia experience different was the fact that, for all the pictures of Mao inside the yurts and the occasional stereotyped lapsing into the jargon we were by now so used to, our nomad hosts were real people, not just puppet extras playing to the visiting foreigners' gallery. They had not been exposed, at least at the time of our trip, to endless parties of Western visitors, nor did they have the party-inspired jargon at their fingertips. On occasion their responses were extraordinarily spontaneous and natural.

Thus, when I asked Pochaı how many times a week she and her fellow nomads took a break to study the works of Mao, she said, 'Whenever we have time.' Pressed further, she admitted that it wasn't often, and a ritual study-of-Mao session we were compelled to film ended with everyone concerned scampering off with obvious relief.

But it was in their relations with our two visiting Chinese escorts that their reactions were most interesting. The Mongol-speaking interpreter was himself one of them, used to life in tents and a good horseman. They regarded him as a natural ally, and he did his best to help us. The Cantonese official, who never revealed his status, but must have had some bureaucratic party function, had never been on a horse in his life, was obviously ill at ease sleeping on a mattress on the floor of a tent, and was unaccustomed to Mongol food. He was miserable, and our nomad friends made constant fun of him behind his back. Our interpreter, Mr. Wuh, adopted an attitude of neutrality, deferring to both.

On occasion we all found it necessary to use tough Mongol ponies to move around on, and the TV team, happily, found such a method of transport adequate (though we scarcely carried it off with the natural elegance of the nomads, who all looked as if they had been born on horseback). But our Cantonese escort simply couldn't keep on even the most docile pony for long. Scared of horses, he became angry with everyone and demanded a jeep. But some of the places we wanted to go to simply weren't suitable even for a jeep, and he started pulling rank, demanding that we revise our program to enable him to keep up with us. This I was reluctant to do—especially since, as time went on, it was obvious that he was exclusively concerned with party orthodoxy and not impressed by the level of the nomads' political consciousness.

The freedom enjoyed by the Mongol nomads was so much greater than that of any other Chinese I saw that I had the impression, several times, that we were in a different country. The commune members were entitled to keep, and trade in, 25 percent of their total sheep, horses, and camel herds, which were their own property, and as a result, they were reasonable affluent. The major decision affecting their work and lives were democratically discussed, and not, I believe, solely for our benefit.

Perhaps it was the proximity of the Outer Mongolia border which caused the Chinese authorities, with considerable pragmatic acumen, to make life so attractive on the Chinese side of the border that any defections were unthinkable. Finally, the degree of freedom granted them may have been in proportion to the hardships suffered through the long, cruel winter. I asked our Mongol-speaking interpreter, who was also an official of some importance, whether the kind of autonomy we witnessed was a permanent feature of all Chinese minorities or whether, little by little, the screws would be tightened. 'We have strict orders,' he said, 'to do nothing—for the moment. We are more concerned with improving the way of life of the nomads than with changing it or turning them into sedentary farmers.'

On the eve of our departure we were compelled to take part in a huge typically Mongol feast. The *pièce de résistance*, coming at the end of a remarkable Chinese banquet by any standards, was the traditional Mongol national dish: boiled sheep's tail. In summer Mongol sheep store in their tails huge quantities of fat, which enables them to survive the lean, cold winter months. The tail, only lightly boiled and resembling nothing so much as a somewhat sheep-smelling hunk of rancid butter, colored white, was cut into slivers, which our hosts piled on top of our rice bowls. It pleased me to observe that our Cantonese escort was overtly appalled by this practice and refused to eat even token portions of this delicacy. My cameraman, Frank Richard, looked at me in mute reproach but nibbled away. I decided that the only way of coping with this unforeseen hazard was to wash everything down with what available alcohol there was. This consisted of mao tai, the somewhat raw 90-proof alcohol, and a Mongol concoction made of boiled milk, whose vapor was captured, fermented, and turned into alcohol by some mysterious process involving a Rube Goldberg contraption. As a result of my necessary but indiscriminate libations, I was able not only to ingurgitate respectable quantities of fatty sheep's tail but also to respond to our hosts' request that we produce a 'revolutionary song' from our respective countries. Richard, to my relief, in a light baritone, struggled through 'Zorro Est Arrivé,' a recent French hit by French musical hall star Henri Salvador. Called upon in turn, I attempted a martial and, I hoped, revolutionary version of 'The Eton Boating Song.' Not since the days of explorer Peter Fleming (brother of Ian and adventurer extraordinary), I reflected in a queasy daze, could this tune have been intoned in the remoter parts of China. At the banquet's very end my hosts responded to my compliments on the quality of the meal by saying they would send for the cook. Emboldened by alcohol, I replied that this was very much the kind of behavior that must have been a feature of the much-decried 'old society.' Rather, I suggested, we should all get up and visit him, which we did. The surprised old man, clearing up in the yurt used as kitchen, seemed genuinely pleased to see me and insisted on pouring yet more fermented sheep's milk. Everyone slept heavily that night.

I was genuinely sorry to leave and have since often wondered about Pochaɪ and her nomad commune. Reports later suggested that during the Cultural Revolution, many of the more autonomous-minded national minorities were 'severely criticized' for their lukewarm revolutionary fervor. Were they compulsorily domesticated, forbidden to stray beyond their new settlements, and sedentarized and their privately owned cattle taken away? Were they so remote that the convulsions elsewhere in China passed them by? Since the Cultural Revolution no foreign visitors have been allowed back into Chinese Mongolia.

We returned to Peking in the same way we had come—first by jeep, then by plane, and finally by train, but this time in daylight. We spent another night in transit in the barracks of the small town we had stopped in on the way out. The only untoward moment came with the hint of bad weather and rain, which threatened to turn the airstrip into mud. What would happen, I asked Mr. Wuh, if our plane were unable to land? With commendable calm he said, 'We will wait here until the next plane comes.' And when would that be? 'In two weeks' time, I am told,' he said. I didn't dare tell my cameraman. In any event the light rain stopped, and the airstrip was dry enough for the Viscount to pick us up.

I became one of the very few reporters to meet Mao informally, and for several hours. This unexpected treat came about as follows: The French government had just staged an industrial fair in Peking, the first since the resumption of diplomatic relations. Several prominent French officials, parliamentarians, and industrialists were in Peking for the fair, and the organizers made a formal request to be received by Mao. As the heads of the only two visiting French TV teams in China at the time, Claude Otzenberger and I also asked to come along. To our surprise, we were told that our request would probably be granted. Emboldened by this response, we then asked whether, by any chance, it would be possible to take our TV crews along, too, to film the encounter. The initial answer from our friends at the Foreign Ministry was encouraging, and we thought, for one giddy moment, that we had a major scoop on our hands, for Mao had—then—never been filmed in close-up or in an informal setting. Then, obviously in response to Mao's own veto, the news came that one representative each from both French TV teams in China could attend, but that no filming would be allowed. No further explanations were given, but there's no doubt in my mind, after the event, that Mao's veto came because he was reluctant to allow viewers to see what he really looked like. At this time all official photographs of Mao showed a smooth-faced Mao who didn't look more than fifty years old. They all were heavily retouched. Also, at this time, Mao had never appeared informally on Chinese TV.

Until the very last moment we didn't know whether our session with Mao would be in Peking or elsewhere. The day before it was scheduled, we were told to be at Peking airport at 6:00 A.M. The French members of the assembled group there included Lucien Paye, the French ambassador in Peking; Jacques Duhamel, then an opposition Radical party politician, and his wife; Bernard de Gaulle, who, as well as being a nephew of General de Gaulle's, was the head of a French electronics firm and a major exhibitor at the fair; and Mr. and Mrs. Guillaume Georges-Picot. He was an ambassador-at-large, a veteran diplomat and organizer of French overseas promotional fairs. She was Russian-born, and had lived in Shanghai before the war.

On the Chinese side, I recognized the expert interpreter, trained at Geneva's interpreters' school, who had accompanied Chou En-lai in Algeria and Africa in 1963. There were two other Chinese with us. One, a tall aristocratic-looking man in his early sixties, was Nan Nan Chen, director of China's Central Bank and organizer of Chinese fairs abroad. A banker in prerevolution times, he had thrown in his lot with Mao and was, I was later told, one

217

of China's best economists and one of the few Chinese close to Mao with a sophisticated grasp of monetary matters. He wore a Mao suit of expensive cloth and the latest and most expensive type of gold Rolex watch. The other official with us was a small, gnomelike man with a humorous expression called Wang Ping Nan. He had been Chinese ambassador in Warsaw at the time of the first U.S.-China meetings there. A student in Germany before World War II, he had married a German woman (who wrote a book, long out of print, entitled *I Fought for Mao* about her experiences in China from 1944 to 1949, after separating from her husband and returning to Europe). At the time of our visit to Mao, he was deputy foreign minister. Both our distinguished escorts later fell afoul of the Cultural Revolution: Nan Nan Chen, according to a number of reports, was either beaten to death by Red Guards or else committed suicide; Wang Ping Nan was removed from office, was presumably sent to reeducation camp, but recently emerged as the leader of a number of Chinese delegations to the Third World, eighteen months after Mao's death.

It wasn't until the very last moment that we learned that we were due to take the regular scheduled flight to Shanghai, to change planes there and alight at Hangchow. When we arrived there, at 11:00 A.M., we were taken, in a fleet of Chinese and Russian-made limousines, to the Hangchow Hotel outside the town, overlooking the lake. A young, intense-looking protocol official said, after lunch, 'You will please stay close to the hotel grounds or in your rooms. You will be given an hour's notice.'

In fact, it wasn't until 4:00 P.M. that we were given our house call, and we gathered expectantly on schedule at 5:00 P.M. in a private sitting room. There followed another hour-long wait, and it was nearly 6:00 P.M., on a cloudy, overcast day, when we piled into our fleet of cars once more. We drove slowly for what could not have been more than seven minutes, skirting the lake. I counted only two policemen on the empty road, but several 'Keep Out' signs. At a

218

driveway entrance, operating a red and white wooden articulated pole, was a solitary sentry. The drive was about 200 yards long and gave on to a compound on the edge of the lake. It was almost dark, but I could make out half a dozen one-storey bungalows, a more modern three-storey building, with a couple of cars parked alongside it, and in the distance the gilt roof of a small pagoda. The largest of the old-fashioned wooden bungalows was ablaze with light, and there, standing on the veranda, was Mao himself, his right hand raised in welcome.

After the introductions and the customary group photograph, Mao led the way to a large drawing room, and we sat in a circle of armchairs. The walls were draped with some dark-red fabric, and there was a thick beige wall-to-wall carpet. It could have been, as I noted at the time, the comfortable, but not overluxurious, home of a middling European executive. But it was unmistakably a Chinese home: There were spittoons, like outsize chamber pots, at the foot of every armchair.

Mao was wearing a baggy light-gray tunic and equally baggy trousers. His heavy brown brogues were highly polished, and his beige cotton socks fell down over his ankles. His sleeves almost covered his hands, his tunic hung in folds around him, and he seemed somewhat shrunken and thinner than I had expected. His hair, meticulously brushed back, was black with scarcely a trace of gray and was almost certainly dyed. His face was much more lined than in any photographs I had seen, but full and fleshy.

Quite obviously he was not in the best of health. As he led the way to the sitting room after the group photograph, an attendant walked beside him, holding him lightly by the elbow. During the evening Mao smoked constantly; his teeth were in appalling condition, blackened by nicotine.

He also had a bad smoker's cough and a distinct wheeze. He had difficulty moving his right arm, and Bernard de Gaulle, whose father had died of Parkinson's disease, said later that Mao seemed to have some of the symptoms of the

219

same disease, in its early stages.

Mao, that evening, was in a lighthearted, almost bantering mood. To Lucien Paye, the French ambassador—who had previously been de Gaulle's education minister—he said, 'I am told you have been education minister in your country. You are obviously a very important man—not like me. I have had very little education. I am just a poor schoolteacher. I never had time for formal learning.'

Paye, despite these opening remarks, was reluctant to depart from a prearranged, formal speech, which he embarked upon at some length. When he came to the bit about France's 'new role' in Asia, Mao, who had been showing evident signs of irritation as the speech was being translated to him, interrupted. 'Since Dien Bien Phu, France has no role in Asia,' he said, speaking softly but insistently. 'And let me tell you something you may or may not know: Many of the gunners at Dien Bien Phu were Chinese.'

There was an appalled silence. Finally, the ambassador, with commendable presence of mind, said, 'Let's not talk about the past but about the future,' and cut short his formal remarks. Another uneasy short silence followed. Finally, Jacques Duhamel (later Pompidou's cultural affairs minister, who in 1977 was to die, tragically, of multiple sclerosis while still in his early fifties) saved the situation by addressing Mao on a relatively uncontroversial subject in a more conversational tone.

During the three hours that followed, Mao reminisced at length about the past. He took obvious pleasure in telling the story of a visiting Japanese businessman who had embarked on a long apology for the crimes committed by Japan against China in the past. 'Not at all,' Mao said he had replied. 'If Japan had not occupied half of China, it would not have been possible for the Chinese people to rise up against the invader. As a result, our army became a million strong. That is how Chou En-lai, Liu Shiao-chi,

Chen Yi, and I learned the art of war. Before that we knew nothing. So I said to my Japanese visitor, "Maybe I should be thanking you."

'We should also thank Britain, the USA, and Chiang Kai-shek for having taught us fundamental things,' Mao went on. 'For instance, the USA gave billions of dollars to Chiang in military aid. In doing so, America was, in fact, aiding us, for we had neither rifles nor artillery. These are *facts*.'

In 1964 direct U.S. involvement in ground fighting in Vietnam was growing but was still on a very small scale, but Mao said he thought that American 'interference' there would last for a long, long time. In the end, however, he added, America would withdraw from Vietnam and Thailand, 'when they get tired of fighting there. Everybody will go home, and that will be the best solution.'

On the Sino-Soviet issue Mao refused to be drawn out. 'Ah,' he said, 'you are trying to get me to say something about Comrade Khrushchev . . . he is inclined to meddle in the affairs of others. He asked me once. "Why do you not take back Hong Kong and Macao?" and I replied, "There are even more problems in your area than Hong Kong and Macao."'

Perhaps his most revealing remarks were his disparaging comments on Chinese youth and the economy as a whole. He referred repeatedly to China as a 'nondeveloped,' poor country. 'We did have a long-term [economic] plan, but it went wrong,' he said. 'Too many ideas were borrowed from abroad. We have less experience than you, and we have not put everything right yet.'

I remained silent but took a number of pictures, including perhaps the only informal photos ever taken of Mao eating with chopsticks and smoking. Suddenly, during a lull in the conversation, he turned to me. 'You,' he said, 'ask me a question. You haven't asked a question yet.'

On the spur of the moment I said, 'What is your opinion of Chinese youth?' I may have struck a sensitive chord, for

Mao embarked on a long and fascinating exegesis on the shortcomings of young people in China, who were 'untried by war' and 'lacked the revolutionary experience of their elders.'

He spoke scathingly of some Chinese university students. 'Not all young Chinese are true socialists,' he said. 'Many are the offspring of landowners and rich peasants and still regret the old days.' This prompted Ambassador Paye to describe a recent visit to Peita University, which he called 'most impressive.' Again displaying his visible irritation, Mao interrupted him. 'It is not a good university,' he said. Paye replied that everyone there had seemed admirably civic-minded. 'What they say does not necessarily correspond to what they do. It is not a good university,' said Mao, obviously displeased at being contradicted. Duhamel then said he had recently visited the Polytechnic University in Sian, 'where everyone appeared to know your works by heart.' Again Mao showed his petulance. 'These people spoke well in front of you, but one must not learn things by rote. Only experience will tell whether they are good or not.'

We had not expected to be invited to dinner, and it was with some surprise that we watched him pat his stomach after about an hour's somewhat stilted conversation, and say, 'I am hungry. Are you hungry? Will you share a meal with me?' This was the cue for his attendants in plain white shirts and blue cotton trousers, who had been listening in on the talks, to move swiftly across the room and whisk away a screen, behind which a circular table was laid.

The meal, with several spicy Hunanese dishes, was both simple and delicious. Mao ate with good appetite, getting through two bowls of rice. He drank only tea and lemonade and barely sipped the mao tai and Chinese wine when ritual toasts to China and to France were made.

He seemed to take a delight in ribbing the unfortunate Wang Ping Nan, who reacted with barely concealed misery

222

to Mao's repeated cracks at him. 'He spent all his youth in Germany,' said Mao, referring to Wang Ping Nan's student days. 'Why, he's scarcely Chinese. He's practically a Nazi.'

As the wife of the seniormost Frenchman present, Tanya Georges-Picot sat on Mao's right at table but said scarcely a word, save at the very end of the meal, when a dark, hot beverage was being served in small cups. 'Tell me,' she said, tugging at Mao's sleeve, 'what is this? Is it tea or is it coffee?' Mao seemed nonplussed.

At the end of the long meal Mao gave the signal for us to leave. 'There are many more things to talk about, but we will do so next time,' he said. Rising, he walked around to where I had placed my camera on the table, peered through the lens, and joked, 'I was never any good at this.' Then, looking at me, bedraggled and sweaty after shooting pictures all evening, he added, 'You work too hard.' As we drove away, after shaking hands, we saw him standing alone in the doorway on the hot, sultry night, his arm raised in a farewell gesture.

It's a measure of the West's ignorance of China at the time of our meeting with Mao that few, if any, China watchers then realized that Mao had, in fact, been relegated to the position of figurehead after the failure, three years earlier, of the 'Great Leap Forward' and was no longer fully in control of events there. Mao himself certainly gave no hint of this, referring with immense assurance to Chou En-lai as 'my prime minister' and dismissing China's recent failures—owing largely to the 'Great Leap Forward' willed by himself—as being the mistakes of others. Partly, of course, the illusion of Mao's power was due to his perfect and detailed knowledge of China's current foreign policy; whether answering questions on Sino-Soviet relations, the status of the Colombo Plan (a stillborn project for economic cooperation then still being considered as a means of solving, too, some of the political conflicts in Vietnam and Cambodia and Laos) or the degree of progress in the then-

223

secret India-China talks over the settlement of the disputed Ladakh and NEFA frontiers, Mao showed, in his answers, that he had facts and figures in his fingertips.

To a very great extent, Mao's isolation during this period from the real levers of command was also concealed by the degree of idolization he enjoyed. Whether Mao reveled in or deliberately encouraged this personality cult—or whether it was a subtle method, utilized by Liu Shao-chi and others to keep him relatively quiet while seemingly enjoying the attributes of absolute power—will probably not be known for at least a generation. It would require someone intimately connected with Mao and the power struggle Mao waged in the sixties to answer this question, and the parallels with Stalin's Russia and the destalinization process are not really valid, for the Chinese tradition of secrecy, of proceeding by allusion and arcane historical and literary reference, scarcely lends itself to any frank and factual exposé. All I can report, from those three and a half hours in Mao's company, was that in response to the fulsome compliments of some of the Frenchmen present, Mao reacted not with self-satisfaction but with what seemed like genuine embarrassment. The most lasting impression I retain, at this fifteen-year distance, is of a wily, somewhat brutal, but jovial peasant patriarch figure, who, as he noisily imbibed his soup and talked at length without fear of contradiction, manifested a certain number of deep-seated and possibly dangerous prejudices. I'm not simply referring to Mao's somewhat simplistic view of history (for him, it appeared as the conversation progressed, nations could be judged and praised only insofar as their attitudes toward China, Mao, and Chiang Kai-shek were concerned, hence some conciliatory words for France's 'independent' policies after the earlier outburst over Dien Bien Phu), but to his complete contempt for intellectuals and his deeply pessimistic view of the future. During the course of the dinner I asked him whether the quality of youthful leadership in China was likely to remain at its current level, and as with the students, he was forthright, gloomy, and cuttingly categoric. 'Not necessarily,' he said. 'They have not known war or armed struggle. They are without experience. They must learn to struggle. Perhaps they will.'

But as I reread my notes taken at the time, my impression is confirmed that Mao's biggest failing, in 1964, was due to the obsession with his own and China's past. There was never the slightest doubt in Mao's mind, from listening to him talk, that the lessons of the Chinese Revolution were universally applicable, that they followed certain immutable laws whose secret Mao himself had unlocked, and that certain social features of China which had, in part at least, been responsible for the revolution were still inhibiting China's progress. At the time of our meal with Mao, regimentation of the Chinese people was complete and had reached a level probably unattained anywhere else in history, with the possible exception of Albania and North Korea. Political indoctrination and the economic leveling of Chinese society had combined to produce a common-denominator robot population, whose acceptance of the new state of affairs was unrestricted and total. Fifteen years had passed since Mao had formally reduced the last pockets of resistance and compelled the discredited remnants of Chiang's armies to flee to Taiwan. A whole generation of young Chinese had grown up with no direct knowledge of the 'old society' or of the exploitation of the landless peasants by landlords and of the intricate and arcane class distinctions which were a feature of prerevolutionary China. The elimination of landlords, bourgeois capitalists, and pro-Chiang officials had been ruthless and thorough, and those who remained were used, as was the last ex-emperor, then still alive and occasionally produced for visiting VIPs, to confess their past sins, underline China's past failings, and extol the wisdom and almost superhuman foresight of Mao himself.

Yet, I was surprised to find, the references used by Mao

in 1964 to explain China's policies and goals fifteen years after the fall of Shanghai in 1949 were still, overwhelmingly, references to pre-1949 China. It was as if, in the absence of a real enemy, Mao had been compelled to pretend that the old enemies were still alive—patently not the case. To what extent Mao rationalized the stresses and strains of internal power struggles by reading into them a continuation of the old class struggles will probably never be known. What is incontrovertible is the seemingly continuous Chinese need to exorcise demons. During our Mao visit the demons were the remnants of the 'old society'; shortly afterward, during the Cultural Revolution, emphasis was laid instead on the evil, privileged party bureaucrats and power holders; later still the real villains, it turned out, were 'traitors' like Lin Piao. Finally, the wheel coming full circle, the latest crop of demons to be exorcised is none other than the Gang of Four—Mao's widow, Chiang Ching, and three other power holders most closely associated with the implementation of Mao's own thought and with the Cultural Revolution of 1966-67.

I left Mao's bungalow in a daze; it had been an enriching and perhaps overrich experience. To paraphrase our first interpreter, 'my spirit was confused.' At the very end of the meal Mao, turning to the French ambassador, had said, 'This conversation is, of course, a private one.' The ambassador had acquiesced. Bernard de Gaulle had then asked whether he might not, nevertheless, 'convey the substance of your remarks to my uncle, the general,' and Mao had agreed. I, of course, considered myself bound by Mao's concern that the talk remain 'private,' though, when a couple of days later our group photograph was published in Peking's *People's Daily* showing us all in Mao's company, I considered it legitimate to describe, in the *Saturday Evening Post*, the circumstances of my meeting with Mao, but not the substance of his conversation, which I began writing about only after his death in 1976.

What followed is a vignette of backstage journalism, as

experienced, I know, by many of my colleagues but almost never written about, partly because there is some reluctance to wash one's linen in public and partly because what we write about for the media necessarily has to take the form of a neatly self-contained package, from which the untidy, not easily digestible jigsaw-puzzle pieces are invariably eliminated.

French Ambassador Lucien Paye was in the first car in our small motorcade back to the hotel. As befitted my lowly status, I was in the last. As I walked into the hotel lobby, I was almost physically set upon by an uncontrollably enraged ambassador. 'You took pictures! You took notes!' he shouted. 'It is intolerable! You will hand over your film and your notes to me right away!'

I backed away from him, and as I did so, I determined that the most sizable scoop in my experience so far was not going to be compromised by an ambassador's petulant and faulty assessment of the circumstances of the meeting.

'No way,' I said with, I hoped, sufficiently firm assurance, not only to get him to change his mind, but also to win over the other members of the party to my side.

Leaving him still shouting at me, I rushed up to my room, locked the door, and proceeded to type out, with as many carbon copies as my portable machine could take, a complete record of the Mao meeting, from my fairly extensive notes. The ambassador's violent reaction forced me to assume that he might try to take them by force. I doubted that he would ask our Chinese friends to act on his behalf, but anything was possible.

As it turned out, this was the most fruitful thing I could have done, for the evening's talk was still fresh in my mind. When I had finished, I concealed the typed sets of notes in pathetic hiding places in my room, including a copy I locked inside my suitcase, together with my exposed film. Carrying the original top copy, as well as my notebook, on my person, I then decided to brave the ambassador's wrath and, in some trepidation, returned to the lobby sitting room, where the rest of the party had remained.

I am glad I did so, for several reasons. In the first place, Jacques Duhamel, who, I felt, realized that the ambassador's stance had been unreasonable, had succeeded to some extent in calming him down. Our trip was not yet over (we were to visit the town of Hangchow the following day, still in the company of Wang Ping Nan and Nan Nan Chen, and I didn't want to be excluded from this and return ignominiously to Peking). But above all I wanted to explain to Ambassador Paye that I had no intention of breaking an agreement between him and Mao and that I would certainly not publish a quoted question-and-answer account of the meeting and dinner I had attended. At the same time I wanted to convey to him certain journalistic facts of life: The first was that if Mao had objected to my taking pictures during the meal, he would have ordered me not to do so from the very beginning. (At one point he had, in fact, toward the end of the meal, turned to me and said, 'You have taken enough pictures now,' and I had immediately put away my Nikon. But this seemed to prove my point—namely, that Mao had, by allowing me to be present and by failing to object in the slightest way to my cameras in the early stages of the meal, fully acquiesced to my picture and note taking.) Then I wanted to point out that since a group photograph had been taken of us for publication in the Chinese press, the fact of our meeting Mao was not to be kept secret and that I was at least free to describe what he looked like, the circumstances of our meeting, and the details of the meal itself.

Finally, I felt that a written record of our three-and-a-half-hour session with Mao represented a valuable addition to our skimpy and imperfect knowledge of things Chinese and that it was in the ambassador's own interest that the details of the conversation with Mao be recorded as accurately as possible. (In contrast, the account written by André Malraux, in his *Antimémoires*, of his conversation with Mao the following year was thought, by many French diplomats and experienced China watchers, to contain more Malraux than Mao.)

Whether I convinced Ambassador Paye of all this or not is doubtful, but in more equable mood, he made no further request that I hand over my film and notes. Instead, he asked me for a copy of my notes (I explained that I had consigned them to my typewriter immediately on leaving him) for his own use. Perhaps, belatedly, he had realized that he was on the point of writing the most important and newsworthy dispatch of his ambassadorial career. Ambassador Paye was not, by nature, an irate or unreasonable man (his nickname, among the English-speaking diplomatic community in Peking, was Sweetypie). Needless to say, a short oral agreement before the Mao meeting on the ground rules for reporting it would have avoided any such unpleasantness, and here I was perhaps as guilty as Ambassador Paye for not having raised the matter before the session with Mao.

Duhamel then suggested that we all sit down and try to remember as much as we could of the meeting and that my notes be used, collectively, by the entire company as a basis for an even more comprehensive written account. Understandably, those who had taken part in the conversation tended to remember best the answers to questions they themselves had asked. My own note taking had been interrupted by picture taking, and I welcomed the opportunity of filling in some inevitable gaps.

The outcome was that on the basis of additional details contributed by others in the party, I rewrote my original account, duly typing it out until late in the night and giving a copy to Ambassador Paye the following morning. I couldn't prevent myself, in the event, from saying as I did so, 'You see, Mr. Ambassador, note taking does serve a purpose occasionally.'

During the rest of the trip Ambassador Paye was unfailingly polite, though I continued to detect a certain reserve, caused, perhaps, by a basic attitude toward reporters shared by other French mandarins of the old school; as all correspondents who have worked in France know, there is, among many of the upper-echelon French technocrats in government service and in key private-sector posts, an innate conviction that all reporters belong, socially at least, to the servants' hall and that their function is merely to report, under the closest control and supervision possible, what the ruling elite considers useful for the implementation of current policy. Such an attitude, not so dissimilar from that surely entertained by Mao himself, cuts across distinctions of 'right' and 'left' and is not simply a phenomenon of age or generation. Some of the most arrogant, and ignorant, would-be manipulators of the media are to be found in young, recent French graduates of elite schools like the Ecole Nationale d'Administration, and it would be wrong to single out France alone for such failings; increasingly, in my experience, British and West German civil servants, particularly ambitious ones who fear that any appearance on the scene of a reporter could jeopardize their unbrokenly successful careers, tend to be as irritatingly supercilious and uncooperative.

I was of course anxious to know whether my color pictures of Mao—taken in dim light, at maximum exposures—had any chance of being serviceable. This I was not to discover until my return to Europe. Miraculously some did indeed turn out to be quite good. One was used in the *Saturday Evening Post*, and my syndicated color photos of Mao were reproduced in major picture magazines all over the world, including *Paris-Match* and *Stern*. Instinctively, to allow maximum exposure without the concomitant blurs, I had propped my camera on the back of the armchair assigned to me, using it like a tripod. Mao had helped by remaining motionless and impassive for long spells at a time. Finally, back in Paris, I had explained the peculiar circumstances under which these pictures had been taken to a Kodak executive, who was kind enough to see that they were developed under special supervision.

But the fate of some of these unique color pictures of the Mao dinner and of the best of the Mao portraits illustrates the organizational shortcomings that can occur in even the best-organized news media. *Newsweek* lost a couple of the best color portraits when I submitted them a couple of years later at a time a cover story on Mao was being prepared, while the *Washington Post* lost the negatives of some of the best black-and-white pictures of Mao using chopsticks at the dinner table—though admittedly I still have the contact sheets. In similar circumstances, my advice to any budding amateur who happens to take striking pictures of value is: Always make duplicates of color frames, and guard negatives with your life.

My final gesture, as I flew from Peking to Shanghai on my way back to Europe, was in retrospect both puerile and irresponsible and can be excused only by prolonged exposure to the restraints and tensions of traveling in the Chinese People's Republic. I had with me, brought in by accident rather than design, a copy of *Playboy*. Suffering from a surfeit of *China Reconstructs*—the only illustrated magazine available on any domestic flight in China—I slipped this copy of *Playboy* in between the hardback *China Reconstructs* folder on the Peking-Shanghai plane and left it there. It was only several years later, in Hong Kong at the time of the Cultural Revolution, that I realized the implications and the possible consequences of such an act. Perhaps it has been the reason why I never again succeeded in obtaining a journalist's visa to China. Perhaps it involved a number of perfectly innocent Chinese in endless, soul-destroying public self-criticism—or worse. Belatedly, in the unlikely event of this ever being read by those with power to grant, or withhold, reporters' visas to Peking, I want to apologize for this characteristically boorish 'foreign devil' act and hope that this small practical joke in the worst possible taste went unnoticed and involved no one in any subsequent hardship. Above all, I want to stress that I

231

meant no disrespect to the Chinese people, those so-called masses whose collective will is still constantly evoked in China by successive layers of power holders but who came across to me then, fifteen years ago, and despite enforced regimentation and 'social engineering' of the most ruthless, brutal kind, as a rich, gifted, varied, and infinitely appealing and adaptable collection of individuals—qualities which, in the last resort, perhaps explain China's astonishing capacity for survival.

VIII. HONG KONG, MACAO, VIETNAM

THOUGH I didn't return to China, I spent almost two years within earshot of it. After leaving *The Saturday Evening Post* to join *Newsweek*, first in Paris and then as its Hong Kong bureau chief (1966-68) I became a moderately competent China watcher at a time when, owing to the convulsions of the Chinese Cultural Revolution, China suddenly began vying with Vietnam as the world's most important foreign news story. Between intervals of commuting to Saigon, I found myself writing about China almost every week.

How could one possibly write meaningfully about China from Hong Kong? It was an old dispute. About to leave for China in 1964, I tended to share the contempt of the proud visa holder for those destined to write about such a vast country at second hand. Once in China in 1964, however, I saw something of the restraints put on the handful of resident, permanent correspondents in Peking and quickly discovered that Hong Kong wasn't such a bad news source after all.

For the lives and the working habits of the resident foreign correspondents in Peking were drab, dull, and frustrated to an unimaginable degree. Except for rare, stage-managed occasions, they were (and still are) unable to leave Peking city limits, except to travel the well-worn paths of the Ming Tombs and the Great Wall; from 1964 on, their very reading was restricted to a limited number of papers and magazines, excluding a wide range of provincial and party papers which had previously provided interesting insights into doctrinal disputes and major policy differences. Not for them the night train to Huhehot or the informal dinner with Mao. To a large extent, all these highly skilled, hardworking, and dedicated journalists could do was translate what papers were made available to them, see whose names came up in the interminable toasts at official banquets, and which were omitted, keep abreast of embassy gossip, and attempt to sum up a national mood from the behavior of Peking street crowds at any given time.

With the Cultural Revolution, of course, their task became both more interesting and riskier. Apart from the physical presence of huge crowds of young Red Guards, wall posters began covering every available inch of space, and the deciphering and comparative study of these posters became a skilled and engrossing science, somewhat akin to cryptography. But as the Cultural Revolution increased in violence, such study became increasingly dangerous: Anthony Grey, Reuters correspondent in Peking at the time of the Cultural Revolution, was confined to a small room under so-called house arrest for more than a year, and the terms of this solitary confinement were so brutal that a lesser man would have suffered a permanent breakdown. Repeatedly, correspondents trying to read or photograph wall posters were hustled away or beaten up.

The same was true for diplomats. At the peak of the Cultural Revolution, Red Guards sacked the British Embassy and roughed up the staff, including the ambassador himself. Japanese reporters and diplomats were slightly less subject to such restraints, simply because they were less conspicuous.

Admittedly, in Hong kong we were unable to sniff the heady revolutionary air of the Cultural Revolution or watch the almost daily marches, meetings, and manhandling of onetime 'power holders,' now dressed in dunces' caps and paraded with humiliating insignia around their necks. Our sources, necessarily, were secondhand. But in retrospect, judging from the more detailed scholarly studies of the Cultural Revolution phenomenon that have been made since, what we reported at the time turned out to be what actually happened.

In the case of *Newsweek*, the reason we failed to make any major mistakes can largely be attributed to Sydney Liu, *Newsweek*'s Hong Kong-based correspondent, himself a former Shanghai journalist with an encyclopedic knowledge of China and a cold, detached passion for factual accuracy.

The weapons at our disposal were not all negligible. There were detailed, almost China-wide, monitored newscasts of all radio programs, issued regularly by the huge United States Consulate General in Hong Kong. There were large numbers of academics, some of them doubtless CIA-funded, making detailed studies of whatever Chinese newsprint came their way. There was a brisk trade in smuggled tracts and some of the smaller posters, and there was our own monitoring of the radio. Finally, there were our own local sources: Chinese refugees, local Chinese journalists known for their links with Peking, and occasional visitors passing to and fro.

I remember, with Sydney Liu, listening to a dramatic speech by Lin Piao at the peak of the Cultural Revolution in October 1966, with Sydney commenting on his unmistakable Fukien accent. Lin Piao, later to be killed 'in an air crash' allegedly while attempting to flee to the Soviet Union with his family in 1971, had emerged as Mao's heir apparent, and in his October speech he praised Mao with such fulsomeness that it sounded, even as Sydney translated it to me as it went along, almost deliberately caricatural. Tuning in to another wavelength on our powerful set, we also heard, on one occasion, clear evidence of the turmoil engendered by the teenaged Red Guards who were converging on Peking and other main towns in the millions. In the middle of a program of revolutionary martial music, a speaker suddenly came on the air to say shrilly, 'Everyone must stay where he is. Nobody must use the trains any more without express permission. Nobody is to take the train to Peking for the time being.'

This is not the place to write about the Cultural Revolution in detail, but in retrospect, the mass movement of millions of Red Guards responding to Mao's direct appeal to them, over the heads of the party bureaucracy, was a masterstroke. Who, in closely regimented China, would pass up the opportunity for such an adventure, for a break in the drab monotony of a routine punctuated with indoctrination sessions and constant repetition by rote of Mao's thought? For those millions of Chinese, now in their late twenties, who took part in the Cultural Revolution, the giddy months of 1966-67 must have been the highpoint of their lives, especially since, with their usefulness over, they were compulsorily sent back to the countryside and banned from the big cities for all time.

The flow of refugees into Hong Kong and Macao accelerated during the Cultural Revolution, partly because pressures on China's last remaining individual non-conformists became intolerable and partly because the very chaos engendered by the 'cultrev' made frontier surveillance less efficient. Most of them told depressingly similar stories of regimentation and general tedium on collective communal farms in the Kwangtung area, nearest Hong Kong. Very occasionally, however, the pattern of refugees strayed from its normal, Kwangtung-peasant variety. Thus, in autumn 1966, a Jesuit priest, Father Ruiz, who ran a Catholic organization to help the destitute in Macao, called the Casa Ricci, and with whom I regularly corresponded, alerted me to the arrival of a singularly motley refugee crew; they consisted of a talented woman painter, the former first violin of the (temporarily defunct) Canton Symphony orchestra, an itinerant vendor of patent

236

medicines, and a minor Cantonese black marketeer.

From individuals such as these, one got not only the flavor of the Cultural Revolution, with its attendant capricious and perhaps understandably childish cruelties, but also an unrivaled insight into the life of a big city like Canton. (Sydney Liu and I later wrote a book about the group's adventures.) From some French and Irish nuns expelled from China and dumped on the Hong Kong side of the frontier after one of their number had died as a result of treatment at the hands of the Red Guards, I also put together a story on the new intolerance prevalent in China, for the nuns, who had stayed peacefully in China throughout the postrevolutionary period, had never proselytized and were engaged solely in hospital work.

Some of the arrivals from across the Lo Wu border, the railway station partly in Hong Kong territory, partly in China itself, were less talkative. I patrolled the station at intervals to talk to likely arrivals, and one day I singled out a tall, burly, well-dressed Westerner whom I took to be a businessman. Since few businessmen were being allowed in, I thought he might have something interesting to say and asked him for his impressions of China. 'I am not in the habit of speaking to the bourgeois imperialist press,' he replied in an unmistakable Australian accent. I had tried to interview the head of the tiny Australian pro-Chinese 'Marxist-Leninist' Communist party.

Other visitors—though less ideologically committed—were equally reluctant to talk to the press, lest this jeopardize their future commercial standing with the Chinese. An old friend of mine, living in Paris, made regular trips to China for an import-export firm and continued doing so throughout the Cultural Revolution. He persistently fobbed off all my requests to describe what life had been like in Shanghai, at the moment of the 'proletarian' takeover there, with: 'I never left my hotel room.'

A party of West German tourists, however, was less

inhibited. From them, including a highly reliable, observant, and surprisingly balanced university professor, we got the first account of large-scale violence and fighting in Canton—a feature of the Cultural Revolution in its later stages, with rival Red Guard factions fighting each other in streets and factories and with more moderate factory workers resisting Red Guard takeovers with homemade (and in some cases factory-made) weapons. The Germans had seen corpses strung up in Canton streets, and though such allegations were queried at the time, later corroborating accounts showed the reports were indeed correct. These were former labor camp and prison detainees, released or escaped from jail during the convulsions, who had indulged in an orgy of looting until rounded up and summarily executed. It was violence of this kind, combined with an almost total breakdown in communications and an alarming drop in industrial and agricultural production, which eventually compelled Mao to give in to army pressure and call off his Red Guards. Again, news of this virtual army takeover came first of all from Hong Kong-based China watchers and was treated with suspicion—but ultimately proved correct.

Understandably, the international business community in Hong Kong eyed events in China with considerable anxiety. But it was in Macao that the impact was to be immediate and irrevocable. Here a minor labor dispute between Chinese laborers and Portuguese authorities escalated, almost overnight, into a mini-Cultural Revolution inside Macao itself. Chinese naval gunboats cruised up and down the harbor, the crews waving Mao's little red book of quotations, by now an indispensable part of any true revolutionary's gear.

I made the mistake of trying to photograph the Chinese boat and was immediately set upon by an angry crowd, kicked, and frog-marched to an improvised Red Guard headquarters, incongruously set up in Macao's Chamber of Commerce. Here I feared the worst, but managed to convey to one of the revolutionaries present a request that he phone Phei Yi Ming in Hong Kong to confirm that I was a bona fide journalist, not a spy.

Phei Yi Ming, editor of the leading Communist newspaper in Hong Kong, was certainly as bourgeois as any of the fat cat party leaders then so heavily criticized in Peking. He was also a former stringer for a group of French papers in Shanghai and sentimentally pro-French. As a result, he was invariably consulted by visiting French correspondents, and I had had several enjoyable meals with him. His counsels must have prevailed, for I was released but told to leave by the first available hydrofoil.

Poor Phei Yi Ming. To closer friends, he expressed considerable fears that the new revolutionary ways in China might indeed lead to a premature takeover by China of Hong Kong and the end of his own luxurious life-style, to say nothing of all the attendant difficulties of assimilating a population of more than 4 million people in what was, and still is, the most aggressively free-enterprise, capitalist enclave in the world. Was it to placate the new power holders in Peking that—in July 1967—the Hong Kong Communists attempted to stage their own Cultural Revolution? For a giddy three weeks the normally industrious colony was the theater of strikes, marches, and violence. An aggressively anti-Communist radio commentator was killed by a youthful gang. Hong Kong real-estate values plummeted. Visiting tourists, suddenly and without warning confined to their hotel rooms in an unprecedented curfew, were unable to indulge in their ritual shopping sprees.

The focal point of protest rapidly became the mansion of Hong Kong's governor-general. For several days columns of marching people, mostly in their teens and early twenties, angrily waved the little red book and shouted slogans, imperturbably watched by police and diminutive Gurkha troops. Perhaps an illustration of the very class and income discrepancies prevalent in Hong Kong came with

239

Phei Yi Ming's own participation in the protests. Instead of marching anonymously with the crowds, he arrived in a spanking new chauffeur-driven Mercedes limousine, stood waving the *Little Red Book* and shouting for a few minutes outside the mansion gates, then sedately got back into his car, which refused to start. Humiliated, he sat as erect as his small size would permit, while I watched humbler demonstrators push it downhill.

Intolerance and downright falsehood are, alas, the almost inescapable concomitants of *engagé* journalism, and Hong Kong's aggressively anti-Communist press was no exception. Covering the riots, for *Panorama*, the well-known BBC news program, was a BBC crew headed by Jim Mossman, undoubtedly the most gifted TV journalist of his or any generation. His cameraman, Ernie Christie, a tough, no-nonsense South African, was filming in the middle of a demonstrating mob outside the governor's mansion when a frail, bespectacled Chinese youth tried to get in his way, holding his hand over the camera lens. Christie, without even bothering to stop filming, swung with his free hand, administering a sharp rabbit punch. The young demonstrator keeled over, losing his glasses. The following day the tabloid Hong Kong *Star* banner-headlined the news: 'BBC TEAM ASSAULTED.'

Whether the Chinese authorities or the precarious and shifting power structure then attempting to control events in China really welcomed the Hong Kong riots as evidence of the universality of the Cultural Revolution phenomenon is in doubt. There seemed to be a strange discrepancy between the cult of violent oratory and action. From the start of the Cultural Revolution, the New China News Agency had constantly referred to the Paris Commune uprising of 1870-71 as a historic example, paralleling the uprising of the Chinese masses. Yet when the Hong Kong Communists decided to act, the Peking authorities became nonplussed. Indeed, the Hong Kong riots ended as abruptly as they had begun, and those who had spearheaded the Hong Kong and Macao 'revolutions' quickly faded into obscurity, if not disgrace. Eventually, the fat cats and the old-timers within the party bureaucracy reestablished control. And the extent to which the wheel came full circle can be gauged from the fact that when the left-wing revolutionary Portuguese officers, after seizing power in Lisbon in 1974, privately expressed the intention of handing Macao back to China, the authorities in Peking were less than delighted. In time-honored parlance, information was conveyed to them that such action would 'not be convenient.'

It has always been a subject of some wonder to me that the Chinese, among the most intelligent people on earth, periodically find it necessary to indulge in the political convulsions of a Cultural Revolution. I could not help reminding a friend of mine, now a correspondent in Europe for the New China News Agency, of this.

The NCNA's news out of Europe, for the entire period of the Cultural Revolution, had been entirely tailored to encourage Mao to believe that his personality cult extended not only to China but to the rest of the world as well. I reminded my friend of an NCNA story I had read on the NCNA wires, in Hong Kong, in 1966. 'Chinese taxi drivers in Lyons, France, love Chairman Mao,' the title had read. How, I asked him, had an NCNA correspondent come up with such a tale? Who were the Chinese taxi drivers in Lyons? My Chinese friend shook his head. 'Very bad story,' he said, adding, softly, 'very bad period.'

241

IX. VIETNAM

In 1967 I at last became one of the several thousand reporters who, at one stage or another of the ill-fated war, became accredited to the South Vietnamese government and to MACV (Military Assistance Command, Vietnam). I was to remain in Vietnam, never a permanent correspondent for more than several months at a time, sometimes returning more than once a year, between 1968 and 1971. In between those years the war went through many stages: escalation of the war and euphoria, at least among Pentagon staff officers, from 1967 until the Tet offensive of January 1968; an increasing awareness of the resilience of the North Vietnamese, despite the bombing and the invasion of Cambodia; then the long-awaited Laos offensive, which should have warned the United States that, left to their devices, the South Vietnamese armies were unable to sustain the might of Hanoi's tough, disciplined, highly motivated troops; finally, the charade of the conclusion of the Paris peace talks, with the 'phony peace,' which, we all knew, was simply a prelude to the North Vietnamese invasion.

Such was the turnover of correspondents in Vietnam that the inexperienced reporter who came into contact with fighting for the first time was a veteran six months later, and most reporters—there were, of course, exceptions—seldom stayed for more than two years. Several generations of correspondents succeeded themselves during my Vietnamese period. For most of the war, any ambitious journalist needed to put in a Vietnam stint simply to be able to say that he had done so.

My motives were perhaps slightly different. True, I very much wanted to report the war at first hand, mainly because I craved to see for myself if it was really as awful and as hopeless as had been described. And I was tired of sitting back in Hong Kong writing about China, while most of my friends were off in Vietnam. Missing out on a war, for a reporter, is like missing out on an invitation to a particularly coveted party. And while I go along with John le Carré's explanation (in *The Honourable Schoolboy*) of why some reporters compulsively risk their lives ('sometimes you do it to save face, other times you just do it because you haven't done your job unless you've scared yourself to death, other times again, you go in order to remind yourself that survival is a fluke. But mostly you go because the others go: for machismo; and because in order to belong you must share'), my motive, in seeing as much of the war as possible, was neither machismo nor a craving for camaraderie (though both elements entered into it) but a genuine curiosity about one of the most enormous aberrations of our time. I knew that the deployment of the huge American war machine, with all its unbelievable technological and bureaucratic ramifications, and in a context more 'colonial' than ever admitted, was a sight that would probably never be seen again in my lifetime, that this was equivalent to the spectacle of the last brontosaurus lumbering about in an increasingly hostile environment.

I don't think many of my fellow reporters perceived the war quite like that, not at least at first. Mostly they were far younger, brasher, preoccupied by the 'hometown' facets of the American involvement, not overinterested in setting the war in its wider context, interested above all, in what, in the argot of the time, was called the 'bang bang,' though 'bang bang,' of course, had another, crudely sexual kind of connotation, too. Until dissent in the United States and the obvious impossibility of winning brought disillusion in its

243

wake, many reporters were latter-day Ernie Pyles, somewhat sentimentally chronicling the lives and multiple tiny dramas within fighting units and almost entirely neglecting the bigger picture. There were exceptions, of course: François Sully, of *Newsweek* (killed in a helicopter crash in 1971), had unrivaled knowledge of the local Vietnamese political scene and of the real—as opposed to the formal—shifts in the power-holding Vietnamese military and civilian Establishment. Gloria Emerson gave Vietnam reporting a new dimension by focusing, as few reporters had done before her, on the disastrous impact of the war on the suffering Vietnamese people, just as, many years later, she wrote, in *Winners and Losers*, one of the most searching reports on those Americans physically, mentally, and psychologically maimed for all time as a result of their Vietnam involvement.

But perhaps it was a little-known underground forces newspaper, *Overseas Weekly*, which, during the years of America's involvement in Vietnam, best conveyed the real, as opposed to the official, picture of the war as it affected American GIs. *Overseas Weekly*, a complete collection of which should be essential data for anyone attempting to chronicle this period of American history, was a true underground tabloid which told of the seamy side of service life in Vietnam: the courtmartials, the fragging of officers, the drug cases—and the occasional race riots. It's a measure of the freedom granted to reporters in Vietnam that *Overseas Weekly* existed at all or was allowed on sale anywhere in Vietnam.

Most reporters, especially at the time I began reporting there in 1967, thought strictly in cliché terms: The Vietnamese generals and the civilian power holders were corrupt, unwilling to fight; the soldiers in the field stole chickens, ran their vehicles into the ground as a result of faulty maintenance, and geared all their activities to eventual survival. Few of us stopped to consider the reasons for such behavior. When I came to discover the abysmally low scale of pay of all officers and men in ARVN (Army of the Republic of Vietnam), I marveled that any individuals could be found to fight at all, especially since the level of pensions for widows and disabled wounded veterans was unbelievably low, too, and the bureaucracy so ill-managed that claims often remained unanswered for years. Similarly, corruption, so loudly decried in the case of province chiefs, was seen by most reporters in the context not of Vietnam, but of current Western political normality. In retrospect, of course, Watergate and its aftermath should make Americans a little less inclined to see all South Vietnamese as villains or, at least, lead to some new compassion. In most cases in Vietnam, corruption and theft were the result of a fundamental survival instinct—not, as nearly always the case in recent United States scandals, the result of efforts to manipulate individuals and to shore up funds to pay for expensive election campaigns. And the reporters who stigmatized the corruption of the South Vietnamese were, most of them, not averse themselves to contributing to the overall corruption by changing their dollars on the black market at a more favorable piaster rate.

There was thus little attempt among most reporters in Vietnam to understand the pressures under which many province chiefs and other officials labored. With inadequate budgets and salaries and with constant demands for handouts coming in from all sides, there was an irresistible urge on their parts to acquire funds in any possible form, for both private and public use, even if this meant padding the roll of the part-time militia forces or siphoning off proceeds from brothels and massage parlors on American bases. Unscrupulous South Vietnamese officials diverted the totality of such funds to their own use. Most spread at least some of it around them.

Similarly, in the darkest days of the Sukarno maladministration, Indonesian museum curators had, some of them, sold off part of their surplus stock of treasures to private collectors, not necessarily for personal gain but to pay their staffs and repair rotting museum buildings—and I never came across an enthusiastic Western collector of Chinese porcelain who refused such deals.

This is not to say that greed played no part in the corrupt practices of wartime Vietnam. One had only to sun oneself around the pool of Saigon's Cercle Sportif or fly from Saigon to Paris in an ·Air France plane packed with the student sons of affluent Vietnamese families, able to avoid the draft (Air France ran a Friday-night special which made a stopover in Nice, where many rich Vietnamese had second homes), to realize that South Vietnamese society was corrupt, class-ridden, and profoundly unjust. But in similar circumstances, how would their American counterparts have reacted? It's arguable that it was only when the sons of affluent American families, hitherto protected by generous deferment terms, became liable for the draft—and Vietnam—that the U.S. Establishment's hostility to the war became irrevocable. For most of my own involvement in the war, fighting infantry and marine units were 50 percent black, Chicano, or Puerto Rican—so much so that the U.S. Army regularly flew those who had acquired American nationality through the necessary terms of military service to the Philippines for oath-taking naturalization ceremonies there—because of a certain reluctance to have such ceremonies carried out on Vietnamese soil!

Many of the appalling features of the Vietnam War could be traced not only to American inexperience and unfamiliarity with the East but also to the short-term assignments of all concerned (except those volunteers who decided to prolong their one-year Vietnam stays). It was fashionable, throughout the Vietnam War, for U.S. generals and senior officials to deride the French for their humiliating Indochina defeat—conveniently forgetting that a French expeditionary force, never more than 250,000 strong, with mostly out-of-date equipment and only a handful of helicopters, had tried to control an area comprising not only South Vietnam but North Vietnam, Cambodia, and Laos as well.

U.S. war gadgetry took many forms; starlight scopes, telescopic rifle sights enabling GIs to find their targets in the dark, have since become standard equipment in armies the world over. Others were less successful. 'People sniffers,' detecting concentrations of enemy troops through unusually high heat radiation, had the drawback of reacting indiscriminately to herds of animals. But 'Puff-the-magic-dragon' was terrifying: from helicopters, sharp steel pellets covering a target area the size of a football field could obliterate enemy concentrations in a single, lethal blast. Sophisticated listening and detection devices were supposed to give advance warning of infiltrating columns but somehow failed to indicate the scope of the Tet 1968 attack. Finally, a huge computerized and supposedly foolproof data system was set up at the instigation of Defense Secretary Robert McNamara to enable the U.S. administration to monitor 'pacification' progress.

It was hardly a coincidence that the system was erected into a dogma under McNamara, who had been in charge of the Ford Motor Company, for it was indeed a perfect system for monitoring the sales and overall productivity of a huge manufacturing company. Its usefulness in subversive warfare was, however, questionable and was a touching, tragicomic example of a fundamental tenet of American faith: that industrial technology, in all its forms, remains applicable to any given situation, including war, with scarcely any amendments.

The scheme was essentially simple. Every week, all over Vietnam, American advisers filled out a precise questionnaire which, when fed into a computer, gave an overall picture reflecting the relative strengths of the South Vietnamese administration and the Vietcong.

But surely, skeptical reporters asked at the time, there

must be a natural tendency on the part of those filling out the questionnaire to 'look good' or at least, in a bad situation, to report progress—even if in reality none occurred? Not so, replied the data specialists, for the questionnaire was laced with so-called control questions, which made any attempt to tamper with the facts impossible. These control questions took several forms: 'Do you travel alone in your area at night, or with an escort?' . . . 'Are you habitually armed during the day?' . . . 'Do you sleep in villages? In fortified compounds?' And so on.

Perhaps, under the West Point honor system, such a compilation would have worked. Alas, as all reporters traveling outside Saigon knew, there was indeed a natural tendency on the part of those providing computerized data to paint a rosy picture of so-called pacification. A story circulating among reporters in 1968 was that using the formidable data available to it, the Pentagon had asked the omniscient computer, 'When will the war be won?' And the computer had replied, 'In 1967.' The elementary caveat—that a computer is only as reliable as the facts fed into it—seemed to be ignored by the White House, the Pentagon, the U.S. Embassy in Saigon, and MACV (Military Assistance Command, Vietnam) headquarters. Only the CIA, with its somewhat more sophisticated alternative sources of information, was more realistically inclined, but even CIA staffers at times grossly underestimated the Vietcong and North Vietnamese potential. A mere six weeks before the 1968 Tet offensive, I remember talking to Robert Komer, then head of all CIA operations in Vietnam. 'Ed,' he told me, 'our information is that they [the Vietcong] can't put more than a company-sized unit into the field anywhere in South Vietnam.' Pentagon-accredited reporters naturally tended to side with Army opinion rather than that of their own reporters in the field. Such arguments, often bitter ones, sometimes spilled over into charges and countercharges of irresponsible reporting and had led, in 1963, to the abrupt resignation of *Time*'s Hong Kong bureau chief, Charles Mohr, whose Saigon dispatches had been questioned back in New York, largely through intense Pentagon lobbying. We were not immune from such internal strife at *Newsweek*, but our editors preferred, when in doubt, to run contradictory stories, emphasizing that a difference of opinion within its own staff existed. From 1967 onward the assessment of the Vietnam situation by its reporters on the spot and the dissenting opinion of its Pentagon-accredited correspondent in Washington were a feature of almost any major story on the Vietnam War.

Returning regularly to Vietnam between 1967 and 1971, I found it frightening to witness the degree of steady deterioration in American military morale. In the beginning the soldiers of 'Big Red One,' the 1st U.S. Infantry Division, with whom I frequently went on operations, were disciplined, gung-ho troops. As time went on, racial tensions grew, there was increased talk of fraggings, and by 1971 some of the units of Big Red One were in a permanent semimutinous state. The drop in morale was brought home to me at the time of the visit to Vietnam of Spiro Agnew, then Nixon's Vice President in the pre-Watergate days. I had spent the day with a unit of Big Red One in the jungles some forty miles north of Saigon without realizing that this was the unit that MACV HQ had decreed that Agnew should visit. I blended discreetly into the background because I was fascinated to discover how such visits were prepared, and I knew that on this particular helicopter whistle-stop tour no reporters would be along. A small group of Secret Service men, highly conspicuous in their wrinkled wash-and-wear suits, arrived at the firebase where I was. They stood talking to each other in low voices. I eavesdropped inconspicuously; in uniform, there was nothing to distinguish me from the rest of the troops there. It was instructive to learn that the Secret Service men were worrying not about the possibility of a Vietcong attack, which was negligible, but about the possibility that a disgruntled GI might use his weapon to shoot the Veep. That same week I attended one of the much-publicized Bob Hope shows specially laid on for the troops—in this case, all available off-duty soldiers of Big Red One. For the first time in Bob Hope's experience, some of his jokes fell flat—and there were catcalls and some booing, admittedly covered by the applause of the majority of the audience.

The biggest change in the Army's behavior from 1967 to 1971 centered on drugs. From the start of the U.S. involvement in Vietnam, GIs had been enthusiastic consumers of hashish, and Vietnamese had soon found that the sale of local marijuana was a rewarding occupation. By 1967 a pall of fragrant marijuana fumes hung like an invisible cloud over practically every American firebase and bunker in South Vietnam, with nearly all officers and NCOs turning a blind eye. Enterprising Vietnamese set up their own cottage industries, with ready-rolled marijuana cigarettes, indistinguishable in their cylindrical perfection from commercial brands, sold in small transparent plastic packs.

Presumably on Pentagon advice, local U.S. Army commanders began issuing stern warnings against the smoking of marijuana, cautioning against its dangerous side effects. Had the Army confined itself to pointing out, as it did, that 'hash' interfered with the fighting GI's reflexes and thus made him less alert and more vulnerable, it would have been on safe ground—and some army posters did, of course, emphasize this fact.

But the GIs continued to smoke, waited in vain for the dreaded side effects to materialize, and smoked some more, gradually coming to the conclusion that here as in so many facets of their Army-dominated lives, the authorities were lying to them. So, when heroin began making an appearance, and the Army reiterated its earlier warnings, only in stronger terms, the general reaction on the part of

250

most GIs was one of disbelief.

Opium, the only drug consumed on a large scale by the Vietnamese themselves, was never a favorite with the GIs, because it required a relatively complicated apparatus: pipes, a lamp, and time to coax the opium into a hot, bubbling, gluey pellet. But many reporters, especially the French contingent, smoked opium regularly, in a variety of opium dens whose addresses were passed on from one visiting batch of reporters to the next.

The most famous was a small, respectable-looking house in the center of Saigon, within easy walking distance of the Caravelle and Continental hotels. Its owner had been opium purveyer to all the major figures of the French Indochina Establishment, including General Raoul Salan (whose nickname, *le Mandarín*, had nothing to do with his physical appearance), and he had an endless fund of stories about them all. His place was virtually risk-free, since many high South Vietnamese officials, including a chief of police, used to visit it regularly. Never was a so-called vice den so innocent in appearance. On the ground floor, past the kitchen, the owner's two little granddaughters could be seen in the evenings, doing their homework and poring over selected French prose of Lamartine or Jean-Jacques Rousseau; the actual smoking occurred in a small, sparsely furnished upstairs room, with endless cups of weak green tea at one's elbow.

But the GIs sought not this leisurely relief from tension but something far more drastic. Outside army bases, in small booths in slum streets, and even in bars, plastic envelopes full of heroin, looking like harmless white powder, began changing hands. The drug came from Hong Kong, Laos, or Thailand, and with millions of items pouring into Vietnam's major ports and airfields every year, smuggling heroin was not difficult, especially since major dealers could afford to be generous with couriers. Why else would a career U.S. Air Force officer, who occasionally flew General William Westmoreland's successor, General Creighton Abrams, to and from Thailand (where the general's wife lived), have agreed to put his career on the line and carry heroin along with the VIPs in his air force plane? He was found out and court-martialed and sentenced to a long term in Leavenworth, but the heroin continued coming in ever-increasing quantities—and dirt cheap.

In February-March 1971, when U.S. forces in Vietnam provided support for the South Vietnamese forces invading Laos to attempt to smash the Ho Chi Minh trail, Khe Sanh, which had been under siege during the 1968 Tet offensive, was reactivated as the main base for the Laos operation, only a few miles away. It was an uneasy time for Army-press relations, but reporters managed to get into Khe Sanh at will, and I had devised a hitchhiker's board to wave to helicopter pilots and hitch rides. On one side were the words 'Are you going to Khe Sanh?' and on the other 'Are you going to Quang Tri?' (where the press camp was located). The pilots would nod, and one would clamber aboard. It was the only way to get around, and the noise from the helicopters was such that talk was impossible.

In Khe Sanh, during this period, I visited a South Vietnamese Army battalion holding part of the perimeter, and since drugs were very much on my mind (I was preparing to write about the GIs' drug involvement), I determined to test matters personally. Rumor had it that the South Vietnamese troops were purveyors of heroin, and I wandered into the South Vietnamese unit's perimeter and, in French, asked a sergeant for some. He summoned another soldier, and soon I had in my hand a plastic envelope with minute quantities of white powder in it. '*C'est de la bonne qualité, au moins*?' I asked. And to try to show some expertise, I added, '*Pas trop de lactose*?'—the powdered milk with which heroin was habitually cut. The sergeant grinned, showing a formidable expanse of gold teeth. '*Lactose cher, héroïne pas cher,*' he said.

That same day, I came across a GI openly smoking

252

heroin through a rifle barrel. I decided on an on-the-spot inquiry. 'How do you feel?' I began somewhat cautiously.

'Terrible, I can't eat, I can't sleep, and I haven't had a shit for a week.'

'Then why do you do it?' I asked.

The soldier looked around us, at the expanse of red laterite dust covering everything, at the helicopters taking off and landing, and said, 'I do it to feel normal.'

During the same Laos operation I remember taking a trip over Laos in a Huey and watching the two side gunners lapse into a veritable heroin-induced coma. Afterward I managed to talk to the pilot. 'Your gunners are totally zonked out on heroin,' I told him.

'I know,' he said. 'That's the only way they can fly.'

There was no doubt in my own mind that the formidable ravages of heroin among the GIs in Vietnam were scarcely fortuitous and the result of more than just a left-handed form of human endeavor, to quote John Huston on crime. It seemed obvious to many observers of the Vietnamese war scene that the North Vietnamese had every reason to encourage the spread of the heroin habit. My own private suspicions went further: For an army with a second-to-none reputation for high health and sanitary standards, the U.S. forces in Vietnam were prone to veritable epidemics of hepatitis, which could not simply be explained in terms of drug addiction (for few GIs mainlined) or operational hazards (for most GIs ate well, except on actual operations, when they made do with C rations). To my mind, the habitual presence, in almost every army cookhouse and kitchen throughout Vietnam, of a sizable force of locally hired Vietnamese dishwashers and assistant cleaners explained why the hepatitis rate was so high. It was significant, for example, that units, like the Green Berets, which refused to admit within their perimeter any Vietnamese civilians of any kind had no such problems. It was even more significant that throughout the war no effort, it seemed to reporters, was really made on the part

253

of MACV headquarters to determine just how hepatitis and other illnesses were propagated.

Perhaps my suspicions, grounded in dim memories of the elementary security precautions taken by my Indian Army unit in Southeast Asia during and after the Second World War, were unfounded. In any event, with the exclusion of the attrition caused by VD cases (the percentage of such 'casualties' was never released), it always seemed to me that the overall health of GIs in Vietnam, including those in the field, was not what it should have been. Neither were standards of cleanliness what I had expected from the most technologically minded army in the world; on more than one occasion I found myself covered with lice after sleeping in U.S. Army blankets.

Prostitution was a subject either avoided by most reporters or written about in the most cliché-ridden terms. Most recurrent was the story about the dreaded 'Vietnam rose,' the supposedly intractable, penicillin-resistant form of gonorrhea. Most stories, it seemed to me, missed the point. To be sure, there were the sordid massage parlors and car-wash booths (where GIs could have their trucks hosed down by South Vietnamese soldiers while they themselves enjoyed a 'short time' with the soldiers' wives or girlfriends), and a major industry, at the peak of the Vietnam War years, was the setting up of 'girlie' bars, where GIs were compelled to buy round after round of 'Saigon tea' in the hope of going to bed with the hostesses of their choice. The real underlying situation, it seemed to me, was this: Not only were Vietnamese girls, brought up, most of them, in a strong family-oriented, puritanical tradition, naturally averse to mercenary sex (unlike the Thais or the Laotians, to whom it seemed to come naturally), but the average GI, too, was very different from the stereotyped version of the swashbuckling, libidinous soldier on the rampage.

Just as the American soldier in Vietnam seemed to have a limitless sentimental attachment for stray dogs that came his way and became adopted pets, so his craving for affection—far stronger than his simple sexual urge—meant that he was unable to indulge in the act of sex with Vietnamese prostitutes without at least pretending to himself that something more than sex was involved.

The 'girlie bar' system, combining the oddest feature of American and Oriental prostitution, also restricted the GI's potential promiscuity. For once he had selected a girl and been to bed with her, it was virtually impossible for him to go to bed with anyone else—at least in that particular bar. Solidarity among the Vietnamese girls was total, as was their strong sense of 'face.' He could, of course, go to other bars, but here again he knew that his choice, once made, was permanent. That many GIs sought companionship and human warmth rather than sexual release was clear from the daily ads in the two English-language Saigon papers, proposing long-standing relationships for the duration of a GI's stay in Vietnam.

Thus, prostitution in Vietnam seldom was the utterly soulless, totally venal, and casual transaction it remains, say, in Hamburg or Amsterdam and on the rue St.-Denis in Paris. On the part of the American soldier, the craving for affection 'humanized' the mercenary relationship. And once such a relationship had been established, the Vietnamese girl involved—who, of course, had similar relationships with large numbers of GIs simultaneously—displayed talents akin to those of the great courtesans of history in keeping her men sentimentally, as well as sexually, satisfied—and unaware of one another's existence. As an observer I witnessed scenes in such bars which would have afforded both Feydeau and Marivaux considerable delight. Needless to say, language difficulties limited communication, but at least communication was attempted. Thus, it was both pathetic and comic to hear teenaged Vietnamese girls, with steady black GI boyfriends, assuming a 'soul' accent and vocabulary and speaking English with an unmistakable black southern

255

drawl. Perhaps the best description of American sex in the
East comes in Paul Theroux's *Saint Jack*; with only slight
differences, the relationships he describes between GIs on
rest and recreation (R and R) in Singapore and local
Singapore prostitutes applies also to Vietnam itself—
though the R and R encounters were probably romanticized
by the GIs themselves.

Girlie bars abounded all over Saigon, but the highest
concentration was to be found on Tu Do (formerly the rue
Catinat), and here, every night, a strange ritual was
enacted. Curfew meant that the bars had to close by 11:00
P.M. Shortly before 11:00 a distant hum could be heard,
culminating in a roar and a rush of Honda motorcycles
circling the street like so many hornets. One minute the
girls in the bars were chatting up the soldiers and egging
them on to buy them glasses of 'Saigon tea.' At the sound of
the Hondas they would expertly gather up lipstick,
sunglasses, and other feminine paraphernalia into their
handbags, rush out onto the street, hop onto the pillions of
the Honda motorcycles piloted by their husbands,
boyfriends, or brothers, and disappear into the night, GIs
running out into the street after them with cries of 'Hey,
honey, where are you going?' For every bar in Saigon
contained a fairly high proportion of *allumeuses* who never
had an intention of doing anything but make the GI part
with his money without ever offering anything in return.
Theirs was a swift getaway, invariably leaving the bar
clientele nonplussed.

There were, of course, other establishments of a
somewhat different nature: dance halls with taxi girls, some
of them outrageously made up, others indescribably
attractive. The 'dates' a GI made with these young ladies
almost invariably ended up with his waiting fruitlessly
outside a rubbish dump or a dentist's office. And there
were disguised brothels, whose inmates wore white coats
like nurses.

There were also a few combination nightclubs and

discotheque-cum-brothels in Cholon, the Chinese twin town with Saigon, though the famous Grand Monde brothel of French Indochina times had since become an army base. From one of these, a distinguished reporter from one of the world's most prestigious newspapers emerged, shortly after the 1968 Tet offensive began, to find himself dodging bullets and black-pajama-clad Vietcong patrols. More dead than alive, he made it back to the Continental Hotel. 'I think,' he told me, 'I've just been laid in Cholon for the last time.'

Some of the Vietnamese bar girls were only a few years removed from childhood and a village upbringing. Many spent their not-inconsiderable gains on futile gadgets, and on eye and nose jobs; it was one of the grotesque paradoxes of Vietnam that a country so lacking in rural doctors had a plethora of plastic surgeons in Saigon itself. But for most of the girls, theirs was an occupation they hated and despised, for all the cunning they displayed in luring Americans to spend money on them, and they indulged in it only to support large families without any other means of subsistence. For all the corruptions and venal glitter of their occupation, many retained a startling beauty.

No recollection of this aspect of Saigon is complete without the inclusion of two stories, one possibly apocryphal, the other incontrovertibly true. The first was the subject of reporters' gossip from 1967 to the end of the American involvement in Vietnam and involved an American army captain (in some cases, the story went, a Green Beret officer) and a Vietnamese prostitute, who, perhaps as an act of revenge or resistance, severely bit him during fellatio. She was arrested. He was hospitalized and in due course awarded the Purple Heart.

The other centers on the small band of transvestite prostitutes who haunted the vicinity of the Continental Hotel in growing numbers in the closing stages of the Vietnam War. (Perhaps one day a sociologist will explain the undoubted correlation between a military collapse and the growth of transvestite prostitution, for this was a phenomenon, almost unknown until the end of American involvement in Vietnam, which immediately afterward assumed extraordinary proportions.) A French reporter acquaintance, who managed to stay on in Saigon for several weeks after the South Vietnamese surrender and Communist takeover, one day watched some North Vietnamese troops, the *bodoi*, rounding up a small group of such transvestites and assumed they were being taken to labor camps. Much to his surprise, they surfaced again, in their usual garb, a couple of days later. 'What happened?' he asked one of them.

'They were very sweet to us' came the reply. 'They didn't keep us very long. We explained that we had disguised ourselves as women as a patriotic duty—in order not to be called up in the puppet army and they let us go.'

For all the suspicions of our editors, who knew full well the range of temptations in Saigon, surprisingly few reporters spent much time in Tu Do bars. These, for old-time Saigon residents, simply faded into the background, just as the sleazy nightclubs and soliciting streetwalkers in Pigalle and strip joints in Soho became an accepted and ignored backcloth for residents there. Most of us were too busy, traveling.

For accreditation to MACV headquarters provided the ultimate in air travel. Space was routinely reserved for the press on the regular daily flights of transport planes from Saigon to the major cities within South Vietnam, and production of the card also ensured space on literally anything that flew in Vietnam, provided there was room. This meant that reporters covering the war were astonishingly mobile; one could leave the Continental Hotel at dawn, report to Tan Son Nhut air base, wait for a plane or helicopter, and find oneself in the middle of a fire fight by midmorning. With luck a plane could be found going one's way back to Saigon before nightfall. (Naturally enough, such arrangements ceased with the final pullout of

258

U.S. troops in 1973. From then onward reporters had to travel by road, by Air Vietnam, and by hitching the occasional ride on South Vietnamese helicopters and planes, and such trips became progressively more difficult and hazardous.)

Many operations were inconclusive, routine affairs, and these in retrospect seem to blend together in one long march through scrub and jungle, with all one's senses on the alert but one's expectations unfulfilled. Occasionally contact would lead to action, and on one or two occasions out of, say, thirty, one might find oneself in a full-scale battle. Two very different stories of operations in Vietnam stand out in my mind: the first a typical patrol with Big Red One, the second a full-scale battle with the 173rd Airborne Brigade at Dak To.

The patrol with an infantry battalion of Big Red One was quintessentially typical of search-and-destroy missions that misfired. A Huey helicopter deposited me within a small clearing in the jungle—the battalion's headquarters. Sometime later I was part of a patrol seeking out possible Vietcong hideouts in an area which was a regular infiltration route. On a previous patrol some VC bunkers and rice caches had been discovered, and these, it was believed, belonged to a 'main force' unit which was known to be operating in the area.

For an hour nothing happened, and our slow progress through the jungle looked as if it would be totally uneventful when a couple of shots rang out; the patrol's point man, or leading scout, had been hit, shot through the eye. From then on, for the next hour at least, a grisly game of hide-and-seek took place. Using the wounded man as a decoy, the Vietcong—skillfully concealed—waited until members of the patrol were close to him, about to treat his wound and carry him away, when they opened fire again.

What surprised me most about the patrol's predicament was that at no time did the patrol commander take the offensive, as British and Indian troops in the Southeast

Asian jungles had been taught to do during World War II, by moving to a flank and attempting to attack the enemy from the rear. Instead, the patrol remained where it had been when the first shots had been fired, and a great deal of ammunition was expended on those patches of the jungle whence the VC fire appeared to be coming. The situation was saved by a U.S. Army medevac Huey helicopter, which appeared above us and began lowering a sling on the end of a steel rope. For agonizing minutes the Huey helicopter hovered immobilely, taking fire from the Vietcong. The wounded man, still conscious and able to grasp the sling, was lifted upward, dangling in the air like a monkey on a string, as the helicopter flew upward and out of the fire zone, to land a few minutes later on the clearing I had myself alighted on earlier. The patrol returned to this base shortly afterward, without making further contact with the Vietcong snipers.

When we got back to the battalion HQ clearing, the medevac helicopter was still there—and unlikely to fly for some time. I counted eighteen bullet impacts in the fuselage, some of which had hit the sling lift. It was copiously leaking oil. From subsequent personal experience, I learned that it's often impossible, once inside a helicopter, to tell whether one is taking fire or not, and the helicopter crew looked at their damaged Huey with awe. They had been unaware, at the time, of the narrowness of their escape.

I then saw something of the extravagant multiplicity of means of the American war effort in Vietnam. Within minutes another medevac Huey came to take the wounded man away to a field hospital. Then a second Huey landed to take the crew of the original wrecked Huey back to their base. Finally, a day later, a 'flying crane' helicopter arrived on the scene and lifted the wrecked helicopter away, to the nearest repair shop. Meanwhile, during the night, B-52 bombers all the way from Guam came and bombed the jungle around the battalion's perimeter, making craters the size of tennis courts. I went on patrol again the following day on a fruitless search for more VC. We came across several of the fresh bomb craters. In one of them lay the only sure casualty of the bombing—a diminutive squirrel.

The other operation was considerably different and made front-page news all over the world. On a Sunday in November 1967 the second battalion of the 173rd Airborne was sweeping the area southwest of Dak To, within a few miles of both the Cambodian and Laotian borders, in search of enemy troops. This part of Vietnam was the southernmost point of the Ho Chi Minh Trail, down which Hanoi sent troops and war matériel, and the Laotian and Cambodian frontier areas had long been under North Vietnamese operational control. The terrain was rugged, with a number of surrounding hills. The battalion was carrying out a routine sweep up the flank of a hill called Hill 875 when it fell into an obviously well-prepared trap.

Just how many regular North Vietnamese troops ambushed the luckless battalion will probably never be known, but they had been there for some time. As survivors later told it, they were in well-concealed North Vietnamese bunkers, with snipers tied to trees and accurate, preplanned mortar fire brought to bear on the trapped American troops. In the first few minutes of the fighting, seventy-one Americans were killed and more than eighty seriously wounded.

This was but the beginning of one of the bloodiest encounters in the whole of the Vietnam War. A young Puerto Rican soldier, both legs shattered, continued manning a machine gun to cover the withdrawal of his platoon to a better defensive perimeter, until he was killed. The posthumous award of a Congressional Medal of Honor—though rumored in his division—never materialized: a good example of the gearing of such awards, for morale and propaganda purposes, to victories rather than stalemate encounters and defeats. The following morning eight medevac Huey helicopters attempting to airlift the wounded out of the besieged zone were shot down, and the battalion remained pinned down, with its dead and dying, for twenty-four hours, with the North Vietnamese keeping up their mortaring and their ground attacks. To compound the tragedy, an American F-100 fighter-bomber, one of many keeping the North Vietnamese at bay with dive-bombing attacks, missed its target, unloaded its bombs within the tiny U.S. perimeter, and killed more Americans, including many of the wounded already herded together for eventual evacuation and most of the medics.

Late Monday afternoon another battalion of the 173rd Airborne managed to fight its way up the hill to link up with the survivors of the shrinking perimeter, but the battle continued. By Tuesday afternoon the first helicopters were able to make risky landings on a tiny clearing within the perimeter, and the first wounded were evacuated to Dak To, along with the first olive-green body bags containing American corpses. Finally, a third battalion was brought in by helicopter to prepare for a full-scale assault on the hill.

Back in Saigon, little had filtered through of the real nature of the fighting, though François Sully, with his nose for bad news, felt that the guarded, obscure prose of the communiqués referring to the Dak To fighting concealed a major story, and on Thursday morning I flew to Dak To to see for myself.

Several reporters were already in the area, and from the large numbers of dead and wounded landed on the base it was clear that we were witnessing, at second hand, a major disaster. I shared a tent with Oriana Fallaci, the well-known Italian columnist and interviewer, and her photographer, a handsome Italian, who kept saying, 'I am not going on the hill.' Neither, to my knowledge, did Oriana Fallaci get there until the battle was over, though I later came across her description of the Hill 875 fighting which—to say the least—failed to make this clear.

All Thursday I had watched the medevac helicopters

come in and talked to some of the wounded, including a medical officer with a hideous hole in his back, caused by a mortar fragment, who described how, in one of the air strikes, all his medics had been killed. Cursed with a vivid imagination, I have always found—whether as a schoolboy waiting for a boxing match or, as then, on the verge of entering a bad war zone—that anticipation made for the most pernicious fear of all. So, still in darkness the following day, I quietly left the press tent and went in search of a helicopter to take me onto Hill 875, where at least I would have something concrete to worry about. Luck was with me. Without difficulty, I thumbed a ride on a supply helicopter which took me to the main fire support base from which supplies were being carried onto the hill itself. Orders had gone out that no reporters were allowed on the hill, but a young black corporal, noting the *Newsweek* flash on my army fatigues, motioned me over and said, 'You're from *Newsweek*? I read it every week. Hide in the bushes, and when the coast is clear, I'll put you on the first chopper going.'

Having made up my mind for me, the corporal was as good as his word, and a few minutes later I was sitting on a load of explosive satchel charges, grimly hanging on for dear life as the Huey swung upward and over the hill. A mere five minutes later, after skimming the treetops, we came down in a clearing at the base of the hill—not the properly prepared landing zone I was used to, but a rough hole in the jungle, originally caused by extensive mortar fire. Nor did we really land. With inches to spare, the helicopter hovered between the trees a few feet from the ground, I jumped out, and the helicopter crew started gingerly tossing the satchel charges to troops below. I had arrived on Hill 875 and immediately felt better.

From then onward, for the rest of Thursday, which happened to be Thanksgiving Day (November 22, 1967), I have total recall. First, as I scrambled from one bunker to the next, trying to reconstruct the overall story of what

263

actually had happened since the beginning of the ambush, my concern became entirely practical: how to keep my notes together, and legible, and how to avoid shedding helmet, pack, and gas mask, which a burly black sergeant insisted that I carry, in case gas was used later on. There was an intermittent thud of incoming mortar shells, but at first this did not worry me. In my haste to accumulate, in the shortest space of time possible, all the relevant sights and sounds of Hill 875, I had assumed that the noise was 'friendly,' and indeed, it was partly concealed by the now-continuous screaming jet attacks of U.S. planes around us. A black sergeant commanded what was left of one of the companies. Many of the troops had dressings, some of them days old, on wounds which normally would have required evacuation.

From the different companies, I pieced together the horrendous total casualty figures. The original survivors of the initial ambush had the hunted, shell-shocked look I had seen so far only in World War II pictures of marines at Iwo Jima and in war movies.

As I arrived, a company was preparing for a final assault on the hill, on which, in well-concealed bunkers, a small group of kamikaze North Vietnamese were still entrenched. 'We're going up that hill. We're gonna get ourselves Hill Eight Seven Five for Thanksgiving Day. Ain't that nice?'

The voice was that of the black sergeant I had talked to immediately on landing and in whose bunker I had spent some time. 'You goin' up?' he asked. I nodded.

The first wave of troops emerged from bunkers and moved up the hill. There was a good deal of cursing and swearing, and one trooper took a vicious swipe at another who was hanging back. I followed at a distance of about twenty yards, picking out the biggest, burliest trooper I could find. But as the line of troops started moving up the hill, the North Vietnamese, from their relatively safe position at least a mile away, started bringing down a rain of mortar fire, regardless of the now-continuous, deafening air strikes on all sides of the hill. There was an explosion ahead of me, and I knew the man I had chosen to hide behind had been killed. Moving at a slightly different angle up the hill, I picked out another advancing rifleman. He too was killed a few minutes later. I suddenly felt very much alone. As I had moved up the hill, it had become a blackened, charred mess, like old World War I pictures of Verdun. The soil was greenish black; trees were twisted and burned black; there were pitted holes everywhere and the remnants of bombed-out bunkers. Unarmed, I now felt intensely vulnerable and dived into a hole. Inside were the corpses of two soldiers, whether North Vietnamese or American I never knew, for I dared not look too closely. Popping up at intervals to follow the progress of the assault, I noted one of the more gruesome sights of the hill: Not all bodies had been recovered during the fighting so far, and many had been blown apart in later air and mortar attacks. I was staring at a greenish grayish hunk of flesh, with bits of cloth attached. From its shape it was either, I decided, a North Vietnamese buttock or perhaps an American shoulder. All around, my bunker was littered with equally grisly, indistinguishable bits of corpses.

Meanwhile, the American assault on the crest of the hill was continuing, and I heard raucous cries, then watched a swirl of red and black smoke from a flamethrower. Gradually the noise abated, and the wounded started coming down the slope. One man carried past me on a stretcher—probably a Chicano or Puerto Rican—was naked from the waist down, though not visibly wounded. He didn't answer when I spoke to him. A shell-shock case, he was stone deaf and simply stared into space. Other stretchers were being carried down, with dead and wounded. Someone said, 'We've got the hill.' No one cheered.

In fiction and in films, once a battle is over, it's over. In real life, things are different. There had been too many

265

counterattacks in the last few days for the survivors to believe that this was the end. Frantically the men began digging in, setting up fresh defensive positions, and taking advantage of what might have been a mere temporary lull to regroup, set up a more adequate helicopter pad, and evacuate all the dead and wounded. An airborne captain, commanding what was left of the brigade, stood in the new clearing halfway up the hill, talking the first helicopters down. He had a huge bloody bandage across both buttocks but seemed unaware of it. An army doctor, who must have come in as a recent reinforcement, perhaps that very morning, appeared to be in shock himself. 'Sir, you've got to help him. He's hit bad,' a soldier kept shouting, motioning him up the hill to a stretcher. Gradually I became aware of more vestiges of the battle: charred helmets, boots, M 16s, but also bandages, first-aid kits, morphine.

Someone gave me a police dog to hold; it's handler had been killed. I turned to another soldier and said, 'Hold this.' My instinct was to get off the hill as soon as possible, to try to tell the story in time for that week's deadline. But the evacuation of the wounded came first. To help speed things up, I became, briefly, a stretcher-bearer helping carry the wounded to the new helicopter pad.

As the helicopters began their shuttle to Dak To, some of my colleagues started arriving. This made me more determined than ever to try to get back to Saigon, but the chances were dim. Luckily the bandaged captain came to my rescue, and with the last casualty, a black GI whom I had helped load aboard, I managed to stay aboard the medevac helicopter, on the pretext of keeping flies off his bloody dressing. Minutes later I was on the Dak To airstrip.

My recurring nightmare is never a simple one involving corpses, blood, and gore. It is, however, closely connected with my Vietnam experiences. I am alone, in the center of a huge concrete airfield, and it is absolutely imperative for me to get away. In a nightmarish setting, part Paul Nash,

266

part early Chirico, I spy a plane at the opposite end of my location and run toward it. There are men stepping aboard, and my chances look good. But the slow jog across the interminable airstrip, because I am weighed down with pack and cameras, is timed to make my venture a hopeless one. I run and run, and as I move imperceptibly forward, the C-130 slowly closes its rear jaws and taxis around in front of me. I scream and wave, jumping up and down to attract the pilot's attention. But the plane revs up and takes off, covering me in laterite red dust.

But for the time being my real-life nightmare involves a search for a plane back to Saigon after the battle of Dak To. Normally I should have gone to the air traffic control center and quietly waited my turn. Somehow I know that if I do this, I will never make it in time. So, relying on chance, I run from one plane to another and eventually find a C-130 about to take off. Miraculously it is indeed going to Saigon. Three hours later I am back in the Continental Hotel. I sit down and complete the longest, most detailed battle story I have ever written, then—about to cable it—try to phone New York. I eventually get through. 'There's no one here,' says the *Newsweek* operator. 'Don't you know it's Thanksgiving Day?'

X.   TET 1968

LONG AFTER the event I asked Ellsworth Bunker, United States ambassador in Saigon during the war years, how he had first become aware of the 1968 Tet offensive, that watershed in both the Vietnam War and American perceptions of it. It was over one of those intimate, yet lavish dinners in the embassy residence in Saigon, where small glasses of iced vodka were served throughout the meal, in addition to superb French wines. The ambassador was a white-haired mandarin whose great age inhibited neither his prowess as a tennis player nor his ardor as a husband, ordering up the embassy plane to fly on weekends to Nepal, where his wife was ambassador in her own right. He was also, despite his United Fruit background and his reputation as a cold warrior, a great raconteur and a humorist. 'If you really want to know,' he told me, 'the first thing I knew about Tet was when a fucking great big black MP sergeant burst into my bedroom in the middle of the night and said, 'Mr. Ambassador, we're going to get you the fuck out of here,' and hustled me away to safety in my pajamas in an armored car.'

As with the Kennedy assassination, all the cast of characters in Vietnam at the time of the 1968 Tet offensive can recall with exactitude where they were and how the event impinged upon them, on that famous dawn of January 30, 1968. The event was brought practically live to the consciousness of the American people through TV news film, notably NBC's. With the time gap between

Vietnam and America, film shot in Saigon at dawn on January 30, flown to Japan, developed in haste, and bounced off satellites, actually arrived in time for the early-morning *Today* show in New York that same day. And behind the event, as always in the case of drama of this magnitude, a host of stories, some funny, some tragic, some farcical, became, for me at least, almost as important and as significant as the main story itself—not least the misadventure of CBS, which got its films mixed up and, instead of transmitting by satellite its film of the Saigon attack on the dawn of the Tet offensive, sent by mistake another film about successful pacification, shot several days earlier.

Shortly before Tet there arrived in Saigon my old friend David Douglas Duncan, the prestigious *ex-Life* photographer, whose pictures of marines during the Korean War had made history. He was back to photograph the U.S. marines, in Vietnam this time, and he still had the old newshound's instinct. At *Newsweek* in Saigon, I had held a short staff conference to decide who should go where and how we should handle what, we knew, was likely to be an event-fraught Tet—though we hardly suspected the scale of these events. Since North Vietnamese and Vietcong strength was greatest in the north, I decided on the eve of Tet to fly to Da Nang, where the offensive looked as if it would be the roughest. David Douglas Duncan was also scheduled to fly to Da Nang to take pictures of the marines at the besieged base of Khe Sanh, and on the day before Tet François Sully drove both Duncan and myself to Tan Son Nhut airport, where we were due to catch the abysmally uncomfortable C-130 air force transport shuttle with undersized canvas strips in guise of seats.

On the way to the airport Sully, who had an almost telepathic awareness of impending crises in Vietnam, talked excitedly, as was his habit, his gloomy prognostications tempered by his manic cheerfulness at the prospect of a major story. 'It could happen right here,' he

269

said as we swung into the fortified airfield complex, having shown our credentials to two sets of vigilant U.S. and Vietnamese guards. 'At this very moment, the VC could be poised around Tan Son Nhut, waiting to seize it.'

'François, you're crazy!' I said. 'This is the most fortified and elaborately defended base in the whole of Vietnam.'

'But think of the propaganda value,' Sully said, 'if they seize the airfield and MACV headquarters, even briefly. It would be the end.'

In the plane, all the way to Da Nang, I brooded over what Sully had said. Little did we know that with consummate skill, meticulous planning, extraordinarily elaborate concealment, and the complicity of thousands of Vietnamese, VC and North Vietnamese teams had indeed infiltrated in dozens of places and were poised to strike, not only around Tan Son Nhut, but all over Saigon and Cholon, and all other major cities in Vietnam. In the semidarkness of the noisy plane, I looked in vain for David Douglas Duncan but assumed, as I did when I failed to spot him among the landing passengers, that such a VIP among correspondents was probably riding up front with the pilot and had been whisked away in a marine general's jeep on arrival.

The truth was otherwise. Deeply impressed by François Sully's predictions, David Douglas Duncan had, at the last minute, slipped out of the still-stationary C-130 as it waited to taxi off for Da Nang, and hitched a ride back to Saigon. He was, therefore, poised to take some epoch-making pictures when, around 3:00 or 4:00 P.M., the suicide squads of the VC began their attack on the U.S. Embassy, only a few hundred yards away from the Continental and Caravelle hotels.

But all through the previous day and night joyous Vietnamese had been loosing off every kind of firecracker, for Tet is their combined Christmas, New Year, Easter, and Guy Fawkes Day, and to the Vietnamese, firecrackers are as integral a part of the festivities as are Christmas trees and carol singing in the West. The noise, needless to say, closely resembled that of battle. So when the real shooting started outside the embassy, David Douglas Duncan assumed that these were simply tardy Tet revelers loosing off their last fireworks and went back to sleep.

My own perception of the start of the Tet offensive was almost equally farcical. The press camp in Da Nang, formerly Tourane, as the French had called it, was in the center of town but on the riverbank, overlooking a huge active harbor. On a nearby metal U.S.-built bridge, American sentries, relayed every few hours, took regular potshots at anything suspect in the water below, to guard against VC or North Vietnamese frogmen. The camp was crowded beyond belief, and there was no army cot for me, though I did finally succeed in requisitioning a stretcher from a sullen black marine.

In Da Nang the Tet offensive came not at dawn but earlier, and soon the night was lit up with huge intermittent flashes: artillery, flares, and streams of dot-dash tracers, penciled into the black sky.

In the initial confusion it was difficult to estimate either the scope of the attack, which seemed to be occurring very close by, in the town center itself, or its degree of success. Confusion and the sense of unreality were compounded by a late-night open-air movie being shown within the press camp as a regular feature for off-duty troops and press alike. The film was one of those gory epics featuring heroic GIs in combat in Europe during the Second World War, and the noise of real fighting blended with the film sound track's studio fire in a strange, unreal cacophony. Throughout the film GIs, American civilians, and women nurses came and went on the outdoor terrace and *ad hoc* open-air movie theater, where they sipped soft drinks and cans of beer and watched the film with relaxed boredom. Inside the press bar, a huge marine sergeant concentrated on making himself a perfect pair of fried eggs. Egg after egg he smashed against the pan in somewhat alcohol-induced

271

frenzy, and he threw away every broken yolk. I recalled the pinched faces of some of the children in the slums of Saigon and Da Nang and reflected that had an Eisenstein wished to convey the contrasts between 'imperialists' and Vietnamese, such a scene—intercut with slum scenes and close-ups of undernourished Vietnamese faces—would have seemed an unjustifiably exaggerated, below-the-belt propaganda sequence.

Tiring of the film and of the marine's waste of food (about a dozen eggs must have found their way into the trashcan) and despairing of getting any sense by phone out of harassed public information officers in various units, who knew no more of the details of the battles than the press did, I decided to try to get settled in. When I got into the press dormitory, a sordid barracks made even more unappetizing by the press corps' aversion to neatness or properly made beds, I decided to take a shower. As I began undressing, another marine NCO suddenly strode into the room. 'Red alert,' he screamed, 'everybody get a weapon.' Stifling an initial reflex to reply, 'You must be joking,' I reflected on what Evelyn Waugh, or his William Boot of *Scoop* fame, might have done in similar circumstances. My own military expertise, once considerable, was limited to Second World War toys: Bren guns, Lee-Enfields, Sten guns, weapons long since confined to museums or penniless Third World armed forces. I had shot pheasants in France and nilgai and blue bull in India with some success, astonishing an Indian friend—and my wife—by dropping a blue bull, at over 300 yards, with a 0·300 rifle devoid of telescopic sights. But I had never actually fired any of the weapons in use during the Vietnam War. As for grenades, an aversion to cricket meant that I had never mastered the art of lobbing and consequently had turned out to be a singular danger on live grenade-throwing exercises.

As a schoolboy Home Guard in the early stages of the war, when we were all half expecting a German invasion, a St. Paul's School classics master and much-decorated First

World War infantry officer, who had become the commander of our pathetic, motley school Home Guard unit, had once said, gently, after watching me lob a practice grenade, 'If you're ever called upon to engage the enemy at close quarters, may I suggest that you use an alternative weapon to a grenade if you wish to achieve even a small modicum of success?' Evelyn Waugh and William Boot, I decided, would have gone ahead with their shower and then poured themselves a stiff drink. I followed their putative example.

Dawn revealed that the red alert had indeed been a close one. Within 100 yards of the press-camp entrance, some forty black-pajamaed corpses lay, mown down in what had quite clearly been a suicide attack. Similar VC dead lay in the center of Da Nang. Gradually, from a none-too-clear phone call to my *Newsweek* bureau in Saigon, and tuning in to my portable radio, I realized that Sully's prophecies had indeed come true, and that all hell had broken loose everywhere.

'Come with me to Hue,' said Catherine Leroy, the diminutive French photographer whose battle fatigues could have come from a stylish Paris store specializing in children's uniforms. 'I'm leaving now, and we could have fun.' She said this seductively, like Charles Boyer saying, 'Come with me to the Casbah.' Catherine Leroy was one of my favorite people in Vietnam, and we had dined together frequently in some of Saigon's less American-influenced 'French' restaurants. She was going by helicopter to a support base and then on to Hue in an army convoy. 'Hue,' she went on, as though making an offer no one in his right mind could refuse, 'is in the hands of the North Vietnamese. It's the biggest battle of the whole war.' I was tempted to pack up and go. But what story could compete with the siege of the U.S. Embassy in Saigon itself? Tet was shaping up to be a cover story of historic dimensions, and as acting bureau chief, I explained, I had to get back to Saigon.

As I sat in the office of the chief public information officer in the press camp, trying to get a seat on any plane returning to Saigon, I witnessed the PIO's colonel's wrath as he discovered that Catherine and a few other hardy souls had actually left the press camp and were on their way to Hue. 'Jesus Christ, Major,' he said to his aide, life imitating art, or rather *M*A*S*H**, 'don't you realize that Hue's in enemy hands?' The incriminated major stood firm, firmly sheltering behind army routine.

'Well, the way I look at it, Colonel,' he said, 'in our book, that is, it says here that a trip to Hue rates as a cultural trip.'

(Catherine Leroy made it to Hue, all right, and got so close to the front that she was actually taken prisoner by North Vietnamese troops. With her inimitable charm and through a complete absence of fear, she not only talked the North Vietnamese into allowing her to take pictures but also got them to release her immediately afterward, to produce what was probably the most impressive photo scoop of the whole Vietnam War.)

Back in Tan Son Nhut, fighting was still going on on the outer perimeter of the airstrip, and there was evidence enough of a close shave. Within yards of our *Newsweek* villa, shooting was still going on. At first I berated the tense U.S. troops for what I assumed was a trigger-happy reflex—until suddenly a kamikaze VC soldier toppled, dead, out of a tree on our very street. The young owner of the Continental Hotel, abstract-painter-turned-hotelier Philippe Franchini, button-holed me in a corridor with undisguised, manic glee. 'Things must be bad,' he said. 'For the first time in my life someone has asked me for a room without windows!'

With almost all major Vietnamese towns under attack and a curfew enforced by trigger-happy 'white mice,' as Saigon's policemen were called, our reporting job was not easy. One veteran U.S. correspondent, famous throughout the Saigon press corps for having spent his long years in Vietnam entirely within the city limits, never once going out into the field, almost tearfully requested help at a briefing session. 'Joe,' said a senior USIA spokesman, 'you're on your own now.'

Because of the curfew, we ran the gauntlet of the police every time we went to the main post office to file—and the possibility of being on the receiving end of a burst of fire from panicky ARVN soldiers or policemen was more frightening than the remote prospect of running into VC suicide squads. In normal times we avoided the post office because it was a slower means of communication than Reuters, which usually handled our copy. But Reuters was saturated with a backlog of correspondents' stories, and though I deliberately and unashamedly kept the Reuters telex operators in food and beer from the Continental Hotel (they had been working around the clock, and some had had nothing to eat for twenty-four hours) to bribe them into taking our copy, we still had to await our turn. So filing from the post office was now our only resource.

On Tet plus one, I had returned to Saigon, and at intervals of touring Saigon and trying to find out what was happening, I took a huge silver-plated Hotel Continental tray piled with roast chicken and rice to the Reuters bungalow. How I lost the tray, and the *Newsweek* car it was in, makes an odd, grotesque story. General Loan, Saigon's police chief, had just distinguished himself by shooting in cold blood a bound VC suspect brought to him on a Saigon street. TV cameras and AP had recorded the scene, which, relayed around the world, immediately became a historic news picture and a symbol of not only Vietnamese brutality during Tet, but of American antiwar feeling as well. I had sent one of our Vietnamese assistants, whom I'll call Mr. Tran, on a tour of Saigon's hospitals to find out the number of civilian wounded admitted since Tet began. Tran begged for the use of François Sully's car, bought some months previously from a departing American diplomat. It still had yellow plates identifying it as a tax-exempt diplomat's vehicle, and while such a car, driven by a 'roundeye,' attracted little attention, General Loan's eye was quick to spot Mr. Tran, a Vietnamese, at the wheel. He immediately had him arrested.

'Worst day of my life,' said Mr. Tran later, with good reason. 'Worse even than yesterday.' And the day before had been bad enough. Mr. Tran, like most Vietnamese, had begun celebrating Tet by visiting his relatives in a Saigon suburb and had not realized anything was amiss until he came under fire from South Vietnamese policemen, defending their police post against a heavy VC attack. He lay behind a tree, wondering what to do next, when a small, terrified ARVN soldier huddled up against him, sobbing with fear. Mr Tran first tried to push him away, but the soldier clung to him. 'Save me, save me,' he kept saying. Mr. Tran waited until some of the firing had died down, then rose and took to his heels, as fast as he could, away from the fighting. The little soldier tagged on behind him.

'Go away,' said Mr. Tran, but the soldier kept following, like a mongrel dog. When he realized he was stuck with him in the now-shuttered, deserted suburb, Mr. Tran said, 'At least take off that uniform. You'll have us both shot.' The soldier stripped down to his underpants. Mr. Tran took the uniform, rolled it up into a bundle, and hurled it over a garden wall. Seconds later the bundle was flung back to him by an invisible hand.

Now Mr. Tran was explaining to General Loan, who ought by rights to have had more urgent things on his mind, how it was that he was driving a diplomat's car. He was locked up, nevertheless, and for some hours our reporting came to a halt as we argued with General Loan. Finally, as I knew he would, General Loan allowed Mr. Tran out—but kept the car and the irreplaceable silver-plated Hotel Continental dish, making Franchini very angry indeed.

I telephoned our driver, Mr. Ma, a French-speaking Vietnamese of Chinese descent, who wore huge pebble glasses and in moments of stress emitted a VHF whine, rather like a defective loudspeaker in a sound recording studio. He lived in the outer reaches of Cholon. Through some extraordinary deal, arranged by François Sully, who prided himself on his ability to cut through Vietnamese red tape, he had been provided with a telephone. 'How are you, Mr. Ma?' I said on the phone cautiously, speaking slowly so he would know who I was. There was a high-pitched snort. 'Mr. Ma,' I went on, 'Don't come into town to see us. And above all, don't tell anyone who it is you work for.'

But Mr. Ma was unusually prolix and, on this occasion at least, both fearless and indignant. 'You bet,' he said in his clear, high-pitched voice. 'There are fifteen VC in my house here right now, and they're eating me out of house and home.'

Reuters was still deluged with copy awaiting transmission, so that evening I had to make another trip to the post office, where a stalwart American civilian crew kept telex lines open at intervals of frequent power cuts. Inevitably, one such power cut occurred before I had finished filing. I busied myself while waiting by reading the mass of cables on ribbon tape piling up on the post office floor, cables that it was unlikely any Saigonese PTT (Posts and Telecommunications) official would paste up and deliver for some time. Most of them were from distraught parents to their soldier and civilian sons, but one struck a different note. 'Frankie,' it read, addressed to a master sergeant, 'if you don't send 500 dollars they're going to repossess the car.'

There were also cables for some of my colleagues, including one, again straight out of Evelyn Waugh's *Scoop*, which read: 'You once again badly failed provide color, personal onscener, fighting narrative. Unwant thinkpieces. Want matcher to opposition's heroic British nurses under siege in Cholon hospital.' This one I charitably tore up.

As I was coming out of the post office with Mert Perry of *Newsweek*, an ARVN soldier guarding the post office gate awoke from a nightmare and simultaneously thrust his sub-machine gun into Perry's capacious belly, accompanying the gesture with a bloodcurdling yell. Perry stood still, and the soldier eventually came out of his nightmare. 'You give money,' he said.

Perry extracted himself from the nozzle of the weapon and said softly, 'The banks are closed, haven't you heard?' We walked away like dowagers avoiding a persistent panhandler, repressing a compulsive urge to break into a swift run.

Our adventures were not over. In the darkness, close to home, we watched the spectacle of a 'white mouse' chasing a Vietnamese around and around a tree, firing as he went, until, as in the denouement of a Mack Sennett chase sequence, the hunted man disappeared inside a building with the policeman in hot pursuit. 'Let's not stick around,' said Perry.

That night, in the Hotel Continental, in the company of fellow reporters including the BBC's Julian Pettifer, I listened to broadcasts made by the Vietcong and beamed at American soldiers, as well as at Vietnamese. A fluent English-speaking, lightly accented voice called on Americans to surrender, while another voice in French urged the inhabitants of Saigon to rise up against their 'imperialist aggressors.' Needless to say, the cynical Saigonese stayed behind locked doors and did nothing. Simultaneously an American woman dissident, broadcasting from Hanoi, was telling GIs in Vietnam to refuse to obey their officers and to 'cooperate with the Liberation Army.' Both voices were loud and clear and proof of the planning that had gone into the Tet offensive.

The U.S. military bureaucracy continued functioning, however, though the staff at MACV HQ emerged for the first time in my experience rather self-consciously dressed in green battle fatigues and wearing revolvers. After only a brief interruption, R and R flights to Hong Kong, Bangkok, and Australia were resumed, and gradually,

PIOs began accentuating the positive: how most of the ARVN troops on special Tet leave had reported back to duty, how nowhere in Vietnam had 'spontaneous uprisings' in favor of the VC taken place, and how, outside of Hue, the combined VC and North Vietnamese forces had failed to hold onto any sizable part of South Vietnamese territory. It was left to General Creighton Abrams, then Westmoreland's deputy, to state what most of us felt. 'Gentlemen,' he said at a briefing I attended, 'we had our asses handed to us.'

Now correspondents were coming into Saigon from the outside, traveling on R and R planes. Among them was Oriana Fallaci. She later wrote a book of reminiscences about her Tet experiences which I found somewhat baffling. According to Oriana, she had had to talk panic-stricken U.S. sergeants into providing her with transport to get to the city. The craven U.S. troops at Tan Son Nhut airport had apparently had to be galvanized into action by this frail but intrepid reporter. 'Are you a man or a mouse?' she asked them.

I well remember the day of her arrival. In common with dozens of other reporters in Saigon at the time, I had driven from Saigon to Tan Son Nhut several times that day to ship film. Convalescing patients, some of them in wheelchairs, at the nearby military hospital were still mounting guard, but the direct threat to the airfield entrance was now over, though fighting was still continuing, and was to continue for some days, around the airstrip perimeter.

Maybe Oriana Fallaci's readers were conditioned to see every manifestation of their heroic girl reporter in cliché, comic-strip terms. Correspondents have a technical term for this kind of reporting. It comes under the generic term hyping. Oriana Fallaci, and a few others, were masters of this peculiar art form, which invariably requires an element of factual truth to which the hype is convincingly added. Thus, Oriana Fallaci undoubtedly arrived in Saigon in the middle of Tet, and yes, she did get to Hue in the middle of the fighting with a number of other reporters. But no sooner did she reach the outskirts of Hue than she had to be put back on the first truck convoy, with a bad case of nerves, by Philip Jones-Griffiths, the Magnum photographer. This proved no bar to her subsequent personal account of the fighting, which—as in the case of the Dak To assault—drew liberally on other reporters' stories.

I was to return several times to Vietnam after Tet 1968, never in circumstances quite so dramatic, though once because of François Sully's tragic death. Invariably, after Tet 1968, the deterioration in the psychological climate was measurable. Tet had robbed U.S. spokesmen of their credibility, whether in Saigon or in Washington. The point made that the Tet offensive, with its horrendous casualty rate among the VC, had robbed the north of its long-term capabilities for months or even years was simply not borne out by the subsequent events. It's tempting, of course, to put the entire blame for the course of the war on the press, and this is what some hawks like General Westmoreland and former Vice President Angew have done, with little success and, I feel, only partial conviction. Nor can I endorse Peter Braestrup's findings to the effect that the U.S. press in Saigon reported as a defeat what had, in effect, been a major U.S. victory. To America's credit, the rules of reporting in Vietnam were not markedly changed after Tet 1968 to restrict correspondents' freedom of action. What had already changed by November 1967, and as a result of my own Hill 875 story, was the American method of accounting for casualties. No longer, after November 1967, were casualty breakdowns issued after every battle, but only on a weekly basis.

The one attempt to prevent reporters from covering a specific event—the Laos offensive of 1971—failed. By this time American morale had slipped, tolerance of the war was lower, even in the field, and we found allies in American troops and helicopter crews who between them conspired to ignore their instructions and smuggle us into Laos.

The Laos operation, in the wake of the then still outwardly successful invasion of Cambodia, involved a massive, complex plan by ARVN to disrupt for all time the North Vietnamese-operated Ho Chi Minh Trail, which ran through Laos into northernmost South Vietnam. Though U.S. ground troops were not directly committed in Laotian territory, U.S. planes and helicopters were. And when the operation proved a costly failure and North Vietnamese units began counterattacking on Vietnamese soil, American troops were naturally involved in the fighting.

My own story of the Laos operation should by rights begin in January 1971 in the Grand Hotel in Calcutta, where I was then working on a cover story of Indira Gandhi. My old friend Larry Burrows, of *Life*, was also there on a difficult assignment; he was trying to photograph leaders of the extreme leftist Naxalite movement, the revolutionaries who were then fairly influential in Bengal. The Laos invasion was about to begin, and Burrows had been urging *Life*'s editors to take him off the Naxalite story and fly him to Vietnam.

'The real reason you want to go to Laos,' I told Burrows, 'is that you're not getting anywhere with the Naxalites.' He agreed. *Life* was extremely reluctant to see Burrows return to Vietnam on the grounds that he had spent so much time there, and taken such risks over the years, that actuarially speaking, the odds were that his luck might not hold. But a phone call from Burrows to *Life* in New York resulted in the grudging permission for him to return to Vietnam forthwith.

I never saw Burrows again. He was in a Vietnamese helicopter near the DMZ when the pilot strayed by mistake over a known North Vietnamese stronghold bristling with antiaircraft weapons and was shot down. The crash was witnessed by other pilots, some of whom tried to talk the doomed helicopter pilot into changing course, without success. No bodies were ever recovered.

By the time I got to Vietnam Sully was dead, too. He had been flying with one of South Vietnam's abler generals, Do Cao Tri, then commanding the South Vietnamese forces in Laos. The general's helicopter took off after refueling at Tay Ninh, near the Cambodian border, and crashed almost immediately. All aboard were killed. Alone of the group, Sully attempted to jump from the burning helicopter on its way down. Suffering from multiple fractures and bad burns, he died, still unconscious, a few hours later.

The circumstances of the crash involved me in a dispute with the U.S. Air Force, as well as with the South Vietnamese, for after the Laos operation was over, I determined to look into the circumstances of the crash and found, scarcely to my astonishment, that while the crash in which Sully died had been an accident, of the unpredictable kind which no air force could possibly guard against, the lack of helicopter maintenance expertise displayed by the South Vietnamese almost guaranteed a horrendous accident rate. *Newsweek* headlined the story 'A Crash Waiting to Happen.' The USAF and the South Vietnamese Air Force took this as a personal slight. My point was not to humiliate them or make them look bad, but to present the facts as I discovered them, from several days' legwork on the major helicopter base at Bien Hoa. The gist of my findings, corroborated, alas, by events, was that in anticipation of a U.S. pullout, the Pentagon was handing over to the Vietnamese more helicopters than they could possibly maintain with any degree of safety.

Despite the deaths of Burrows and Sully, the atmosphere in the Quang Tri press camp, the northernmost base in Vietnam and the main rearguard base for the Laos operation, was that of a multinational, high-spirited summer camp. The Vietnamization of the war was apparent in the new composition of many TV crews. Now almost all cameramen and sound engineers working for U.S. networks were either Vietnamese, Japanese, or South Korean. They brought an exotic note to our foul Quonset hut, since they supplemented tasteless U.S. Army food by cooking their own on Primus stoves. No one had the courage to object to the pungent smell of Korean kimchi, and the Japanese brought out plastic-wrapped fish bought in local markets in what appeared to be an advanced stage of decomposition. A cooking party, to my intense discomfort, took place directly beneath my own upper bunk in the two-tiered army cot I had managed to occupy.

As the only woman correspondent present, Gloria Emerson had to use the all-masculine facilities of a communal toilet, and she did so with aplomb. One night, from the totally blacked-out, neo-Turkish privy came a bloodcurdling yell. A reporter, in the darkness, had cautiously made his way to the toilet. Slipping down his trousers, he groped for an adequate squatting position—and found himself sitting in Gloria Emerson's lap. The yell, it should be noted, came not from Gloria, but from the embarrassed man.

I determined to spend as little time in Quang Tri as possible, and commuted successfully to Khe Sanh, using my hitchhiker's board ('Are you going to Khe Sanh?'). There a curious hide-and-seek game was being played between the Army and the press. I overcame this hurdle by moving into a friendly bunker, occupied by some helicopter pilots. It provided a unique listening post from which to report the progress of the Laos operation and contribute to the *Newsweek* cover on 'America's Helicopter War.'

My first flight from Saigon to Khe Sanh during the Laos operation was memorable for two reasons. First, during the actual flight a large field gun we were carrying almost broke its moorings, nearly causing our plane to crash. We hastily landed somewhere to put the load to rights. Then, on arrival in Khe Sanh, the unit of ARVN paratroopers I had been traveling with waited for further instructions, and while they waited, their American military adviser, a major, out of good manners, strayed off into the bushes to relieve himself. There was a loud thud. He had stepped on a mine, probably an American one left behind at the time of the first Khe Sanh siege. Soon the major was on a stretcher, his leg hanging by a few shreds. Away he went in a medevac helicopter. I calculated that his entire stay in Khe Sanh had lasted seven minutes and made a mental note to stick to well-worn paths within the Khe Sanh perimeter.

We were deployed, four *Newsweek* correspondents in all (Maynard Parker, Kevin Buckley, Tony Clifton, and I), to report on America's helicopter operations. I chose to report on the riskiest of all missions: the medevac helicopter crews. The bravery of the medevac teams was legendary, and the speed with which, thanks to them, the wounded were evacuated was, to anyone with World War II experience, little short of miraculous.

As the Laos operation turned sour, helicopter casualties increased, and demoralized ARVN soldiers added to the pilots' difficulties by flinging themselves on helicopters at all costs to flee the battle zones. To keep the ARVN at bay, U.S. helicopter crews belted the unfortunate Vietnamese and stomped on their fingers to make them let go. Some clung on regardless, and some dropped from great heights and died a horrible death. One member of a U.S. helicopter crew, a Hawaiian, marooned on a besieged ARVN firebase in Laos for several days after his own helicopter had crashed, won a Silver Star for helping the ARVN organize their own defense. The true story of his bravery was a little more complicated. One of the reasons he remained so long on the besieged firebase was that he looked too much like a Vietnamese. A particularly daring helicopter pilot ran the gauntlet of enemy fire to land on the firebase and remove the survivors of the first crashed U.S. helicopter. But when our Hawaiian hero tried to scramble aboard, a crew member from the rescuing helicopter hit him right between the eyes, toppling him to the ground, and shouted, 'No, not you, you fucking gook.' The pilots in my temporary bunker were entranced by this example of black humor and told the story again and again.

As the Laos offensive petered out, revealing the many weaknesses of ARVN, the baffling U.S. military bureaucracy machine pursued its own course, seemingly with a life of its own. On the one hand, as the operation was being wound up, Americans were dismantling everything they could find in Khe Sanh to take back to Quang Tri and Saigon. At the same time, within a few days of the total evacuation of Khe Sanh, fresh supplies were being unloaded there.

I was waiting for a plane to take me out to Khe Sanh for the last time when in came a C-130 with huge wooden crates, which were promptly off-loaded. Curiosity made me take a closer look. For reasons best known to Pentagon East, the U.S. Army's headquarters in Vietnam, the plane had just brought in several tons of Uncle Ben's Rice.

By now the North Vietnamese were shelling Khe Sanh with almost Germanic regularity, and the day's incoming mortar shells invariably landed at 2:00 P.M. The rice-carrying plane had landed at 1:45. Two minutes later I was aboard, somewhat anxiously awaiting the loading of a huge electric generator aboard the plane. As in some giant intelligence test, it seemed designed not to fit into the plane except at an odd angle—an angle the sergeant tried in vain to find. We looked at our watches, sweating. Finally, the pilot himself must have lost patience, for he revved up and took off, with the generator still on the ground and the sergeant waving his fist.

Back in Saigon, I found myself embroiled in a typically Vietnamese imbroglio. At Sully's funeral an ARVN officer had made a short speech, praising Sully and adding, as an afterthought, that François had given tangible evidence of his love of Vietnam. He had, said the officer, left his entire estate to an ARVN orphans' fund. The Army bid to lay claim to Sully was not the only one. He seemed to have promised marriage to a number of his Vietnamese girlfriends, who gathered tearfully around his coffin. 'I loved him,' said one, paraphrasing the call sign of the U.S.

Armed Forces network call sign, 'from the Delta to the DMZ.'

Eventually, years later, Sully's estate in Saigon was disposed of. Car, cameras, records, hi-fi set, and other personal possessions were auctioned off. But when the American lawyer dealing with his estate asked that the proceeds be transferred, the bland South Vietnamese lawyer entrusted with the arrangements in Saigon promptly sent in a bill for her services which—surprise, surprise—neatly corresponded, within a few thousand piasters, to the total amount of Sully's Saigon estate.

The story came as no shock to those with experience of living in Saigon. Taking advantage of Americans had been refined to a level of a fine art; this perhaps explained why many Americans wives preferred to shop at the American PX rather than at the superb, colorful Central Market. Some of them spent more than a year in Saigon without even visiting it. The Saigon 'thieves' market,' in another part of town, also, at the height of American involvement in the war, gave some idea of the scale of theft from American installations. One could buy anything there, including a M-16. Stolen Nikons were offered for sale at a third of their real value—as I knew, for two of my cameras had been stolen out of my pack and I searched for them in vain in the 'thieves' market.' Permanent residents could also take advantage of another kind of service: Old Vietnamese ladies displayed not stolen goods, but whole Nikon, Akai, and Canon catalogues. One could order what one wanted from the catalogue, as in a mail-order firm. The brand-new cameras or hi-fi equipment were delivered a month later, from pilfered PX installations. No amount of security could, it seemed, prevent such rip-offs.

Some Vietnamese institutions seemed, however, specifically designed for American approval. One of these was the oft-visited 'Revolutionary Development School' of Major B. at Vung Tau, formerly Cap St. Jacques. Major B. never tired of telling how, as a disillusioned Viet Minh, he had defected, with the idea of applying Communist methods to come to the aid of the anti-Communist regimes of Ky and Thieu. Some cynics claimed that Major B.'s school was nothing more than a convenient repository of middle-class students anxious to avoid the draft, and others hinted that it was penetrated by a 'gay' Vietnamese cell. Both allegations may have been true, at least in part. On my only visit, as I sat in the back of a truck on its way to Major B.'s residence, a young, somewhat simpering Revolutionary Development cadet sat uncomfortably close to me. He put a slim hand on my knee, slipped it gently up to my upper thigh, asked me where I was spending the night, looked shyly over the top of his M-16, and said, 'You number one!'

Like Major B., most South Vietnamese officials displayed a strange ambivalence toward the American presence. They sought American approval but at the same time needed, above all, to preserve 'face.' Any evidence of condescension, any imagined slight, caused ripples of unease and undisguised hostility. French-educated Vietnamese were even more susceptible, displaying French as well as Vietnamese prejudices toward Americans. Any reminder, however unintended, of South Vietnam's ultimate dependence on the United States was enough to throw a durable pall over any conversation.

The relatively uncomplicated, optimistic nature of many Americans was a further drawback to understanding. In the late sixties Vietnam was visited by large numbers of businessmen and economists, corralled into making the trip to Vietnam by President Lyndon Johnson. After a brief trip to the Delta they would return to Saigon with glowing accounts of progress and prosperity: 'Ed, you've no idea! They're all turning into capitalists! Everyone has a Honda, even in the boonies' (for they were quick to pick up GI slang). 'The rice farmers have never seen so much money in their lives!' This breed of optimists conveniently overlooked the fact that such prosperity was almost entirely artificial. Some of their predictions were as glowing as those of stock-market tipsters on the eve of the Great Crash of 1929, and indeed, they lived in a similar environment, for the United States, during this period, had entered its own boom. Reporters, by definition Cassandras and purveyors of bad news, could hardly compete with glowing graphs of mushrooming Honda sales and farmers' incomes. What this breed of visitor lacked was any insight into the fragility of the regime, its dependence on the American presence, and the profound passivity of most South Vietnamese. Needless to say, certain areas of the admittedly prosperous Delta, buoyantly carried by a rich, extravagant war economy, became Potemkin villages, while few visitors went to I Corps, the zone closest to the DMZ.

And not all such arranged visits to areas outside Saigon generated optimism. I recall attending the official opening of a veterinarians' school, in the company of a group of visiting Americans, at a small town in the Delta.

In the middle of the ceremony, attended only by low-level Vietnamese officials—for a Cabinet minister had promised to come but canceled his trip at the last moment—a clump of VC mortar shells landed uncomfortably close. We all hit the ground. A young AID official, who had helped fund the project, whispered to me, as we lay prone before awkwardly and somewhat gingerly resuming our spectator stance, 'Do you think the minister knows something we didn't?'

William Colby, later CIA director under Nixon and the ranking CIA official in Vietnam, would occasionally take a reporter with him on a trip to the provinces, which he regularly visited. One weekend in 1970 I flew with him to Quang Ngai, just south of Da Nang, a very 'black' (i.e., VC-penetrated) area indeed.

The province chief we spent the day with was a Protestant convert, and an extremely active one. There were only a few days to go until Christmas 1970, and our schedule included endless church services and hymn singing. The GIs attached to the province chief's HQ were also, by some strange coincidence, Baptist Fundamentalists, and the result was that we seemed to be in the midst of a singularly well-armed, militant, and uniformed missionary outpost. One evening Colby and I had hymnbooks pressed into our hands and prepared ourselves for yet another interminable service. Inevitably one of the hymns was all about 'Peace on earth' and 'goodwill towards men.' Our singing was entirely covered by the regular sound of artillery shells being fired off into the surrounding jungles only yards away from the school building the service was being held in. 'Don't you think,' I hissed to Colby over my hymnbook, 'that there's something particularly grotesque about all this?'

He looked at me with astonishment. 'No, I don't,' he said. 'What's wrong with it?'

It was easy—after some months in Vietnam—to become insensitive to situations of this kind, so much so that I invariably advised newcomers to soak in as many impressions of Vietnam as they could within the shortest period, for after that, I claimed, we all gradually lost our sense of the absurd. Partly this blindness was a consequence of the arrogance of power, of manipulating the extraordinarily complex but unsuitable war machine brought to bear in Vietnam and unconsciously shelving unpalatable facts. It also stemmed from a racist attitude toward the Vietnamese, who, in official army jargon, were not people, but only OHBs or 'Oriental Human Beings.' All this was brought home to me during a visit to Vietnam of Lyndon Johnson as early as 1967. He was shaking hands with GIs, seeking reassurance in bear hugs and bodily contact, while an aide kept looking at his watch. LBJ was due to see President Thieu that afternoon, and the aide was afraid that he might be late for the appointment. Finally, the aide managed to detach him from the GIs, and LBJ made for the nearest helicopter. The aide checked him. 'Mr. President,' he said, 'that's not your helicopter. *That's* your helicopter over there.'

LBJ looked at him, patted him on the shoulder from his sizable height, and said, in his much-imitated southern drawl, 'That's all right, son. They're *all* my helicopters.'

But the story that puts the whole American incomprehension of Vietnam into perspective occurred during the same trip. LBJ was on his way to one of the largest American bases and was bowling along an asphalt road, in an air-conditioned black Cadillac, one of at least twenty heavily guarded limousines. Suddenly the President spotted a little old Vietnamese woman trotting by the side of the road. He turned to Ambassador Bunker and said, 'Does this little old lady know that the USA built this mighty fine road she's walking on?' The answer was noncommittal, but LBJ was in one of his manic Texas moods. The President ordered the whole convoy to come to a stop. He said, 'Someone go over and ask her who built this road?' The command was transmitted from ambassador to general to aide to colonel to a junior officer interpreter, who went up to the terrified old lady and said, 'Who built this road? The President of the United States wants to know.'

The little old lady went down on her knees, sobbing, rolling in the dust, and saying over and over again, 'I don't know. I didn't do it. I didn't have anything to do with the road.'

XI. SINGLE GENTLEMEN PREFERRED

'SINGLE GENTLEMEN preferred' was a formula to be found occasionally under the 'furnished accommodation to let' section of certain British papers, and it can still be seen in some window displays of some of the cheaper London estate agents. It's also a qualification most editors, in their heart of hearts, would dearly love to apply to their foreign reporting staff. If editors had their way, they not only would like their foreign correspondents to be single but would prefer them teetotal, completely devoid of any sex drive, and animal haters as well.

Unfortunately few foreign correspondents live up to this description, having normal, if erratic, sex drives and a penchant for alcohol and being perhaps more prone to marital troubles than most categories of employed adults, with the possible exception of punk-rock groups, racing drivers, and crews of nuclear-powered submarines.

This means that much of an editor's time, unless he has delegated such responsibilities to someone else, is taken up with arcane logistical and personnel considerations which have little to do with putting out a newspaper or magazine. These can range from deciding whether to send X, who is first-class, to Hong Kong, where he will require an apartment for himself and his large family costing at least $1,300 a month, to say nothing of hefty school fees, or Y, who is inexperienced but childless and could make do with a smaller apartment. Or whether the cost of maintaining

Z's two dachshunds, unhappily and expensively quarantined in southern England, is a legitimate item in the foreign news budget.

Such issues are sometimes decided on precedent or by applying State Department rules (where Americans are involved) or—if the foreign correspondent happens to be a star performer—in favor of the reporter, even if some claims are regarded as extravagant. There are twilight areas, however, which seldom come under State Department consideration. A bachelor, suddenly appointed to a far-flung foreign correspondent's post, suddenly turns out to have a girlfriend in tow. For reasons both complicated and irrelevant, they are not about to marry but are equally determined not to be separated. Should she be 'carried' on the paper's travel budget, and if so, will she demand, and obtain, a regular round-trip ticket back to New York or London at the company's expense as a quasi-marital right? And if this is 'exceptionally' authorized, how many single correspondents will get to hear of it and surface with hitherto anonymous and invisible companions in tow, making similar demands and serious inroads into an already overburdened travel budget? And with sex equality, could such privileges not be extended, in time, to the boyfriends of women correspondents?

Diplomats have immunity. Journalists don't. Expulsion is a frequent threat, and any editor is bound to have ambivalent attitudes over one of his correspondents who happens to be expelled, even for the best of motives. Unscrupulous totalitarian governments know this and shamelessly exploit it. How far, in ordinary court cases that may arise from time to time, should editors intervene to back their men in the field? Most do so generously, even when the correspondent may be in the wrong, but some are notoriously callous. I shall never forget the exchange of messages over the Reuters wire after its resident correspondent in Saigon, in the fifties, had been charged with injuring a passerby in a Saigon traffic accident and arrested. 'On no account bail out X,' the message ran, 'till all facts are known.'

When *Time* posted me to New Delhi in 1962, I was in the middle of a protracted divorce but determined not to leave without Christiane, who later became my wife. She too was technically married to someone else, but the fact that we had been living together for more than a year prompted me to press *Time* to consider us, for practical purposes, man and wife. *Time* agreed, but someone in the travel department balked at the fee involved in transporting Max, our large golden retriever, from Paris to New Delhi. The expense was not enormous, but it was unprecedented for *Time* to pay for the cost of transportation of correspondents' pets when the correspondents were theoretically single. Presumably, somewhere in the *Time-Life* infrastructure, was a cost accountant figuring out how much would have to be added to the yearly travel budget if, at one fell swoop, all of *Time*'s single reporters were suddenly to acquire golden retrievers.

Then there was the problem of immigration. Since Christiane was not married to me and was not even British, Indian immigration officials would not give her a permanent resident's permit, compelling her to leave the country every three months. The regulations concerning foreigners in Hong Kong were equally drastic. Christiane has since charged me, not entirely in jest, with having married her in Hong Kong in 1967 solely to rid myself of a nagging bureaucratic problem.

Diplomats' wives roughly know, even before their husbands' first overseas posting, what to expect in the way of routine social chores and local environmental problems. Journalists' wives—especially those posted abroad—should be aware of only one thing: that they will never know, from one day to the next, what their husbands are really up to.

I once took off on a replacement stint in Vietnam which

was to last two weeks—and stayed there for more than four months. The possible result of such prolonged absences can lead to inevitable and formidable marital tensions, for several reasons.

A returning reporter, once back at home, wants above all to immerse himself in a family routine he has missed. He is sick of hotels, of restaurant meals, even of glamorous out-of-the-way places, aspiring only to a kind of uxorious ease in familiar surroundings. His wife, especially if young and not long married, will on the contrary look forward to the very type of outing and excitement that, to him, has become a prodigious bore. And it's difficult, in such circumstances, for wives to believe that their journalist husbands' assignments had not included more than their fair share of luxury and wild amorous philandering. They would endorse Rimbaud's famous line: 'Women nurse these fierce cripples after their return from the tropics.'

And reporters are themselves such odd creatures that they cannot return home without at once longing for the kind of assignment that has just ended. Sitting in a beleaguered Belfast hotel several winters ago, a world-famous war photographer outlined this dilemma in an apt, if somewhat crude, stream-of-consciousness monologue. 'All I want right now,' he said, 'is to be in my semidetached bungalow in Surbiton'—he was deliberately over-emphasizing the modesty of his home life—'surrounded by my dear wife and three screaming children. And when I'm there, I know that what I'll really want is to wrestle with that marvelous little whore who used to share my nights when I was last in Vientiane.'

Wives invariably assume their departed journalist husbands are unfaithful whenever they leave town, and some believe that they lead double lives, actually departing with glamorous girlfriends after kissing them good-bye. They will be correct in only a minority of cases. As any philandering journalist will very soon find out, the strain of trying to do one's job in an unfamiliar country and of carrying on an affair at the same time is the surest path to both professional oblivion and cardiac arrest. 'He travels fastest who travels alone' remains a valid axiom.

The philandering foreign correspondent will also have to take a number of embarrassing security precautions unless he intends to flaunt his extramarital adventures, like ensuring that his hotel bill remains sufficiently vague so as to leave in doubt the issue of double occupancy. This in turn means that the most pusillanimous will forgo breakfast. He will also have to convince his companion not to answer the phone in his absence—an act which is liable to arouse her suspicions, especially if he has conveniently forgotten precisely to define his own marital status. Finally, there's the need to avoid his colleagues, who are watching him like hawks and, through some contrived or genuine indiscretion at a later date, may well betray him. For all these reasons, extramarital adventures in the course of a reporting stint are to be discouraged, except, perhaps, in the event of the leisurely, timeless kind of reporting that *Life* used occasionally to encourage and that is now very much in abeyance.

There are other questionable practices, with editors and not correspondents in the role of the philandering villains. Thus it's not unknown for an editor to send away on major and, indeed, irresistible assignments reporters or photographers on whose wives and girlfriends he has designs. The practice, from personal experience, while not unknown in the United States, is more prevalent in France and Italy. And foreign correspondents themselves, let loose in faraway places, will notoriously stray, though usually only once their stories are filed. The familiarity of most correspondents with so-called girlie bars all over Southeast Asia is notorious, as is the specialized knowledge of newspapers and magazine office politics of the young ladies concerned, as witness the following true story: A well-known foreign correspondent was making love to a Filipino bar girl in his Manila hotel room when she suddenly blurted out, 'Is it true they're sending Tony from Hong Kong to Beirut?'

There are, of course, some happy and productive husband-and-wife teams, probably the only way of combining a foreign assignment with a minimum of felicity. But such teams are the exception in foreign correspondents' households for obvious reasons, and they too occasionally break up, after logging millions of miles together. Like poker games and manning a small yacht, the insight gained of one's companion during a harassing trip—especially one involving discomfort, sudden changes of plan, and one's own sudden and prolonged absence—is invaluable. Should a foreign correspondent stumble by chance on someone who will not object when he sets his alarm at 5:00 A.M. to type his story noisily in a cramped hotel room, who will uncomplainingly pack in the middle of the night to go to some completely unforeseen destination, who will refrain from nagging if he receives stateside calls at four in the morning, my immediate advice would be: Hang onto such a pearl, and if not already married, marry her forthwith.

If, on the other hand, you find yourself in Bangkok with someone who insists on visiting the floating market, the palaces, museums, and silk stores and will sulk if you fail to go along with her at a time when you should be running from ministry to ministry and meeting informers in seedy cafés, if, in short, you find yourself neglecting your assignment or facing nagging recrimination and tears if you return to your hotel room at midnight, having promised to be back at eight, or if, worse still, you find that your beloved has—against all advice—strayed alone into a North African medina wearing a short skirt and a see-through blouse, thereby encouraging small boys to pinch her bottom and perhaps steal her purse, then you should draw your own conclusions. If you are head over heels in love, I suggest you opt for some alternative means of earning a living.

It is not only wives and girlfriends whose presence on an assignment may lead to disaster. Anyone who has taken a TV crew to foreign parts knows the delicate balance between success and failure, largely dependent on morale, which in turn depends on small things. In their way, TV crews can be as demanding, as unreasonable, as inclined to complain as any number of spoiled children or nagging wives. To bring up this aspect of a reporter's preoccupations may appear churlish, for who has not witnessed the extraordinary stamina, skill, and courage of TV crews on various war fronts in Vietnam, Cyprus, and the Middle East? Nevertheless, there is a certain type of TV crew whose inclusion in a team can be an almost guaranteed recipe for disaster. The French TV crew that expects, as a natural right, red wine and a grilled steak, even in the middle of a teetotal state and sulks in a remote part of India, if denied this is a case in point. So is the union-conscious sound engineer who is aware of his rights, as defined by his guild, to the exclusion of almost everything else ('we're entitled to a hot lunch'). Almost in a similar category I would put the sound engineer whose standards are so meticulous that he will balk at working in anything but a studio atmosphere, the cameraman who will interrupt proceedings whenever the slightest cloud appears on the horizon, the electrician whose prime purpose appears to be to blow the fuses.

Having said all this, I'm remorseful, for I recall taking a Swiss TV crew to India and putting this bunch of Lausanne gourmets through the most appalling experiences, including several days in an ashram where the only food to eat was vague vegetarian messes spread on banana leaves and eaten with one's fingers; I remember the French TV crew I spent some time with on the Micronesian islands, fighting a losing battle against oversize rats in our rooms, becoming lice-ridden, and spending days in a longhouse on a staple diet of coconuts and crabs roasted over a fire—all without complaining.

Most of all, I remember the TV crew, part French, part Swiss, that accompanied me to India in 1967 to make a one-hour documentary. Our plans included filming for a few days in a village so remote that it was almost inaccessible, with the surrounding open fields as toilets. Their conduct was exemplary, and their morale never flagged. The trip was memorable in many ways. We talked to a village moneylender. I asked him whether he did not agree with me that his yearly interest rate on small loans (about 50 percent a year) was somewhat usurious. 'These are poor people,' he said. 'They cannot pay more.'

But when I think of the horrors and hazards of TV crews, I most vividly remember a story, admittedly told me at second hand, but true, of the British crew in Nigeria filming there shortly after the collapse of the Biafra secessionists. A wave of robberies was being repressed by the government in the most brutal way possible—by capital punishment—and the crew was filming an execution. The unfortunate victim, convicted of some particularly modest robbery, had been tied to a tree and blindfolded. A priest had administered the last rites. An army squad, its rifles loaded, took aim. At this point the proceedings were interrupted by the sound engineer. 'Stop everything, please,' he said. 'there's something wrong with the set.'

The execution squad commander courteously obeyed; the troops grounded arms until the tinkering with the recording machine was completed. 'Now let's have a test,' the sound engineer said, completely oblivious of his surroundings. 'Okay, you can go ahead now.'

XII.   GETTING THERE
IS HALF THE FUN

TRAVELING ON reporting assignments for Reuters, *Time-Life*, the *Saturday Evening Post*, and *Newsweek* has involved me in almost every conceivable form of transportation, from Mongol pony to requisitioned sandbagged army train, but the mainstay has always been the airline. Reporters get to be shrewd connoisseurs of the vagaries of different, exotic and little-known airlines: Air Zaire takes off and lands to the sound of paeans of praise for President Mobutu from recorded Congolese folk song groups; Air Ceylon has the most spectacularly beautiful air hostesses in the world; traveling by Royal Nepalese Airlines was, in the sixties, almost as hazardous as playing Russian roulette.

Terrorism has also made us highly conscious of the different forms of body search indulged in at different airports. In West Germany it's a brisk, impersonal, but thorough operation with the hint of a heel click when it's over; at Kinshasa's airport passengers are searched by customs on leaving as well as on arrival, but this is mainly so that the customs officials can squeeze the last few banknotes out of harassed and by this time desperate travelers; at Madrid airport once, in Franco's day, the body inspection was so thorough, and so equivocal, that I wondered whether the searcher was attempting to discover whether I was 'dressing on the left' (as the London master tailors put it) and whether this was not, in the Spain of the time, a political offense.

The hijacking wave has given the lie, of course, to the airlines 'honored guest' routine, for how can this fiction survive the expert frisking of passengers, even those traveling first class? It's rather like telling a weekend guest, 'Come again, we love you, but first open up that suitcase so we can see whether you've made off with the cutlery.' As a compulsive reader of airline ads I long ago ceased to be amazed at their credibility gap. And I was always something of an anomaly among my fellow reporters because I professed to enjoy working in India. Sometimes I wonder whether my fondness for that country didn't conceal a deeply masochistic streak. For to be a reporter in India is to make extensive use of Indian Airlines—surely one of the main contributory causes of the shortness of journalists' lives. (I'm not impugning their safety record; the hazards are solely in terms of nervous wear and tear.)

For Indian Airlines is one of the few airlines in the world to apply the International Air Transport Association (IATA) rules to the full, and this involves imposing fines on passengers who change their minds at the last minute. For changing or canceling one's flight within forty-eight hours, one is liable to a fine representing 20 percent of the ticket's total cost. The fine shoots up to 50 percent if this happens within twenty-four hours of departure. Reporters are notorious ditherers, usually for reasons beyond their control, but the rule is inflexible, and all that is needed is a cancelation within twenty-four hours, made on two successive occasions, and you have no ticket left at all. The first time you find this out can be a memorable occasion.

Needless to say, the corollary of this brilliant bureaucratic tyranny is that experienced travelers in India seldom make reservations in advance. The net result at almost any Indian airport is pandemonium.

Don't for an instant believe, however, that your troubles are over once you have fought your way to the airline counter. I remember traveling with a French TV crew from

Trivandrum to Bombay. I handed over four tickets at the counter. There was a long wait, and then the clerk looked up and asked, 'There are four of you?' I nodded. 'Where is your other ticket, please? You have given me only three tickets.'

Having counted the four tickets seconds before handing them to the clerk, I felt that a search of his desk would produce the missing one. But I made the fatal error of implying that he had been at fault for mislaying it. 'Three can go,' he said with Brahminical dignity. 'The fourth person will have to buy a ticket.'

The argument that followed almost ended in bloodshed, for at no time would the clerk agree to go through the morass of papers on his desk, which was in fact awash with tickets, one of them presumably ours. But it was his turn that day to drive a traveler (preferably foreign) to the breaking point, and he succeeded. A year later I still was engaged in correspondence with Indian Airlines on the matter. Finally, on shrewd advice, I wrote to say that I now figured I must have lost the ticket. Reimbursement came, along with a little homily about being more careful next time.

As it happened, our trip from Trivandrum to Bombay aborted that day when we were forcibly removed from the plane upon landing thirty minutes later in Cochin. 'You did not actually make reservations from Trivandrum to Bombay, but merely requested space,' said the Indian Airlines man in Cochin (this was an arrant lie). 'You were firmly booked only from Trivandrum to Cochin.' We asked when we might be expected to continue our journey. 'Cochin to Bombay is another story,' he said equably. 'Tomorrow we shall see.'

Compelled to spend the night in Cochin and already on a tight schedule, we behaved so menacingly the next morning that seats were somehow found for us aboard the first Bombay-bound plane. A young man from the Peace Corps was not so fortunate. He was gibbering, much as I had gibbered the day before, and his inarticulate rage was such that I felt compelled to ask him what was wrong. 'Nothing wrong, nothing wrong,' interjected the Indian Airlines man. 'He is in a good position. He is number three on the waiting list.'

The young man howled with rage. 'What do you mean, number three? Yesterday I was number two!'

A week later, after some harrowing filming in Calcutta, we turned up at dawn at Calcutta's Dum Dum Airport to board a plane for New Delhi. I had previously warned Indian Airlines of our 400 pounds of excess baggage (mainly TV equipment). Nothing was said as we piled our equipment and our luggage on the scales. The Indian Airlines man took our tickets (but this time I held onto them as he did so).

'You can go,' he said, looking up, 'but your baggage cannot go.'

'What do you mean, our baggage can't go?'

He turned and pointed to a huge pile of luggage reaching up to the ceiling of the cavernous airport building. 'You see this baggage here,' he said with great patience, as one would address a moronic child. 'It is baggage from yesterday's plane. It has not gone either.'

There are times when the low cunning of reporters, driven by desperation, knows no bounds. Instead of throwing a tantrum, I decided to play it cool. Taking aside one of the more senior Indian Airlines staff, I asked him confidentially for the real reason of the 'hold' on luggage. The answer was that Indian Airlines was also carrying some urgent freight on the plane and that passengers' luggage would simply have to fly later. 'That's slightly unfortunate for me,' I said, 'Indira Gandhi, your prime minister, is expecting us at her residence this afternoon for an interview. If we say that we have to cancel the appointment because Indian Airlines wouldn't take our stuff, she won't be very pleased, and it could be awkward for you later on.' It was a typical Moghul ploy—threatening a lower official

302

with the wrath of a remote, higher official and bringing to bear one's influence. Luckily I had with me correspondence from the prime minister's office relating to our interview (I only hoped, of course, that he would not read it too closely, for we had in fact already interviewed the lady), and like a magician, I brandished it casually so that he might see the official prime minister's office letterhead.

'I'll see what I can do,' he said, adding, 'Whatever you do, don't come near the counter or be seen to have anything to do with me before the plane leaves.'

Out of the corner of my eye, I watched our TV equipment loaded onto a separate trolley, which then disappeared. A good sign. Then, a few moments later, the waiting room was made hideous with German oaths and a furious argument, some of it in German-accented Hindi, some of it in English and German.

A big blond man, surrounded by his wife and three small children, was on the verge of apoplexy. 'Three months ago I these reservations made had,' he shouted. Speechless rage choked him. 'You . . . you . . . impossible . . . I will my consulate call.'

What happened was simple: In order to take us and our TV equipment aboard, our friendly Indian Airlines official had bounced an East German technician returning home after three years in Calcutta. The choice of victim led me to believe that the gesture was politically motivated.

During the period (1962-63) I was *Time-Life*'s bureau chief in New Delhi, I was puzzled to discover that while seats on Indian Airlines to Katmandu, Nepal, were always difficult to obtain, Royal Nepalese Airlines planes always had seats available. Then I learned that what I suppose could be described as 'consumer acceptance' of Royal Nepalese Airlines was sadly lacking. The story was that after a series of crashes, which had left it with only one serviceable plane, a DC-3, the Nepalese government had asked the United Nations for technical assistance in the form of a multiskilled pilot instructor, master mechanic,

303

accountant, traffic manager, and meteorological expert rolled into one. This rara avis had been found and sent out to Nepal, where he worked hard for several months. When the time finally came for him to leave, he left by jeep.

Then there's the fun of dealing with bureaucrats in post offices and at telex counters all over the world. Some are wonderful; others leave one so frustrated that one retires, shaking, to the nearest bar—if there is a bar. At the time of the Algerian War I was compelled on occasion to send my stories from Morocco by post office telex. The procedure was always the same: I would provide a word count. Then the post office clerk would count the words, with agonizing slowness. His tally, of course, would invariably add up differently. I would then beg him to accept his, usually inflated, word count. But with imbecilic courtesy he would start counting again, interrupted at intervals by other customers, buying stamps, having their savings books endorsed, or sending shorter telegrams of their own. After each interruption he would lose count and start afresh. At last he would arrive at an acceptable figure. 'And now,' he would say, thrusting the cable back at me, 'please add up the number of erased words.' I would do so. When I would return to the counter, it would be closed for the day.

There are also hotels which become a correspondent's nightmare for the simple reason that their switchboard operators believe that attack is the best line of defense, that a go-slow policy will successfully discourage one from placing any further calls. Thus, at one famous Rabat hostelry, one asks the operator for a number. One bathes, shaves, breakfasts, reads the papers. Time elapses. The call is almost forgotten. One picks up the phone again in panic. 'Line engaged,' says the operator, before one has uttered a word.

I never dared calculate how many weeks of my life have been wasted waiting for phone calls to come through in hotel rooms as far afield as Dakar or Peking. But my worst single phone experience owed nothing to the hotel operators. I was in Tananarive, capital of the Malagasy Republic (then Madagascar), desperately trying to call the Paris office of *Time*. After what seemed like days of confinement in a Turkish bath of a post office phone booth, I finally heard the distant but unmistakable voice of our Paris switchboard operator.

'This is Edward Behr calling from Madagascar,' I said brightly.

'You can't talk to M. Behr, he's in Madagascar,' she said, and hung up.

XIII. UP THE STREET
AND ROUND THE CORNER

ONE DAY in August 1968 I received a phone call in the middle of the night from the editor of *Newsweek*. 'You may not be aware of it yet,' he said, 'but the Russians have just invaded Czechoslovakia. Nobody knows where Dubcek is. I want you to display some of your well-known ingenuity and get to Prague—today.'

The Russian move was not entirely surprising. Alexander Dubcek, the liberal Czech premier, had increasingly irritated the Soviet Union by playing fast and loose with orthodox Communist principles, which threatened to undermine Soviet influence over the rest of Eastern Europe. For some time Soviet troops had been concentrated at Czechoslovakia's borders.

Getting a visa from the Czech Embassy in Paris was no problem. The staff was handing them out to all comers, only too aware that these might be the last for some time. In the visa section at least, they were still Dubcek partisans to a man.

I flew to Munich, hired a car, and tried my luck at crossing the Czech border at a place called Zelezna Rula. Cars containing scores of my colleagues, some with TV equipment, were forlornly waiting on the West German side. 'You don't stand a chance,' said a BBC reporter I knew. 'They're not letting any journalists in.'

I thought I had a slight edge on them all. On my passport, my profession was listed as 'corporation representative,' which was, in the widest sense, true since *Newsweek* is a part of a corporation called the Washington Post Company. And I had worked out what, in retrospect, seems a wildly improbable story. Apprehensive but displaying what I hoped was an unconcerned smile, I drove up to the border checkpoint. Having made it through the West German side, I moved forward a few yards and smiled sweetly at the grim middle-aged Czech border guard officer on the Czech side. 'What is the purpose of your visit?' he asked, in good English, with a look that meant: 'I know who you really are, you scum.' I explained that, as a representative of the Wellcome Corporation, a Hong Kong-based company (whose name I had just invented), I was on my way to Pilsen to place a large order for Pilsen beer, a beverage which was very popular in Hong Kong.

Even as I was explaining this, I realized how unconvincing I sounded. The Czech officer heard me out, expressionless. 'Where is your correspondence with the Pilsen brewery?' he asked, fingering my passport attentively and pausing before the numerous pages obliterated with exotic Vietnamese visas. 'My good sir, I don't keep my files with me when I'm traveling,' I said. 'They're back in my Hong Kong office. Besides,' I added unwisely, 'everything is on record at the brewery.'

He moved a few muscles in his cheeks, a wintry, post-Dubcek smile. 'And what,' he asked, 'is the name of the export manager who has been dealing with you and whom you intend to see? This you surely must remember.'

I went through the motions of consulting my diary. I should, of course, have had a common Czech name, like Stepanic, at my fingertips, but caught on the spur of the moment, my mind was a dreadful blank. Alas, only one name came to mind at that fateful instant, and I was fool enough to blurt it out. 'I believe his name is Schweik,' I said. *The Good Soldier Schweik* is, of course, a Czech classic—and perhaps the only Czech book title foreigners know.

He handed me my passport. 'Back,' he said, adding sotto voce, 'Good try.'

The other reporters cheered ironically as they saw me reverse and return to the German side of the frontier. But by this time the challenge to get into Czechoslovakia had become an absorbing game, and the following day I made another attempt, this time from the Austrian border, after building myself a more convincing cover story. Shortly before the Soviet invasion an industrial fair, with participating firms from all over the world, had been due to open at Bratislava. This fair had now been canceled, owing to the Soviet invasion. I decided that my imaginary Wellcome Corporation was the kind of firm to send exhibits to the Bratislava fair. What more natural than it should make semiconductors for Hong Kong's booming transistor industry? So, under the horrified eyes of *Newsweek*'s office manager in Vienna, unused to such duplicity, I sent myself a fake telex message, purporting to come from Hong Kong and ordering me to proceed to Bratislava to supervise the crating up of the fair exhibits for a safe return to Hong Kong. This time, at the Znojmo checkpoint on the Czech side, the somewhat soiled, dog-eared telex had the desired effect. I was allowed in. While I was brandishing my faked telex message, *Newsweek*'s Arnaud de Borchgrave was crossing the border in equally surreptitious fashion—hiding under the seat of a train with the connivance of some scared fellow travelers in his compartment.

But my troubles weren't all over, though my sense of elation was great. The patriotic Czechs had torn down or deliberately misplaced all road signs in order to confuse the Russians. Luckily I found willing helpers not only to guide me on my way but to help me avoid Soviet checkpoints, through the use of country roads. Some of my guides, when they discovered I was a Western reporter, insisted on coming aboard and on traveling with me to make sure I didn't get lost. They must have spent hours walking home but refused to take any money for their services, and in

broken English or German all wished me luck, un-
equivocally damned the Russians, made the V sign, and
even, on occasion, kissed me emotionally on both cheeks.

My only hazardous moment came late at night, within a
few miles of Prague itself. Suddenly I was flagged down by a
Soviet Army officer. Behind him, as far as the eye could
see, stretched an interminable tank column. (Later I was to
count 150 of them.) The officer scrutinized my passport,
searched the car, and stole my Michelin road map. From
some of his pidgin German questions, it was clear that he
assumed he was north of Prague, whereas, of course, he
was some distance south. I had two young Czech
hitchhikers in the car with me, and they swore in Czech at
the officer, shook their fists at him, and made as if to take
on the whole tank column single-handed. Speaking slowly
in English, a language one of them understood, I told them
to stop, threatening to leave them on the road with the
Russians unless they ceased their patriotic, futile, and
dangerous antics.

Such con-man approaches, questionable in themselves
and used only in dire emergencies, were sometimes the
only means of getting around otherwise insuperable
obstacles. Thus, during the terrorist hijacking of Israeli
athletes at the Munich Olympic Games in 1972, I got
through a police cordon keeping out reporters and
bystanders by waving an old press pass and shouting out,
'*Sicherheitsdienst*' ('security'), in my best German accent.
It worked and enabled me to get so close to the scene of the
hijacking that I was able almost to touch the buses on which
the doomed athletes were being taken, prior to their
departure to the airport, by the arms-toting Palestinians.

Sometimes any old card would do. In different
circumstances John Gale of the London *Observer* was
equally resourceful in extricating himself from a
particularly nasty corner in Rabat in August 1955. Partisans
of the returning Sultan Mohammed V, who had been exiled
by the French, were busy roasting alive some of the

supporters of his pro-French predecessor, Ben Arafa, within the palace grounds. John Gale, mistakenly assumed to be a Ben Arafa supporter, was in imminent danger of being equally roughly treated. Surrounded by crazed Moroccan tribesmen, Gale showed them his red MCC (Marylebone Cricket Club) membership card. They immediately fell back. 'And yet,' said Gale afterward, 'they didn't look as if they knew much about cricket.'

In the late sixties Prince Sihanouk was still in control of Cambodia, then a quiet and delightful country, and the prince was intent on keeping all reporters out of the country unless he personally invited them in. It was not difficult to sympathize with Sihanouk. With some VC and North Vietnamese units firmly entrenched in his own country, with American bombers surreptitiously bombing these VC concentrations within Cambodia, and, I'm convinced, with the prince's own tacit assent, and with a full-scale war going on immediately to the south of Cambodia's frontiers, it was a feat of tightrope walking to keep Cambodia neutral and outwardly uninvolved in the war. This, however, Sihanouk managed to do for some years, with considerable diplomatic skill, until the Lon Nol coup in 1970 forced him into exile in Peking.

Needless to say, Sihanouk's aversion to journalists was seen, by the press, as a challenge, and for some months I found a way to beat the ban. I discovered that the Cambodian diplomats in New Delhi, a capital I frequently visited in those years, were not taking their jobs too seriously. In fact, they were almost never in their offices. All visas there were issued by a Sikh clerk, who was aware of Sihanouk's rule that all reporters' visa requests should be addressed directly to him. But since my passport described me as a 'corporation representative,' and since I invariably applied for a short tourist visa, it was assumed that I was going to Cambodia for a vacation, and I managed to make several trips in this fashion. My contacts in the capital, Phnom Penh, were well aware that I was defying

Sihanouk's ban, but since I never filed any stories until I had left the country and never wrote in the first person as if I had just visited Cambodia, I was able to keep this up for some time. Interestingly, I was eventually betrayed not by a Cambodian but by the ambassador of a small Western country who had developed an emotional hero-worship cult for Sihanouk. He came across me on a Phnom Penh street one day and asked, 'Does His Highness know you're here?' He soon did.

I cannot, in retrospect, feel any shame at such innocent deceptions, partly because the games we tried to play on Sihanouk were nothing compared to the games he played on us. For Sihanouk's obsession with what the press said about him and about Cambodia was limitless. No article ever appeared in any paper without provoking a lengthy critique or rejoinder, and the duties of the Cambodian diplomatic missions abroad were almost entirely confined to providing Sihanouk with a detailed press survey of everything that was written about Cambodia around the world.

In his prim, schoolmasterish way, Sihanouk could be almost insufferable. At one press conference, to which all senior Asian hands were summoned (and who could turn down a summons by Sihanouk when he so rarely accorded entry visas?), he lectured the press, interminably, about its shortcomings and abysmal ignorance of all things Cambodian.

'The press refers to "small Cambodia," to "tiny Cambodia,"' he said, in his impeccable, high-pitched French. 'Now I will read you a list of all the countries that are smaller than Cambodia.'

Sihanouk also took a delight in publishing a monthly press digest containing all the articles written about Cambodia around the world in the previous month, with his lengthy annotations. In my case, he went one stage further: After one of my visits, a licit one this time, he published, in his press digest, the text, not of my article on Cambodia as it eventually appeared in *Newsweek*, but of my original cable to New York, as deposited at the Cambodian post office. We all knew that Sihanouk read all outgoing reporters' dispatches, but to have him publish them, in their unabridged form, took some doing.

'I am not a red prince.' Sihanouk was fond of saying, 'I am a pink prince.' But while his views were indeed 'pink,' i.e., populist and left-wing, he never gave up his insistence on rigid court protocol, thus enjoying the best of both worlds. He could also drive visiting reporters to extremes of frustration. During De Gaulle's state visit to Phnom Penh in October 1966, for instance, reporters and photographers, clamoring for passes to attend a highly formal concert to be attended by both De Gaulle and Sihanouk in Phnom Penh's main theater and having been warned in advance that tuxedos were to be worn, were flummoxed by a Sihanouk aide, who announced, 'His Highness has changed his mind. You must now wear spencers.' To those, like myself—until that afternoon at least—who may be ignorant of the finer points of court dress, a spencer, or bum freezer, is the short ceremonial jacket of the kind worn by army officers in Hollywood movies set in the nineteenth century. Needless to say, we submitted to this latest prank without demur. 'You are sure you have a spencer?' the suspicious palace aide asked each reporter in turn before handing over the coveted invitation cards. 'Of course,' came a chorus of replies. 'Never travel without one,' said a particularly hard-bitten AP photographer. One inexperienced young French reporter— less versed in Sihanouk's ways—almost gave the game away. 'I don't have one,' he started to say. 'I don't even know what they are.' He was promptly pulled to the rear of the line by the rest of the press, cuffed, and told to shut up. Needless to say, we all appeared in tuxedos, and nothing further was said about *les spencers*.

However infuriating Sihanouk could be to reporters, he was never dull, and his genius for publicity would have made him a fortune on Madison Avenue. He undoubtedly saw himself as a truly Renaissance Oriental prince, priding himself on his gifts as composer, saxophone player, actor, writer, and film director. His protean gifts were taken extremely seriously by his scared and docile court. During the De Gaulle state visit, in between some remarkably graceful Cambodian traditional dancing, a Cambodian symphony orchestra played excerpts from Mozart—and Sihanouk. In his last year before the Lon Nol coup, Sihanouk spent a great deal of his time making movies, in which he himself starred. The plot was nearly always the same: Dashing officer in the Royal Khmer Forces (played by Sihanouk) unmasked a dastardly plot fomented by American imperialists and their CIA henchmen. Such films were regularly entered in the annual Cambodian Film Festival, where, scarcely surprisingly, Sihanouk walked off with the first prize for directing, acting, scriptwriting, and composition. One ambassador once confessed to me that keeping a straight face during the projection of these interminable films was the best possible test of a diplomat's propensity for concealing his true feelings.

Jacqueline Kennedy, who accepted Sihanouk's invitation to visit Cambodia in October 1967, soon discovered that her 'private visit' was unashamedly being used as a vehicle by Sihanouk to promote Cambodia. He waived all bans on visiting reporters, and his embassies throughout the world issued scores of visas. The result was that Jackie, wherever she went, found herself not only cheered by thousands of Cambodians but also filmed, relentlessly, by scores of TV crews.

After a particularly grueling ceremony, held under the blazing sun with TV crews in close attendance within the palace grounds and marked by interminable speeches, presentations, and exchanges of gifts, Sihanouk grasped a microphone and announced, 'And now Mrs. Kennedy will feed the sacred elephants!' As though by magic, the crowds parted, and huge painted elephants appeared in a cloud of dust, their trunks curled upward in a gesture Kipling would certainly have approved. Jackie Kennedy retained, to her credit, a slightly strained but still dazzling smile, but the microphones picked up her despairing groan of 'Oh, no!'

If Sihanouk indulged in endless cat-and-mouse games with reporters, his cheerful craving for favorable publicity on his own terms was so open and unabashed as to be almost endearing. But I had already had a less endearing example of such single-mindedness a few years earlier, when Richard Nixon came to Paris, as a temporary fellow journalist, in 1963. I was then European contributing editor for the late *Saturday Evening Post*, whose editor, Clay Blair, had asked me to meet Nixon at Orly Airport and give him any help he might require.

I saw Nixon and his family into a suite in the George V Hotel and asked whether there was anything I might do for him. 'Ed, there is something,' said Nixon. 'I'm having lunch with de Gaulle, and I want a picture of us together.'

My heart sank. The ways of the Elysée Palace were very different from those of the White House, and though a horde of photographs chronicled de Gaulle's every public appearance, there was no in-house, resident Elysée photographer on hand to take pictures of de Gaulle's private guests. Indeed, de Gaulle was known to have a tantrum when a press aide once suggested that he might adopt this American habit. The fact that Nixon was traveling with a *Post* staff photographer didn't help matters either. I could easily arrange for the photographer to be at the Elysée on the morning of Nixon's lunch appointment. But getting him into the lunch was out of the question, and having de Gaulle and Nixon pose together inside the Elysée for the *Post* photographer also presented grave problems.

I tried my best. What were the chances, I asked a de Gaulle press aide, of having a *Saturday Evening Post* photographer take pictures of Nixon and the French president shaking hands? 'This is a private visit,' said the aide icily, 'and no such photographs are usually taken.'

Would there be the remotest chance of General de Gaulle's coming down from the floor of his office to see his visitor off, so that both were in full view of the photographers waiting in the courtyard outside? 'Monsieur,' said the aide, 'protocol limits such appearances to visits of heads of state.' Would there be an Elysee photographer on hand to record the meeting? The answer was an unequivocal no.

It was my sad duty to return to the George V suite and tell Mr. Nixon that while a fairly large crowd of reporters would be waiting for him to emerge from the Elysée building, the chances of getting a picture of him and de Gaulle together were negligible. Nixon's hitherto friendly countenance underwent an immediate change. 'Surely there must be *someone* who can fix this?' he said in what, for all its cliché use, I can only describe as a snarl.

Alas, my further attempts were equally unsuccessful. 'I know Mr. Nixon places great importance on a picture with the president,' another aide said archly, 'but it's not the general's habit to allow a photographer in for a private meeting.'

Nixon took this news badly, as I knew he would, and from then on, for the rest of his stay, he was coldly remote. I had failed him, so I was the enemy. The lunch went well, and there were large numbers of photographers and reporters outside the Elysée Palace doors when Nixon emerged. He was interviewed at length by French TV reporters, while the then U.S. ambassador in Paris, the late Charles Bohlen, twisted his features in grimaces of undisguised boredom and loathing. At the airport, on his way to Berlin, Nixon shook hands with me. 'Pity about those pictures,' he said, adding, with obvious irritation, 'There *must* have been a way round that situation somehow.' Years later I watched Nixon get a head of state's greeting from Charles de Gaulle on his first trip to Paris as President after his November 1968 election victory. Hundreds of photographers and serried ranks of TV crews were on hand to record the formal handshake and greeting.

This, I thought to myself, is Nixon's revenge.

But then, Nixon's single-minded pursuit of a picture of himself with de Gaulle, useful for his future political career (at a time when most people had dismissed him as a has-been), was simply an instance of the politician's instinct at work. For politicians, as most professional reporters will admit, are not people or, at least, not like most people. The inescapable servitude of the politician's life, the boredom of routine meetings, of speeches told and retold over and over again, of time spent on necessary but uninteresting and hideously time-consuming visits, dinners, inaugurations, and election addresses, the fake bonhomie and the rigidly crammed timetables, the frittering away of energies, and the complete curtailment of any unplanned leisure, to say nothing of the absence of any really private life, would be quite beyond the inclinations of most people.

Reporters, compelled to chronicle the day-to-day activities of major politicians, are constantly baffled by such behavior. Can power be such an aphrodisiac that its lure justifies such a life? For only rarely do political leaders, in a democracy at least, succeed in avoiding such routines. The late Georges Pompidou, promoted from aide to prime minister overnight, did skirt such an arduous apprenticeship before his premiership but adopted the politician's backbreaking routine afterward. The same holds true of Raymond Barre, appointed French prime minister by President Giscard d'Estaing without any prior experience of cut-and-thrust politics. But such examples are so rare that they confirm the rule: In a democracy, a politician's life is, to an outsider at least, a form of private hell.

Dictators prove hell for others. In their different ways, both Idi Amin Dada of Uganda and the Central African Republic's Emperor Jean Bedel Bokassa make Caligula look like Gladstone. Idi Amin's fantasies are those of a small, military-crazed boy given to dressing up; in his language, bearing, and mannerisms, he has successfully aped the middle-class British African society he caught glimpses of in his youth, a society, one might add, not so different, in its worship of self-assured middle-class truths, from that of 'white' Rhodesia.

Jean Bedel Bokassa has acted out a more complex, literary pipe dream. By having himself proclaimed emperor, with the travestied pageantry of Napoleon's crowning, complete with earldoms for his officers, Bokassa has concretized some quintessentially French fantasies. Their antics are best known because they provide reporters with regular copy material. For all the unbelievable brutality of the Ugandan and Central African regimes, reporters tend to stress the tragicomic element in both men's schizophrenia. But are they all that exceptional?

When I first met Habib Bourguiba, the Tunisian leader, he was a persuasive, moderate nationalist leader whose campaign for Tunisian self-government had led to house arrest, where he promptly charmed his jailers into allowing him a greater measure of personal freedom and seems to have won most of them around to his thinking. In the course of subsequent years I saw a great deal of Bourguiba. As his country's 'Supreme Guide,' he remained, for some time, astonishingly informal. He prided himself on his talents as a cook and once cooked me a fish couscous in his country home, then still a modest establishment.

But in the sixties he began dotting Tunisia with a series of unnecessary and expensive state palaces in excruciating taste, furnished in Louis XVI-Arabian Nights style. In his later years he would regale docile audiences with interminable tales of his early life, including details of a most personal nature, such as his discovery that he only had one testicle.

Not surprisingly, many French reporters who once sympathetically chronicled his struggle for independence have since become persona non grata, and the rest have had to resist, with differing degrees of success, becoming part of an Oriental court around this remote, autocratic figure.

317

Journalists are in a very special quandary, for their success depends, to some extent at least, on enjoying a cozy relationship with politicians and power holders. Deep down, however, they know that they are tolerated only for the favorable image and public exposure they can at times guarantee their subject. The fatal tendency for reporters is to start believing that they are admitted into the intimacy of the great and powerful not simply because of their usefulness, but also for their wit, good company, and friendship ties based on common past shared experience. This, of course, is nonsense, as anyone who has abruptly stopped being a well-known reporter can testify. Politicians are the only people, apart from journalists themselves, who regularly read the mastheads on magazines listing the names of the staff, and they do so for one very good reason. They want to be sure that when they see X or Y, they will not, as one of them put it to me crudely once, 'be wasting my time.'

Not that I am suggesting that any but a tiny handful of reporters are either corrupt enough or snobbish enough to be regularly and consciously manipulated. But manipulation takes several forms, and some of it is very dirty pool indeed. At its most ruthless it involves the denial of facilities, the withholding of visas or confidential information. How many reporters have put their careers on the line by speaking out, in the knowledge that this would lead to closed doors and banned entries, and how many, to ensure a continuing access to people and places, have neatly tailored their writings accordingly? In such circumstances it's something of a miracle that a Watergate scandal ever gets exposed, and it's probably fair to surmise that had the Nixon administration not adopted a systematic confrontation attitude toward the media, thereby goading the press in turn into fighting back, the chances were that it would have been buried forever. Indeed, the United States was just about the only country in the world where such an investigation could hope to succeed. In Britain the security-blanket 'D' notice, forbidding any press mention, would have effectively stopped any reporting on the subject. As for France, the methods used in Washington by *Washington Post* reporters Woodward and Bernstein would, very probably, have caused them, under French laws, to end up in jail.

And yet, for all the abuses and imperfections of the so-called free press, for all our occasional questionable tactics in obtaining information, for all our shortcomings, including our abject pandering to prurient public opinion, our tasteless pornography, and our emphasis on crimes of violence, anything, even the grossest abuse of freedom, must be better than its loss. For only through an even imperfect free press can we hope to expose the human folly of our times and to make the world more aware of the growing totalitarianism in our midst. Satire and ridicule, as in Orwell's *1984*, are wonderful but at best limited weapons. In the end the reporter's quest is for facts, all the facts, not just the selected facts that would slant a story in a given direction. Facts are in the last resort the humanist's only weapon, against which the doctrinaire bully can only attempt outright suppression.

The search for facts, as I hope I have shown, can be an odd, enriching experience. It can also, on occasion, be dangerous, hilarious, time-consuming, and oddly unsatisfactory, since the armchair editorialist will philosophize with an utter disregard for facts, statisticians will say that facts can be made to fit any interpretation, and totalitarians will claim that fact-finding is a bourgeois alibi.

But the reporter's quest for facts brings rewards of its own, which only partly have to do with being proved right in the end. The truly addicted reporter (and most of the other kind drop out of the game sooner or later) will never tire of joining in the chase, watching the adrenaline flow, and bringing all available ingenuity to bear on a situation which, like life itself, is never tidy, finite, or simple. The sport is all, the consequences sometimes hilarious, sometimes tragic, often frustrating, but never boring. Our attitude toward time itself is not that of most people. While others think of it in terms of family occurrences and personal office promotions, our conception of time is entirely bound up with salient world events.

I am writing this on the terrace of my house in Ramatuelle, in southern France, overlooking some of the most beautiful countryside in the world. Vineyards merge into fields which end at the edge of the Mediterranean. Two dogs and a cat, a household the very picture of domestic bliss, all but lull me into a state of not caring what may be happening in the rest of the remote world. But I know that all it takes is a news flash, a phone call, the distant lure of some distant crisis, however calamitous or bloody, to send me on my way with no regrets for all I am leaving behind me. And this despite a growing conviction that at best the latest adventure will contain moments of almost caricatural frustration and at worst moments of sheer abject terror. For despite the terror, there is a curious compulsion to go up the street and see what's around the corner, even if ultimately, at that last corner, we shall never know.

A SELECTION OF NON-FICTION FROM
HODDER AND STOUGHTON PAPERBACKS

CHRIS BONNINGTON

☐ 41426 X   The Everest Years   £2.95

LIONEL BLUE

☐ 41371 9   Bolts from the Blue   £1.95

MICHAEL LEAPMAN

☐ 41107 4   The Last Days of the Beeb   £3.50

All these books are available at your local bookshop or newsagent, or can be ordered direct from the publisher. Just tick the titles you want and fill in the form below.

Prices and availability subject to change without notice.

Hodder & Stoughton Paperbacks, P.O. Box 11, Falmouth, Cornwall.

Please send cheque or postal order, and allow the following for postage and packing:

U.K. – 55p for one book, plus 22p for the second book, and 14p for each additional book ordered up to a £1.75 maximum.

B.F.P.O. and EIRE – 55p for the first book, plus 22p for the second book, and 14p per copy for the next 7 books, 8p per book thereafter.

OTHER OVERSEAS CUSTOMERS – £1.00 for the first book, plus 25p per copy for each additional book.

Name ....

Address ....

....